To Sandy
with love and
sweet memories of time we've
shared —
Hope this will both
bless and challenge you
as you continue your walk
with our Lord.

Ruth

But...Where Do You Really Live?

Ruth Garde

authorHOUSE®

AuthorHouse™
1663 Liberty Drive, Suite 200
Bloomington, IN 47403
www.authorhouse.com
Phone: 1-800-839-8640

First published by AuthorHouse 5/4/2009

ISBN: 978-1-4389-6856-8 (sc)

Printed in the United States of America
Bloomington, Indiana

This book is printed on acid-free paper.

Copies of this book may be obtained by e-mailing ruthgarde@windstream.net or calling (704) 788-6085.

Contents

Acknowledgements

I have to try, but I do not have to succeed.
Following Christ has nothing to do with success
as the world sees success. It has to do with love.
Madeline L'Engle

Writing this book had been a daunting challenge. Attempting to tell this story of how God worked in my life it was impossible to include the many people who profoundly touched and blessed my life. Please know because you aren't named doesn't imply you are not in my heart.

To my cherished editors and computer coaches, hope you realize how much the part you played is appreciated. thank you for your patience and willingness.

To my cheerleaders my constant encouragers thank you for being there.

Introduction

Love those cardinals. I was privileged to have two different pairs visit morning and late afternoon in my Connecticut home to enjoy the stocked feeder put out for them. I had the perfect spot on my couch looking out my picture window indulging myself with my view. It doesn't take any talent to spot the male... that flash of brilliant red catches your eye. He stands out in any setting garbed in his crimson splendor.

But I soon found greater delight in watching for the female. Sometimes she would follow briefly after her mate and at times she would precede him. But consistently the pair would feed together.

Her warm brown feathers with hints and tinges of red on her crown and feathers, along with her matching black face and red beak were pleasing to my eyes. So many folks miss what she has to offer because her counterpart is so spectacular. Watch out for that subtle one however, she's a quiet beauty, with strength and potential. She has all kinds of adventures and surprises ahead.

The Long Ten Years

The shock of the last few days was slowly, but surely sinking in. The need to face a new reality that had been thrust on me was now my agenda. It was the end of May and I had run to my beach house on the Jersey Shore.

I had gone alone to the beach after my husband of twenty years, had told me he was leaving and wanted a divorce. Was I really to be single? While I walked along the sandy shore pouring out my heart to God, I was struggling as I processed the shocking events and attempted to discern my future. With each step the realization that if my twenty year marriage was truly over, in spite of obvious negatives there were some pluses. If I was to be single, no longer yoked, there would be a freeing in that. When my sons went out on their own I probably would be only fifty. What I chose to do with my life would be up to me, the decisions would be mine to make. That was both scary and intriguing. In the walking.. and the talking.. and the crying.. I sensed the Lord telling me words I didn't understand... but carried hope. It wasn't an audible voice and yet I knew the Holy Spirit was revealing to me, to my heart and mind, things he wanted me to hear. There was that whisper in my ear, the Lord telling me to trust him. There was something very special for me in my future that was beyond my understanding. Little could I realize what that would be. Whatever might that involve? Lots of questions...

Those years were tough. There was much grooming and growing that was essential so that I would be equipped for the life ahead. First job was to learn to be single and to appreciate that being alone was okay. One is a whole number and that took work to become whole and healthy again. My three teenage sons needed a stable mom and have a safe haven until they were ready to go out on their own.

For years I had been plagued with an inner ear problem, Meniere's. Dizziness, nausea, sensitivity to noise all led to fatigue. This was not a good combination for an elementary teacher managing a classroom of active kids. Usually at the end of a school day I would come home exhausted sending me to my bed and adding to my loneliness. In the isolation I learned to draw closer to the Lord and find rest in his arms. There were times when the dizziness would be more intense and I would have to stay home. The quieter I became, the more relief I found. My patience was deepening, my turning to and totally relying on God was steadily developing. I used to tell my classes at the end of a school day that I couldn't wait to get home and listen to the quiet. That was a concept that totally puzzled them. One of my favorite B.J. Thomas songs started with the words, "I need to be still and let God love me." Definitely I was learning to be still and experience that love.

After many doctors and many prayers I was told about a surgeon in New York City who was having success with inner ear problems. God was leading and after two surgeries on my ear in 1977 and '78 the problem was relieved.

During these years many thoughts of that promise on the

beach would come to me and it made me wonder, what was that all about and what would be involved. Serving in a variety of ways in my local church had always brought a deep satisfaction to my life and with each opportunity I felt useful and fulfilled. It was time to begin exploring possibilities for places of ministry and begin to see what was out there. Both of my older sons were now on their own.

Also, the time was rapidly approaching when Dan, my youngest would leave home. He was close to being halfway through his college years. Now that the surgeries were behind me I sensed I needed to begin checking out what options were out there. What was that something special the Lord had promised me and when was it going to happen? I received some reassurance and a chuckle from a quote from one of my favorite authors, John Ortberg in his book, "Love Beyond Reason."

> *God does not lead his people in a roundabout way.*
> *He does not move hastily. He is never in a hurry.*
> *It is one of his most irritating qualities.*

While reading a Christian magazine I read about a service named Intercristo. An individual was asked to complete a questionnaire about themselves and they would strive to match them with available positions that included work in churches as well as mission related opportunities. That drew my attention and I decided to offer my information and check out what they listed as available. My experiences of working in various capacities in my local church after putting in a full day's work had been frustrating. There was a longing to have the privilege of giving "the cream" of my energies in ministry rather then the "leftovers" of my supply of energy.

I began to discover Christian Education Director positions were not all that available. Churches weren't looking for a divorced fifty year old to lead their staff. Plus, there were lots of applicants for these positions. As a public school teacher I had enjoyed working with student teachers, interacting with them, sharing insights and encouragement. I wondered whether I might be able to get a position where I would be working with prospective teachers at a college. Quickly I found that you had to be in the process of working on your doctorate. I had successfully completed a master's degree in education, but knew investing time and work in graduate studies was not for me.

Missions certainly was an interest, but that required raising your own support and that would create a barrier. Hm, feeling somewhat stymied. "Lord... I've knocked on some doors... please show me what's next."

a new church...

As a young child, I had attended a Presbyterian Church with my aunt and my impression brings the words cold, dark, formal, somber to mind. Later, in my college days, while working summers at the Jersey Shore I had conversations with a Presbyterian minister whose beliefs were alien to mine. He believed the world was gradually evolving into a new and peaceful "one world". That exchange with him had made me very uncomfortable as he said other things that were contrary to my beliefs. My limited experience had left a negative impression.

We were blessed when new neighbors from the South moved in next door. They were part of the small group who shared a vision of starting a new Presbyterian church in my home town. After a few conversations with them, I knew they were solid in their faith. My son had gone to their church one week and started to receive the church's information in the mail. I was only attending the Worship Service at my present church and wanted to contribute much more but there didn't seem to be any doors to ministry, except you guessed... the nursery. The start-up church was about to have a retreat and that drew my attention for I knew that was a great way to make significant connections. After some conversations with the Lord about the matter I felt led to attend a service and found the young pastor to be warm and caring. His sermons were stimulating, stirring up longings in the deep recesses of my heart that brought hopes and aspirations to the surface. I couldn't put a name to these at that time, but I was dreaming dreams of an unknown future. Jim was more liberal in his theology than me, but I sensed the Lord was calling me to step out of my comfort zone and open myself to a mission field I had never imagined.

Entering this new arena I attended the retreat and then joined a small group study. I enjoyed these new connections with folks. Listening while people shared their spiritual journeys I became aware my evangelical language needed some adjustment. Their experiences were just as valid as mine in spite of the fact they weren't using my lingo. Terms like saved, born again, justification that are so casually used among evangelicals are not typically used in mainline churches. I began to listen with not only my ears and mind but also my heart. The stories of hurts and bruises, inflicted by well meaning witnessing Christians, grieved me. "Christianese" created barriers. I was remembering the sensitivity God had taught me in my neighborhood Bible clubs of the value of using understandable words with people from different backgrounds.

I was growing and stretching in other ways, too. Different styles of worship all had value I soon discovered. Printed prayers, music, order of worship are not the critical thing, *it's always the condition of the heart.* Am I engaged or just thoughtlessly going through the motions. This challenge faces us all, whether our church is charismatic or liturgical, big or small.

One day a leader of the church approached me saying, "We

would like you to serve on our steering committee and when we are chartered become an elder." Now that was a biggy, I mean I grew up in a fundamental church and Baptist churches where only men filled these positions. Okay, Lord, now what am I supposed to do about this issue? After praying about it, I sought some trusted counsel from mature Christians. The feedback I received from a former pastor, who had been there for me when my marriage came apart was, "God has gifted you and you are responsible to use those gifts in the ways he calls you to". And so, I accepted the responsibility. Christian Ed was where they needed someone and I certainly had a heart and experience in that ministry. I confess that when I served communion the first time, that being a woman, I just might be struck dead.

My involvement grew and quickly I found there was much more to learn. I still painfully remember teaching an adult class on prayer in this new church and overwhelming everyone with much too much stuff. Their glazed looks made me both wince and chuckle at myself. One of my strengths and joys as an elementary teacher was the ability to size up my new students each year, discerning where they were in their learning experiences and determining the best course of action for them to progress. Now I was discovering a greater need for this in my ministry.

volunteer ... VIMs

In conversations with my new pastor, I shared the longing in my heart for full-time ministry. I told him of the breakup of my marriage, that divorce had never even been in my vocabulary. Certainly I expected marriage would be challenging and there would be tough times, but in those difficult stretches you hang in there and work on the problems. I shared my beach story and the promise God had planted in my heart. I had heard the Lord telling me, a forty year old, words I didn't comprehend at that time... words that carried hope of something very special...

beyond my understanding... that would come out of all of this. Little did I dream of the adventures that were in store as I kept my eyes on the Lord.

As we continued our talk, Jim asked me had I ever considered a volunteer position. He explained that Presbyterian USA had a Volunteer In Mission program that provided a wide range of opportunities to go and spend a given amount of time in a variety of places and areas of service. Being new to the denomination, I hadn't known about the program or that it had evolved as a response to JFK's Peace Corp.

Different churches, camps, colleges, projects could write up a request for volunteers to serve X number of months or years doing a specific job. Some were house parents, secretaries, maintenance crews, camp councilors to name a few. The volunteers came from recent college grads as well as early retirees. I didn't fit either mold. The descriptions were printed up in a brochure each year and he had the latest in his office. I realized while skimming over the material that there was no financial compensation. I blurted out, "You know Jim, I expected a pay cut but do you mean I would be working for nothing?" We both laughed and he went on to explain that my needs would be met. Room and board and a small monthly stipend, usually fifty dollars would be given.

After looking at the brochure I folded it up and returned it to Jim. A seed had been planted but needed time to germinate. God had more work to do in me. In the following months while reading my Bible, a chapter in Isaiah jumped out at me. I often say the Holy Spirit lights up a verse or a portion of scripture and you know the Lord is speaking to you.

> *Come, all you who are thirsty and you who have no money,*
>   *come buy and eat!*
> *Come, buy wine and milk without money and without cost*

Why spend money on what is not bread
and your labor on what does not satisfy?
Listen, listen to me, and eat what is good and your soul will
delight in the richest of fare. Isaiah 55:1-2

The words that practically jumped off the page were, "come all you who are thirsty" and "why labor on what does not satisfy?" I had loved being a homemaker, a wife, a mom, an elementary teacher but there was a longing, a calling, a sense that had been blessed but there's something more out there. Whatever would it be? Wherever would it take me?

the big three …

In the Spring of '81, I received a mailing from Emmanuel Gospel Center in Boston describing their desire to have Backyard Bible Clubs in the summer. They were seeking staff to work in this area. I had enjoyed significant ministry in clubs, initiating, training and conducting my own in middle-class neighborhoods and in the housing projects. That announcement caught my eye and touched my heart. I called a friend who was on staff at the center seeking more information, little realizing what was unfolding. Charles was quick to invite me to come and stay with the family. They lived in the inner city, had two kids, and a room in the attic. I had always been involved in ministry part of my summers and this opportunity excited me.

My application was eagerly accepted and I soon found myself packing my bags and driving north to Boston. It wasn't difficult to fit into the family and find my space in my "penthouse". This was a tough neighborhood and the week I moved in, a car had been stolen from off the street. I was a proud owner of a "new" three year old Honda Accord and very concerned with its safety. It was quickly evident that Boston was a tough place to drive in and I was learning that it was necessary to tell the Lord the car was his and not mine.

I was part of a team that would go door to door in designated neighborhoods in the inner city, pass out a flyer inviting the children to join us and told them where and when we would be having a club. Most met daily for a week. I played a very basic guitar that caught their attention as we sang lively songs. We had spiral teaching books that showed pictures of the Bible stories we told. Each meeting a "chapter" was told from the life of a famous missionary. These were a hit as the story was continuous with a new episode each day. The team made learning Bible verses fun. We also played some games and had some surprises each session. Our clubs would vary in number, one location, only five kids showed up but usually we would run from the teens into the twenties.

Each club had its own characteristics. One of my favorites was in a Black Portuguese neighborhood. We were told that we could not have the club until late afternoon because the children had to stay in their apartments until their parents returned from work. The families would keep the kids up late so they would sleep in most of the morning. The oldest child was responsible for the kids. The first two days of the club we were checked out by the elder men. They wanted to make sure we were "safe". We must have passed their inspection since they stopped coming after the first days. This community impressed me.

Another club was at a project that looked like a prison. We had more than sixty kids come every day and sit on concrete steps. Our timing was bad as our club met as the garbage trucks came rolling in to pick up the trash. The kids tended to sit there like statues, expressionless. After three or four days of singing "You're Something Special, you're the only one of a kind", they began to respond, first with some eye contact and then finally with a smile. The team felt the children had held back because of all the broken promises and disappointments in their young lives. I was so glad that a neighborhood church was going to follow up with their own program after we moved on. Actually all our clubs had different churches ready to continue the ministry.

Questions began to fester pertaining to traditional evangelistic techniques. Often children are asked to raise their hand or stand showing they wanted to ask Jesus into their heart. Kids are such people pleasers and my concern was and is that was their motivation. If after we left and they didn't experience change in their own heart would they then doubt and dismiss the whole experience? To help remedy this, I began telling the children if they wanted Jesus to be in their lives that when the club was over they should approach one of the leaders and they would explain what this was all about. Everywhere we went children came forward and talked to one of the leaders. I felt this was more effective.

My home situation was special. It was great being part of a family. In addition it was a joy to have this time with Charles and Candy. His mother and father were very special to me as was their sister and I relished this time with them. I appreciated their interest in me, the many stimulating conversations, as well as having fun with the kids. I loved being able to go up to my attic room when I needed to be quiet. Of course this also gave the family some space and created a delicate balance that worked well.

Exploring Boston was a blast. Before venturing out on my own Charles would meticulously draw a map showing me how to reach my destination. After looking at it with him and thanking him I would begin to go when he would say, "but wait I need to show you how to get home." Boston is famous for its narrow streets (old cowpaths) and a multitude of one way roads. Invariably it seemed upon my return I passed through the "red light district". I'm thankful the Lord was always with me.

Quincy Market was great fun doing the shops and watching the various performers, music, mime, juggling, you name it they did it. American history has always been an interest for me so I loved revisiting historic sites Old Ironsides, North Street Church and seeing a few that were new to me. Of course I enjoyed a relaxing harbor cruise, delighting in viewing Cape Cod from the water as well as viewing the city as the boat circled back.

The primary mission at the Gospel Center was to provide support, training and inspiration to the local churches. One of my highlights that summer was a Worship Service with leaders of every color, church affiliation, style, and music. What a joy to listen to Hispanics singing in Spanish while playing their Mexican instruments, a refined British gentleman singing a classic hymn, Blacks presenting their music sharing their hearts and soul, all contributed to rich and unique Worship time. Each one was affirmed and appreciated creating a rich foretaste of heaven where artificial man-made barriers will not exist. It had been an absolute feast, each course absolutely delicious.

Little did I know then what the Lord had called me to. This was a prototype of what God was planning, an opportunity to try it on to see how it fit. He was preparing me for what he had in store . laying out "The Big Three", the ingredients I would have and need in my approaching adventure: finding family (being connected), the excitement of exploring new places, and most importantly ministry that satisfied my deep longings to serve my Lord.

When I reflect, I see how God had orchestrated opportunities in my life where I had an option to take a risk or say no. Each step led to another. Thankfully, I listened and said yes, at times with fear and trepidation, but yes. How terrible it would have been if I had let fear stop me. What a loss if I had missed all those blessings.

Returning home it was time to tend to my house and get myself prepared for a new year of school. When I read my Bible and spent time in prayer and reflection, I found myself assessing things. How good God had been to me, but along with a thankful heart there existed a questioning, a wondering and a longing. I was getting itchy about my future. The waiting... the wondering... the wishing... how long Lord...

Back to the routine I found the school year evaporated quickly in spite of the questions brewing within. The summer of '82 arrived and I volunteered to direct a children's program at Harvey Cedars Bible Conference at the Jersey Shore. I was free in the afternoons and loved watching the kids with their families enjoy the sand and surf together. Later, I spent a few weeks with friends in New Hampshire, conducting Backyard Bible clubs in neighborhoods. Once again I was staying with a family, very dear to me. Once again I found it comfortable, finding my own space and giving them theirs. It had been a satisfying summer, but I found I there was an eagerness building. I sensed and hoped that something good was soon to happen. My youngest was now one year away from college graduation.

getting close...

Labor Day weekend marked the start of a new school year. I found myself not only curious about volunteering but actually pursuing my pastor, asking about the new brochure for Volunteer In Mission candidates. When I got my hands on it I eagerly poured over its contents. The northwest attracted my attention. I had long dreamed of seeing the Pacific Ocean, eager especially to visit the beaches of Oregon and Washington. There was a church near the Washington coast that was seeking a person to help with their Christian Ed program. That caught my eye. Another church in New Mexico also drew my interest.

No ocean, but they were seeking an assistant to the pastor and that was intriguing. I was getting ready to take steps and begin the application process.

About the same time I was experiencing distress with a weird "bug" that made my sensitive ears even more troubled. Exposure to lots of noise was difficult and I was finding it affected my nervous system. I was forced to take a few days off to rest and savor the silence. It was almost Christmas and the break was a relief. It seemed ironic to be considering going off on a grand adventure while I found myself incapacitated, not knowing whether this would be eased or continue to trouble me. But I also experienced a sense of expectancy.... a readiness for the unknown.

The early part of the new year, I completed my application and identified my references. Progress was in the making. The moment had arrived for me to rank my project choices. With lots of prayer but no clear leading, I wrote down the one in Washington as my first choice.

It was difficult waiting for an answer. I felt vulnerable when checking the mailbox. While I reflected on how difficult it is to wait. I thought of how challenging that must have been for Jesus. After all his ministry didn't begin until he was thirty and in that culture Jesus would have been considered a man for a long time. I wonder if he asked his Father why are we waiting, "let's get on with the program".

I had already enjoyed a positive conversation with my principal filling him in on my explorations. He was thrilled along with me and was more than willing to request a year's leave of absence from the Board of Education if an opportunity opened up.

Finally the answer arrived encased in a very thick envelope. I eagerly opened it up and read the cover letter ..."sorry but we are unable to have a volunteer on the staff at this time." Whoa, that was a blow! In the envelope were copies of my applications and my references. These of course should not been returned to me but I was to find that the reference that had been written by my principal was included in the papers. Don had written that, "Ruth would thrive on new challenges" and that, "she truly "walks with God, daily." This especially blessed me since tragically he died of a heart attack just prior to my receiving this negative answer.

I phoned the VIM office in NYC. The director had received the notice from the church and was upset too. She suggested sending my application to a church in Mount Lake Terrace Washington. I had already poured over the brochure wondering where that was, but had been unable to locate it on my map. She informed me it was just north of Seattle. That sounded great to me. I wanted to be on the west side of the mountains, near Seattle, the Puget Sound and the ocean. My next concern was that the description of the job sounded like they were wanting a social worker and although I had interest in that I lacked any experience. She answered she didn't think that would be a problem so we agreed she would put my information in the mail.

This time the reaction was the complete opposite. Within a few days the phone rang and when I picked up the receiver I heard, "hello, this is Dick Gibson calling from Mount Lake Terrace in Washington." He was eager to pursue the possibilities. One of my first questions was how far is the beach. He laughed and told me about fifteen minutes away, but then informed me that was the Puget Sound, the ocean was a good three hours away. My reply was that's just like here in Connecticut. I shared my concern about the job description and he told me that when the leaders had written the blurb about what they were looking for had been a few years ago and those folks had moved away. Anyway the church would want for me to bring my unique gifts and interests and come and be myself. That sounded great to me. The church, Terrace View, had about one hundred members of all ages, many were active and vital. He would share with the leaders my credentials and anticipated they would be excited about the opportunity of my service and he would keep in touch.

All this of course led to conversations with my sons, close friends and my parents. Folks were excited with me, the only exception was my mom. That surprised me since she always seemed to be the adventurer, the one pushing the limits. She was facing a second heart valve replacement and dreading that. I can't help but think that colored her reaction.

leaving home...

The practical side of me kicked in and I began to consider what to do with my home. Should I leave it empty, rent or sell it. After much thought and prayer, my decision was to sell. I would strip down my belongings to put in storage anticipating when returning, I would seek a condo. My needs would be different as Dan would be leaving for seminary in Kentucky and I would really be alone, an empty nester.

A vivid memory from my childhood affected my decision. I remember sitting in the middle of the back seat of the car. It was dark and Dad had stopped to pick up the rent from his tenants. As he climbed back into the driver's seat he spoke softly to my mom telling her that the tenants didn't have enough money to pay him. He had tears in his eyes and was worried not knowing how he was going to be able to pay the mortgage. There were only a few occasions that I recall seeing Dad cry or with tears so that scene remains in my heart. This reenforced my looking to sell. I didn't feel comfortable strapping my oldest son with that responsibility. John had a wife and baby daughter to care for.

Early in my marriage we moved to Texas. After two difficult years in the Houston area, my husband and I moved to Connecticut a few hours away from our families. John had been able to get a transfer at work to the company's research lab. We both wanted to move back to the northeast. Since we had requested the transfer we had to foot the bill. My brother Rodger pulled one trailer and we in our totally renovated '36 Ford coupe pulled another with our modest belongings. We were returning with two little guys, one had just turned two and big brother was almost four. We moved with little money and no expectation of buying a place. God knew better.

In God's tender way, he opened up through my dad a way of buying a home and within a month of driving away from Texas we were moving into our home in Bethel. We knew we had experienced one of God's many miracles. Our third child, another boy was born the next year making our family complete. For twenty- five eventful years that remained my home. It was a modest Cape Cod house but more than adequate. The boys had room for their train, models and activities. We all loved the holidays, Christmas especially, and loved decorating and entertaining family and friends. My home was well used as I led many Bible clubs and studies, conducted meetings and entertained missionaries and ministers. Our family dog must be in heaven because she heard the gospel over and over. I had undergone many transitions as we all do, some anticipated and others totally unthinkable.

But now the Lord was calling me to leave my nest. It was a place that was God given and where his presence permeated every room. I loved taking care of my home, creating a welcoming and enjoyable place. Even as I became single the memories did not prevent me from finding my home to be a source of comfort and strength, a precious haven no matter what the storm.

The reality of how huge these decisions were began to sink

in. How does one who had been reasonably "normal" all of their life decide to leave it all behind? I'd be saying goodbye to my house with a mortgage paid in full, the security of a teaching job as well as the comfort and love of my family and friends. The familiar verse in Matthew came to mind.

> *Anyone who loves his father or mother more than me is not worthy of me; anyone who loves his son or daughter (or granddaughter) more than me is not worthy of me; and anyone who does not take his cross and follow me is not worthy of me.*
> *Whoever finds his life will lose it, and whoever loses his life for my sake will find it.   Matthew 10:37-39*

Now the challenge to live this verse at a much deeper level was before me.

Fortunately I'm blessed with solid organizational skills. Having a home with neither an attic nor a basement and only a small outside storage enclosure that had a workbench and limited space for tools and lawn needs was a blessing because it was a necessity to weed out things you really didn't use or need. My work began in earnest as I went through everything in my home making hard decisions about what to keep and what to discard. What would be needed when I returned and set up housekeeping again. The storage areas in the upstairs now were scrutinized and emptied. Some items were placed in a container designated for a yard sale or storage. The Salvation Army became a frequented destination.

all systems go...

The news came from Terrace View and was an enthusiastic yes. I was wanted and welcome. The Session in their meetings had quite a discussion talking about how they would provide my room and board. The elders thought it would be great if different folks invited me to move in with them for a month enabling them to get to know me better. They were hoping that arrangement would be okay. My reply was positive. When I shared this with my pastor I laughed saying that maybe I won't have to do dishes I'll always be a guest. However, it didn't quite work out that way.

When I shared with Pastor Dick that I was selling my home he was concerned and called my pastor. Jim reassured him I was a very thoughtful person and had seriously considered this move. Now that the commitment on both ends was made, Dick shared with me that he had an extra car, a VW Rabbit and I would be available for my use.

It was time to contact a real estate agent. Making these major decisions alone I was finding both do-able and comfortable. The momentum was building.

farewells...

As the school year was ending in June the teachers threw me a farewell party complete with gifts. A footlocker was one that I still have as it traveled many miles with me before retiring to my present home. Everyone was excited with me.

During the summer months I made my circuit, first going down to North Carolina for a short visit with my son Jim and Denise. Then I headed north to Vermont and New Hampshire to say farewells to dear friends. Mom and Dad, siblings and their families all were visited. Sadly, Mom had a stroke the end of May and never recovered or returned home again. I don't think she was able to grasp what I was about to be doing.

Dan, my youngest, left home in August for seminary, to major in music in Kentucky. We were able to say our farewells at the Jersey Shore. The house had sold and the timing was perfect.

Summer had been packed full of goodbyes, pruning and packing. I was expecting this to be a once in a lifetime year of adventure and then return, buy a condo and try to be normal again.

On my last Sunday, the church gave me a special farewell. Jim had a commissioning service and I saved a copy that still thrills and challenges me. One question especially stands out:

> *"Ruth, will you allow yourself to be surprised by what God can do through you, surpassing your own hopes and expectations, and will you be open to the growth that God calls from you?"*

I have found myself pondering those prophetic words as I humbly found them to become a living reality. What a great God, I am in awe of how he has lead me and how he has poured out on me blessing upon blessing.

The moving van had come and taken the designated items that would be stored. The next morning I sat on my lone chair with my cup of coffee and reread John 21, a favorite of mine. In this passage Jesus asks Peter three times if he loves him and tells him to feed his sheep. Remember thinking, yes, I love you Lord more that anything. Use me. Yes, another one of those occasions, those "Kleenex moments". Some men came to take my bedroom furniture and a few items, that I donated to help support a local Cambodia ministry.

My son, John and his wife and baby had come to my now empty house for our last goodbye. We sat on the living room rug together saying our farewells to John's childhood home as well as to each other. My heart ached while I held the nine month old Kristen in my arms knowing what I would be missing out on. Talk about a tough one. Even now, I experience the pain and some tears.

Letting myself out of my home, I felt somewhat numb while

backing out of the driveway for this final time and driving to my friends, Bob and Ruth, where I would spend my last night. I was finding that it was necessary to feel the pain but also critical to focus on the adventure that awaited me. Of all crazy things, my pastor, also a committed Dodger fan and I were treated by folks in the church to go to see a baseball game featuring my favorite Dodgers playing the Mets. We had seats behind home plate. Our team won!

Early the next morning Jim drove me to JFK for my flight to Seattle. After arriving at the airport and hustling my footlocker and two large suitcases through the check-in process, we sat down for a last cup of coffee together. He looked at me with a big smile and said, " You're ready for this aren't you. I can see it in your eyes."

We hugged, I took a deep breath and then turned and proceeded down the long corridor looking for my gate. When I approached it, there was a woman in a wheelchair and I cringed, feeling guilty, thinking how can I leave my mother in her condition. But then my mind was filled with those challenging words that anyone who loves his mother or father more than me is not worthy of me. This was followed with a beautiful peace and a whisper to keep going.

You're where I want you to be.

Boarding the plane I found my window seat and fastened my seat belt ready for a flight that would greatly alter my life.

> This little female cardinal was
> about to embark on an adventure
> not knowing she would never be the same.

Cardinals are typically seen in pairs... this one was a single.
Cardinals don't live beyond the Rocky Mountains... this one was about to break the mold.

2

Terrace View '83

Genesis 12:1...Leave your country, your people and your father's household and go to the land I will show you.

This flight to Seattle would be the longest one I had ever experienced. Years before, I had flown to Minneapolis to attend a writers' conference at the Billy Graham Headquarters that stimulated an interest in writing. Also, I had been treated to two short flights in private planes. I admit to some nervousness about flying but not enough to keep me from loving it. Now I was flying west to a part of the country that had always attracted me. This was a lifetime dream being fulfilled. Having a window seat, I spent most of the flight with my face glued to it. I was impressed with our country's size and variety, spotting the Great Lakes, the flat expanses that seemed endless, and then the Rockies, awesome. At last the Cascades, Seattle, the Puget Sound, the large lakes that dotted the landscape. Wow, was I excited anticipating the adventures that awaited me !!

As promised, two women from the church were at my gate. One was to be my hostess for the first month. We squeezed my gear into a Honda Accord. Rather ironic since I had left mine behind to be sold by my son. My first glimpses of Seattle as we drove north on I-5 were a delight. Cities have always interested me and I eagerly anticipated exploring this one.

We arrived in Mount Lake Terrace and pulled in the driveway of the house that would be my first home. It was small, cozy and inviting. Alice had to have been handpicked by the Lord as I quickly discovered she was a committed Christian and a great support for me. She was a solid member of the church, respected by all and well acquainted with the people. She had found both a home in the church and a caring pastor. She appreciated his attention, cheerfulness, affirmation as well as his pop-in visits.

My room was her well stocked craft room. She was highly invested in the lovely creations she created. I slept on a pulled out couch, surrounded by a sea of stuff. After months of making difficult decisions, eliminating many possessions, simplifying my life this overabundance disturbed me and called for an adjustment on my part.

Being eager to meet people, I was pleased when Alice told me we were invited to dinner at the home of Larry and Georgie, active members of the church. The pastor, Dick and his wife, Christine were also present and it created a most comfortable introduction. Good vibes and pleasant conversation marked the evening. I sensed Georgie would become a special person in my life.

Terrace View was within walking distance. The area had an abundance of churches including several other Presbyterian ones. With so many to choose from, the result was small congregations.

I liked immediately the contemporary building with its open and inviting entrance. The sanctuary had windows that went from the ceiling to the floor and lined two of the walls making it light and airy. The view was pleasant, lots of green grass, trees, birds and even an occasional squirrel to entertain.

The church had a big capacity to love and to give, coupled with a willingness to risk and to be vulnerable. Both the pastor and the congregation were warm and welcoming. Often in later years when thinking back over my experiences it was obvious the Lord had called me to the most suitable place to launch me in ministry. When I was invited to come as a volunteer staff person, the people understood the relationship was one in which they could expect to receive, but also one they needed to take responsibility in giving of themselves to me. In the many churches that followed, this concept was never as fully grasped. There were always some folks that put into practice that two way giving and receiving.

Dick had told me on the phone that before I would be officially introduced I would be treated to a camping weekend at Tall Timbers. This would be an awesome trip in the Cascades. The ride was my first experience in the mountains and I found it thrilling. While our little car climbed up to the top of Steven's Pass, my eyes were popping as well as my ears. When we reached the summit, approximately five thousand feet, Alice pulled off the road so we could get out of the car and take in the grandeur. Standing there I was awed noting that there were mountains around us that soared even higher. The descent was lovely as the road followed alongside a rushing mountain stream. The tall straight pines reaching for the sky formed a lovely backdrop.

When we arrived at the campgrounds and started unloading our gear, I paused a moment overwhelmed with the camp's spectacular setting, it sat on a tableland complete with mountains soaring upward in all their splendor.

It was Family Camp, always held on Labor Day weekend and was a great way to meet many people from the church. I enjoyed singing around the campfire, eating delicious food and multiple opportunities to connect with people. One of the campers was a women who was going through a painful divorce. She and her kids had arrived later than the rest of us, but we began a conversation that led to a wonderful relationship. She became one I could count on in a wide variety of ways.

A definite highlight was a ten mile hike, a real workout. The walk created a new appreciation for me to the mountains. I felt a connection as I realized that was a reward that happens when you get out on the trail and experience firsthand the grandeur. The mountain becomes a part of you. Philip, one of the young teenage boys, stuck close to my side the whole hike. He was quite the chatterbox and quickly realized I had to keep trucking up and down the paths in order to get back to my cottage and end the "conversation."

The next day I was invited to go into Leavenworth just a few miles outside the campgrounds with a few of the gals. We poked around the charming shops enjoying the Bavarian flavor of the town. Observing people "having" to buy things they really didn't need, I felt dismayed. I had to acknowledge how although generally a thrifty person, there at times I had found myself buying not needed items. With this new challenge of a limited income, I would have to consider more carefully how and when to use my money.

the work begins...

Labor Day found everyone packing up and heading for home. Upon our return Alice headed for the beach in Edmonds, where the ferry comes in to dock from Kingston located on the Puget Sound. We munched on fish and chips while the sun went down behind the Olympics. I fell in love with that spot and couldn't tell you how many times I returned. My cup runneth over.

Tuesday, I met with Dick and we spent several hours together. I was more than eager to find out just what I would be doing. This was the first of many meetings where we shared, worked and planned together. Dick also presented me with the keys to a VW Rabbit that he was giving me to use while I was at the church.

Thursday we went to Synod offices in Seattle where I was

interviewed for their publication. Guess I was making news in my role as a Volunteer In Mission. Then it was time to wander down the hill, to explore the waterfront to my heart's delight while Dick spent his day in meetings. In my ignorance I kept looking for Mount Rainier not knowing it isn't visible from there. I spent a fascinating time people watching, struck with the rich variety, Scandinavians, Asian, Native Americans and some Eskimo. Hearing the Australian accents in some of the shops gave me a kick.

At that time the Alaskan ferry docked in Seattle and there were several Native Americans wandering around the area. The slump of their shoulders combined with a lost look made me wonder how staggering the big city must be to them. It made me curious... what their stories were... where in Alaska were they from... what brought them to Seattle.

I hopped the trolley that runs up and down the waterfront and the tall, good looking conductor put on a show. To the tune of "Sixteen Tons" he sang his own words complete with his Norwegian accent. He was quite the character. Another delight.

Dick and I met at our designated spot and he drove over to the locks that connect Lake Union with Elliott Bay. How fascinating it was watching some boats make their way through the locks. But viewing the salmon ladder and watching the determined fish struggle to climb it filled me with awe and respect for these creatures. I had seen my first salmon spawning in the stream at Tall Timber Camp. That had been a more peaceful experience for the salmon had reached their destination. The contrasting experience in both settings was something to witness. What an absolutely marvelous day in Seattle.

With the Cascades Mountains to the east and the Olympic Mountains west across the Puget Sound knowing what direction you were going was a breeze.

A few days later I drove to Edmonds and treated myself to a ferry ride in the lovely evening. When the ferry pushed away from the dock and moved out into the Sound my eyes and mouth opened wide as I got my first look at the snowcapped Mount Rainier. She was "out" in all her glory. What a sight, the mount is so massive even from that distance. Talk about overwhelmed, awed, speechless I was all of those and more. It was an instant love affair that continues to this day.

At one of our early meetings, Dick asked was if I would be comfortable visiting people in the congregation. Per usual, I said that it would be fine, not letting on I was shaking in my boots. And so a visiting ministry was launched which proved to be most interesting and challenging, demanding a significant piece of my energy. Anyone on the church list was fair game. When walking up the path feeling nervous and shaky, to knock on the door of a person who was just a name to me, it didn't take me long to realize that yes, I can do this! How special it was to visit folks in their own home. One gains much insight into the person and a bond quickly forms.

What a rich diverse group, I found. Some were active and others hadn't darkened the church doors for years. I began to pick up various facets of how Dick was seen by his flock. In the mix of what I was hearing, there were some reoccurring themes. He was certainly liked and was always there when people were in difficulty. There where both positive and negatives comments which made me wonder what was I do with this information. All were curious about me and I found my interest in what they were all about, growing. Along with much information about who they were, I began to hear more and more about Alaska. The stories stirred my heart and made me wonder... was this a beginning, the early stages of a call, a mission. A vague longing and curiosity was brewing...

School had begun and for the first time in my life I wasn't a student, a mom or a teacher. I was experiencing a freedom in my routines and delighting in some unstructured time enabling me to drive down to the beach in Edmonds, walk and soak up the beauty of the Puget Sound and the Olympic Mountains. Nevertheless, even though I wasn't confined to a classroom I sensed in many ways I was still a teacher. The challenge was to get connected with folks, listen to their heart cry and stimulate new growth. That was familiar territory, a task I savored immensely.

I sensed it would be of value to seek out a confidant, someone who was not in the community and one I could share openly my joys along with my concerns and frustrations. Fortunately, in a multistaff church in north Seattle when I called and shared my need the church receptionist directed me to Pastor Wes who filled that void for me.

Dick was always alert to including me in on most of his activities expanding my insights and understanding. He took me to "Impact". This was a group of mainline pastors that met weekly, brown bagging it and sharing their "stuff" with each other, a mutual support system. There were weeks when I would shake my head in disbelief and check with the Lord asking did he really want me there. Often I was the only woman and usually the only evangelical. I had my foot in two worlds and was challenged as they described what they felt was an arrogance in fundamental churches in their claim that they were the only churches that preached the gospel. It was confusing to them as they acknowledged that those churches seemed to be the ones that were growing but were somewhat perplexed as to the reasons why their congregations were stagnant. In a few one-on- one conversations I found satisfying, some genuine dialogue pertaining to the different perspectives. I would have welcomed more opportunities.

One of my first ventures was to started up a morning exercise group. I had purchased an exercise video that we all enjoyed.

This was followed with a Bible study with the women. This was met with great enthusiasm as connections and friendships were beginning. Later, I initiated a women's evening group using the "Edge of Adventure Series", featuring Bruce Larson and Keith Miller. On the tapes the authors spoke candidly about their faith experiences which created a safe place to begin genuine conversation. In my Connecticut church I had been part of a small group that used this series. Fortunately I was able to borrow the somewhat costly series of tapes, materials and books from the nearby University Presbyterian Church in Seattle. This was a bonus for a small church with a limited budget.

The first Session (this is the governing body in Presbyterian churches) meeting was intriguing. We shared a meal upon arrival affording opportunity for social exchange before the meeting began. My strongest memory of the event was observing the frustration and stress of the clerk. Her duties were to record items discussed as well as motions voted on. I couldn't help but wonder whether she was in the wrong place. I questioned Alice about her when I got home. She chuckled and reassured me that I would find the clerk to be more than capable as well as a lot of fun. Both were definitely true.

The vibes were positive and I felt very welcomed. We shared a common curiosity about what this adventure would involve.

We all had stepped out on a limb, taking a risk on each other.

Sunday morning service Dick usually had me involved. The children's message came naturally for me and I was pleasantly surprised with lots of positive feedback from the adults. I often read the scripture and led in prayer.

a dream is fulfilled...

Being an ocean lover, I had always hoped some day to see the Pacific. In my dreams I wanted to especially experience the Northwest coast. If there was time and money, California would also attract me but Washington or Oregon was to be first. September 22nd, my youngest son's birthday was to be the day I would embark on a trip that would fulfill that desire.

I drove south to Olympia and then turned west toward the coast. My route took me through Hoquiam, a locale I had first applied to only to be told they weren't seeking a volunteer anymore. I couldn't help but feel gratitude again for a God who was surely directing my path as I sensed that would have been a very difficult place due to the isolation and huge amounts of rainfall.

Continuing my westward drive I soon caught my first glimpse of the Pacific. I quickly stopped to walk out on the beach at Ocean City, taking it all in and filled again with thanksgiving and wonder of what God was giving me. Continuing north up the coast, I stopped at Moclips and found a modest motel right on the beach. Being off season, there was no difficulty getting a room complete with windows facing the water. Quickly, I plopped my luggage in my room and made my way to the beach. When I began to walk on what appeared to be an endless stretch of sand, I spotted a perfect sand dollar. It didn't take long to discover that Moclips is "sand dollar heaven" and people could pick up as many as their heart desired.

Returning to my room and settling in, I enjoyed the view while sitting on my bed. I decided to splurge and treat myself to dinner at Ocean Crest, a well known restaurant that sits on a bluff overlooking the beach and ocean, complete with a full view of the setting sun. I found myself thinking how special this would be to share the experience with a special man. The little girl in me was often wondering and looking for that knight in shining armor who would ride up on his white horse and sweep me off my feet. It was now more than ten years of being single. After indulging myself in this fantasy, I took a deep breath and set that aside, focusing on the lovely spectacular view and absolutely delicious salmon dinner. Thankfully, I was able to receive the blessing of knowing my Lord was not only present, but was more than pleased about where I was in my life and that was comforting.

I enjoyed two nights and did some exploring of the immediate area. When I drove to nearby Taholah, a Quinault Reservation, I was stunned, never anticipating what I saw. Junk, trash, discarded appliances, cars marked the area. Here the tribe sat located on an absolutely beautiful ocean front but it appeared that they took no pleasure or pride in the natural beauty of their setting. Poor, shabby, depressed homes with yards that were in need of major cleaning up and repair. There was nothing that reflected their rich culture only the trash of ours. What a stark contrast of Native owned property. The one, Ocean Crest was of the highest quality while the other filled me with a deep sorrow. I came away digesting the two extremes in my first exposure to the coastal tribes.

Next phase of my adventure took me up the coast through a long section of towering trees lining the roadside. Felt like I was in a cathedral as they stretched upward to the Lord and found myself deeply moved by their quiet splendor as they focused my thoughts on my Creator, my God.

In Washington, while driving north along the coast there are long stretches where Route 101 takes you inland as you proceed around Indian Reservations. When the road opens up again you are treated to long views of the beaches dotted with a wide variety of rock formations that are named sea stacks. There are places where between the highway and the beach there are lots of trees so you find yourself peeking through the forest to view the water... so many treats for this east coast girl to discover. What a completely different coastline.

Back in the car, my little Rabbit, I was finding that the

road was turning east a little and away from the water. I drove through the small town of Forks and followed the signs to La Push. Alice had mentioned this beach and how lovely it was. When I entered the Quileyute Reservation once again I found myself deeply saddened by the village and a developing concern in my heart about these people.

I parked the car, just outside the village and followed the signs that directed me to Beach 2. Proceeding up the path through the forest I found myself more and more intimidated by the signs warning me about the safety of my car. Probably the impact of the adventure, going into new territory on my own for a few days and the not knowing of what the return trip would entail, all factored in to my turning around and heading back to the car. Little did I realize that the beach would be come one of my all time favorites.

Now I headed east, the return side of going around the peninsula. The rugged mountains seemed to be all around me and soon I was delighted when just ahead I spotted a crystal clear lake, Lake Crescent that extended for miles. I was smitten with its beauty and relished the treat of driving the curvy road that kept part of the lake hidden.

Port Angeles was the first city I came to. Needing to make a stop, I parked at the waterfront and viewed the docked cargo ships and some Coast Guard boats. They looked like giants sitting there in the water. Back on the road, the next "city" was Sequim. I had noticed signs telling about the Dungeness Spit and wondered about that, but I drove through the small town with one, maybe two traffic lights continuing on.

Highway 101 continued for a while and then I left it and headed to Kingston and the ferry, which would take me back to the mainland. Another special place awaited me first and that was the Hood Canal Floating Bridge. What a fantastic view as

I drove across the bridge while seeing the San Juan Islands off in the distance .

My way home from the ferry was easy now, I was well acquainted with how to do that. Alice warmly welcomed me and asked me if I had gotten to La Push and what did I think? "Wasn't it gorgeous?" My reaction was how sad it made me to see how poor the Indians were. I was weary, drained and emotional about the whole excursion and was totally taken back by her reply. Growing up in the Dakotas, she nurtured a strong bias against Native Americans. She had been exposed to much negative behavior, such as drunkenness and laziness. It wasn't easy to swallow hard and really listen to a totally different point of view, but I gained great insight into the American dilemma.

intro to projects...

The fall season progressed and more and more boxes of dry goods lined first the hallway and then extended into the sanctuary. The main storage area was located in the basement of an adjacent home that sat on the corner. The Food Bank was an integral part of the church. It was Dick's baby, his pride and joy. It was housed at Terrace View and serviced the other churches in south Snohomish County. He was the in-charge man for the operation. The pastors cooperated with each other in keeping tabs of people seeking help/handouts. Dick opened my eyes that there were some who liked to work the system, so I was not to ever give money, a voucher system was in use. Also, he cautioned me to avoid people knocking on the church door when alone in the building.

There were an impressive team of volunteers, many from Terrace View and some from the surrounding churches. They put in hours of service behind the scenes as well as those upfront on Food Bank morning. I never quite got used to seeing people lining up on Tuesdays waiting for the doors to open. I spent time during my two years at Terrace engaging waiting folks in conversation. There was an almost desperate need to tell someone why they were seeking food and I soon learned that most had a legitimate sad story. Jobs, food, homes can and are lost, sometimes in a twinkling of an eye. This led me to appreciate more, how much I had to be thankful for and realized one should never take anything for granted.

One of the Food Bank volunteers, Dolores invited me to dinner at her house. Later on, I stayed with her and Philip, sharing many good times together. She originally was from the east coast and told of a time she brought a salmon home in her suitcase to treat her dad. Unfortunately, her bag was delayed and when delivered the next day the fish was no longer a treat. The fish had made its presence known with its odor permeating all her belongings.

A particular incident of a Food Bank morning stands out for me. It was a cold and chilly day and folks were lining up anxiously waiting to see the doors open. A man came to the door urgently asking to use the men's room and was let in. He took care of his needs and rejoined the line. Another person went to use the rest room and came out gagging telling us some one had vomited all over the floor. Out of nowhere it seemed, Dick appeared and ran down the hall getting a mop and bucket to clean up the mess. That impressed me for it clearly demonstrated that servant quality in this pastor. He could have easily requested one of the volunteers, instead he chose to take care of it himself. In our times together, I was learning to appreciate that Dick's keen interest in social issues was the real thing. God had equipped and called him to that. We both were cultivating a deep respect for each other.

Another project Dick was deeply involved with was the Synod Self Development Committee. Presbyterian Church USA is divided up geographically into synods and presbyteries. Several presbyteries make up a synod and the one we were located in was Pacific Northwest which included Alaska. This Synod was the largest in area due to the spareness of churches.

My heart resonates with the concept of encouraging people to be independent, seeking to improve themselves with creating a job or project that with a little outside support might prove to be of worth. I looked forward to the meetings when the committee would examine the different projects people were hoping to start. We often traveled to interview first hand these folks. That led to many interesting experiences. One of the criteria was that the project was required to become self sufficient within a year or two dated from it startup to qualify for funding.

some unique experiences...

Early in the Fall, Dick took me out to Neah Bay, a Makah Reservation on business. We visited the tiny church enjoying a pleasant conversation the pastor and his wife. The small fishing village was similar to what I had observed in the other native coastal villages. My reaction again was of sadness and heavy heartedness.

Next we went out to Cape Flattery. It boasts as being the farthest northwest point in the lower forty-eight states. We tramped through a bit of the rain forest in order to reach it. On a rock we stood looking out at the Pacific to the west and to the north the starting point of the Strait of Juan de Fuca. Awesome!

My interest in the native people was intensifying and I was hungry for more information. Dick shared with the minister who was the head of a presbytery committee on native affairs. This led to an invitation to join a group that was going to Neah Bay to celebrate the church's anniversary. One of my unforgettables!

A marvelous spread was served, a delicious salmon dinner with all the trimmings.

The next morning the oldest elder, a honored and revered leader in the church and community, met us at the door of the Makah Museum. She was a small lady probably one you wouldn't even notice. She unlocked the door and welcomed us in. Then she turned to the wall removing a tom-tom. When she began beating it, chills ran up and down my spine and for the next hour the entire group's attention was riveted on her every word. We proceeded to follow her as she walked us through the museum telling the stories of her people. Believe me, I stayed glued to her side not wanting to miss a word. No way could anyone miss the pride she had for her people and her heritage.

In November, Dick and I in the Sunday service gave a dialogue on stewardship. I didn't dream at the time, that this would lead to my doing sermons. The preparation process was particularly stimulating, starting with deciding what God was calling me to say, next studying the scriptures and then developing the message. The combination of being scared, but exhilarated and deeply blessed in presenting the message to the congregation was a treasure. Dick and I did a lot of brainstorming as we prepared our joint venture. I found that a most useful tool in working out a message, implementing that technique on repeated occasions. When we presented the dialogue it came across as being spontaneous and people enjoyed it in addition to being challenged.

The Presbytery, that fall had hired a woman minister, a native of the Philippines to be a liaison between the tribes and the church.

The committee felt she would be more readily accepted by coastal natives due to her background and even her appearance. The two of us became buddies and she took me along on some of her visits. Early in December we drove north to the Tulalip

Reservation near La Connor to attend their annual Candlelight Ceremony. The tribes in western Washington and British Columbia are small so many joined together for this event.

After feasting on more salmon, fry bread and other Native treats, we found seats in the bleachers. The gym floor was cleared and covered with a huge blue tarp. Two long tables were set up and placed at one end. The only other white face in the crowd besides me were two Catholic priests that served in this community and were participating in the ceremony.

Many of the men from the tribe had painted their faces to look like black masks. Two men from the tribe solemnly read a long list of those who had died during the year. When a name was read a family member would come to light a candle in their honor. The priests stepped forward and one explained the significance of the ceremony. The fire represented the love in our hearts for our departed ones. The priests then circled the bleachers sprinkling water that represented the baptism we all have experienced and we all will have when we pass on. The priest then spoke passionately of his own brother who had died that year. He shared the great emptiness in his heart and knew the ceremony would help to fill the void. Then the more than seventy candles were extinguished and removed as well as the tables.

The grieving priest then let out a wail and the men started to pound on the tom-toms. He then proceeded to move the entire length of the floor crying out in agony while he danced. His countenance and movements all demonstrated his deep grief. When he completed the circle some men grabbed him assisting him to a seat. This was followed as one by one other deceased members honored a family member and would step out and begin to dance. While circling the bleachers other family members would join.

The evening progressed and I found myself responding to

the beating of the tom-toms. What started out as a keen interest gradually grabbed hold of me emotionally. I was strangely and deeply moved. The ceremony marked the end of the grief and a time now to celebrate the future. I think of my culture and ponder how little we understand the grieving process. I've found people who stay stuck in their grief. Suspect we have many things, we could glean from our brothers... the place of community... that oneness with each other, the knowing of someone coming along side being there for you... the strength and comfort that brings. The ceremony continued for a few hours and when we slipped away, both Thelma and I were exhausted emotionally. Another unforgettable experience, one I feel privileged to have been a part of.

back home...

Mother's health was failing. Early in December I received a phone call from my dad asking me to come home. My home church had given me a plane ticket to come visit at Christmas, but he felt her death was imminent. Heavy hearted I traveled home uncertain what I would find. Mom looked frail, so extremely weak. It was painful to see her like this how unlike the vital woman she had been. I couldn't help wonder if she even was aware of my visit. At least, I was certain my presence brought some comfort to Dad.

As planned, I returned again for the holidays and on Christmas Eve found myself with Mom and Dad in an emergency room. The hospital was full and mom was placed on a bed in a hallway in the ER area. That was painful for us, especially Dad. He was so dejected and sorrowful as we stood by her bedside. It didn't feel like Christmas to either one of us.

A few days later I was able to celebrate with my sons and family. Of course being with my only grandchild, who was now thirteen months, was a delight that provided more than enough holiday joy.

Mom died in January and when I received the news from my sister I remember thinking my mom is beautiful again. It had been so painful to witness the dramatic differences in her appearance. For financial reasons mostly, I did not go home. Folks at the church were caring, but I learned that an important part when a dear one dies is to be with people that knew and loved that person. The telling of stories all helps dealing with the grief and aid in the healing process.

Questions, wonderings were churning and questions emerged... What about next year... Should I return home to teaching and settle into a new place? There was a growing sense that my call to ministry wasn't done yet. During the early weeks and months there were many thoughts of how absolutely satisfying I was finding this experience. The numerous adventures, the personal growth as I discovered strengths and weaknesses. Was this to be a one year hiatus or should I consider staying for a second year. Would Dick or the church even welcome that?

Also back home, I didn't have a clue whether I could get a second year leave of absence for my teaching position. Obviously there was lots of conversation with my Heavenly Father. Show me Lord what do you want... where do you want me to be... While home at Christmas, I stopped in to visit the superintendent of schools to run my thoughts of a second year by him. He was supportive of my desire, but wasn't sure if he could sell it to the Board of Education. Next I needed to know what Dick would think. I did not want to mention anything to people in the church until we discussed it first.

what a house...

Meanwhile Linda had approached me asking if I would be interested in house-sitting. My first reaction was no. Living with people had proven to be a vital piece of my ministry and felt I shouldn't stray from that. She proceeded to explain that the doctor she worked for, lived in Edmonds overlooking the Puget Sound. He and his wife always went to Mexico for three weeks in February and would be very pleased to have someone in their home. I was about to turn her down when I felt one of those Holy Spirit nudges and whisper telling me, "HELLO, I have something very special for you. Don't blow it!"

Thankfully, I listened and come February moved into an unforgettable home. The couple invited me over to show me around prior to their leaving. Their home was lovely and I felt like maybe this was a dream, it was so unreal. The kitchen was inviting. The lady of the house was short like me and being a person who loved to cook, ordered counters that were lower than normal and comfortable. She had a fascinating array of cook books to browse through. The family area was open to the kitchen complete with fireplace, TV and very inviting couch and chairs.

The dining room was elegant with a crystal chandler hanging over the massive table. While dining, you were treated to an incredible view. The house sat on the hill in Edmonds facing the Olympic Mountains and the Puget Sound and in the evening while the sun was setting behind the mountains the sky was painted with spectacular hues of red and pink.

I loved watching the ferry going to and fro to Kingston as well as delighting in the occasional train that runs along the Edmond's waterfront. Hearing that train whistle evoked memories of college days when I had commuted. I remember those giant steam engines that pulled into the train station belching smoke. Unforgettable. That melancholy sound stirred some homesickness in me.

Having my "own" home provided me with a great place to entertain as well as host committee meetings. What a delight to share this fabulous treat. How thankful I still am, so glad I learned to listen.

One evening, I invited Dick and Christine to dinner. When we sat down to eat he was about to ask the blessing when we all burst out laughing over how outlandish this was for us to be seated at this elegant table. I had already talked with Dick about a second year and after his initial surprise he enthusiastically took it to Session.

One day, while I was sitting on the couch looking out the windows at my incredible view I jotted down some reflections about this house sitting experience.

House sitting........at the Shaws

Hey, little girl... my but you are having a good time playing house

How much fun to actually live out a fantasy, a dream with substance, not just an exercise of your imagination.

What in the world are you doing in that ridiculous bed. King-sized with all kinds of push buttons for the electric blanket and TV.

How absurd your closet is more spacious than some of the rooms you've lived in.

And the kitchen,, you've used both ovens plus microwave to prepare your company dinner.

The appliances are like yours were and feel like old comfortable friends. How good that feels.

The dining room .. unreal, the chandelier, the glass walls, the huge table, with the lovely linen tablecloth, elegance for sure.

My favorite spot is the family room due to its comfy coziness. It feels like home , sitting on the couch feet up of course an looking out at all that space. The sound that goes across to the peninsula and then joins the Strait of Juan De Fuca out to Neah Bay and the Pacific.

*The Olympics, that play hide and seek, showing off their
majestic beauty*

*The evening sky at sunset with all each shades of pinks and
red. What a vesper service , dear Lord , I love your
handiwork.*

*Hey, little girl, what are you doing in the lap of luxury? VIMs
are expected to experience a subsistence life style.*

*Dear Father, I see the twinkle in your eye. How like you to
bless me with delights, treats, surprises.*

*And when night falls and I view the twinkling lights below
and relish the crackling fire that warms me, I also am
keenly aware of the warmth of your great love.*

This was a day off, my day to savor. Blessed with solitude
and privacy I was experiencing a void, an emptiness, a feeling
of not really belonging even though I was so deeply invested.
At times I attempted to fill the void or to plug up the rush of
feelings. Other times I would deny them, stuffing them, a bad
habit of mine and one I needed to eliminate. There were times
of sorrow of missing home and family. Times of longing for
a mate someone to love and who would love me. Was all this
really worthwhile? I'm grateful when in those quiet times the
Lord drew me near and quieted me making me secure again in
his love.   I was beginning to appreciate those quiet alone times
during those long waiting ten years. I had learned how precious
they could be.

more challenges...

There was a new thought stirring around in me, something
needing to be expressed. This unique volunteering experience that
was stretching and molding me in new ways. When sharing this
with Dick I was able to identify my need to share these insights
in a sermon. The whole experience of learning to receive needed
to be told. He was per usual, supportive and for the first time in

my life I was in the pulpit. Believe me this gal never expected such a privilege. My message was that learning to receive wasn't easy. One has to relinquish control and humbly accept what is being offered. Giving had always been a joy for me, but I was discovering that one robs others of that joy when we hinder their giving to us. Read somewhere that grace is something you can never get, but only be given. You can't work for it or earn it, you need to receive it.

I also continued to learn how essential it was to be open to each situation. When feeling homesick, I found if I dwelled on what was missing instead of receiving what was offered, the pain intensified. I learned that when I appreciated and savored the many blessings God provided, it became possible to handle the sadness and maintain a heathy balance.

Lots of precious memories flood my mind and heart now as I recall dear folks that enriched my time at Terrace View. Moving in with folks is a quick way of becoming family. Listening to their stories and sharing your own is such a blessing. One of my homes was with an older couple that had a large family, all grown up and out on their own. Bill played the piano, but was hesitant to play if he thought someone was listening. I discovered that if I slipped into the house and went quietly downstairs to my room I enjoyed the treat of hearing him play. He was such a loving man and often shared his concern about my being so far removed from my family. He found it difficult to understand that that was all right for them and me because God had called me to this place.

One of my early homes had been with the Gibsons. Dick and Christine took a trip back East for part of the month. I stayed with the kids, all teenagers at the time. Barb, the middle child was talented with numbers and finances. Her older brother when short of cash would come to her and ask if he could borrow some money. She was always willing and also ready to charge interest on the loan. Smart gal! Living in that house was always lively, never dull.

Each month I experienced moving into a new home. I found the variety challenging and delightful. I quickly adapted to the new environment and learned to absorb the uniqueness of my new domain. Usually it only took me my first overnight, morning shower and coffee and I was settled in. Never learned to like the leaving and at first I wanted to find the perfect gift to honor my "home givers". When I looked at my finances, I quickly realized that would not work on my very limited income. While browsing through a Christian book store, I spotted some inexpensive magnets and was delighted to be able to leave behind a thank you. It was fun when visiting later on to see "my magnet" prominently displayed on the "frig".

Dottie, when she found out I loved to walk, took me out to many different places for good vigorous workouts. If anyone takes a walk of any length in the Seattle area they will find yourself going up and down many hills. I quickly learned to let her talk when we were on the upward climb. One early chilly morning, Dottie took me to the zoo for our walk. Noticing the animals waking up, flexing their muscles preparing themselves to begin the new day. There were very few visitors at that early hour, just staff beginning their daily chores. That added to my pleasure and made the whole experience special.

Many people in the church treated me to a wide variety of events. Loved my first opera, ballet and listening to the symphony. A group of us went to an Andy William's Concert. I was delighted with seeing a performance of the Nutcracker. Felt like a little girl again as I got caught up in the magic of the story. At intermission I got a kick out of seeing little girls all dressed up in their velvet dresses, white stocking and black patented leather shoes.

Two different people whom I had lived with, had a Catholic

background. In talking with them they expressed they felt a void attending a protestant church. It had been difficult to leave the church they had grown up in. They felt the need to go to Mass and chose to go Saturday nights, freeing them to attend with the family, Terrace View on Sunday mornings. I definitely was experiencing growth in accepting a variety of Christians. I don't think God ever intended to pour us into static molds.

In May I indulged in another adventure that took be into Canada to visit Vancouver. I made the trip on my own and stayed at a Seminary where Dick made arrangements for me to have a room. My visit coincided with Queen Victoria Day and when I walked up the steps and knocked on the massive door I felt just a little intimidated.

The door opened slowly and I was faced with a most grim person who invited me into a large empty hallway. She led me down the hall to the elevator. Each of our footsteps echoed creating an eerie feeling and I wondered if there was any one else around. She showed me to my room, handed me a key and gave some instructions and then hurriedly left me to check out my room. It was rather austere with a single bed a desk and a chair. When I checked the view I had to climb up on the chair to see out the window.

After getting back into the car I drove to Stanley Park and was delighted when I spotted some men garbed in white, complete with knickers engaged in a cricket match. How British is that! Later I located a zoo and other attractions. I love the picturesque city with its cosmopolitan atmosphere finding many delightful places, particularly Granville Island and the market there and Oil Town.

California, here I come...

My first summer was approaching rapidly and in talks with Dick it was decided that I could take the summer off.

Church programs typically take a vacation along with the folks in the congregation. I was eager to spend part of it in ministry somewhere. He suggested that I might like the challenge of volunteering at the Watts Community Center. He knew the director and would call her and find out if there were possibilities. That intrigued me and so a most unique opportunity unfolded, one that put me in Los Angeles the summer of '84.

The plane was descending, preparing to land at LAX. My instructions were that I would be met by someone from the Community House. This whole experience was rather intimidating since I was about to be submerged in a different culture, I would be serving in Watts. For me that name was synonymous with riots. What was I doing here? Lord, guess I need to trust and not be afraid.

Quickly I connected with my driver who escorted me to the center and then onto my home in Compton. Little did I realize that during the next month the only white face I would see would be when brushing my teeth or when I got to do some touristy things.

July of '84 was an eventful month In Los Angeles. The summer Olympics preparations were in process. My driver had shared his great concern that the "brothers" might cause problems and bring shame down on the Black community. Another source of pride and excitement was the anticipation of Jesse Jackson's appearance at the upcoming Democratic Convention as a presidential nominee .

I quickly discovered the LA area to be different from what I was used to in the northeast. The Black area was vast and totally segregated. After the riots I was told, all "whites" moved out of the area creating the probability that a kid growing up would only see black faces in business places, medical facilities etc. Their only exposure to other races would be in the classroom and there the turnover of teachers was high.

My home was in Compton, a city next to LA. My hostess told me her home was in a stable and safe neighborhood. Folks had lived there and owned their home for twenty years or more. Inez was a fascinating person and knew a wide variety of people. She would take me out in her little low slung car and do "popcorn" visits. We popped in on the mayor and were greeted at the door by an Asian maid. We also went up to visit her relatives in Baldwin Hills. They had a lovely home overlooking the city. A baby grand piano graced the living room as well as some lovely art pieces. Out on the patio was an in-ground pool. Typically, I found in our visits that it was assumed that because I was white I was well educated and well to do. I definitely felt outclassed as they were talking about trips to various places that I had never dreamed of.

First day at the community house, sitting in a large gym, I found myself looking out at a sea of young kids wondering how will I connect... my white face... my age... my background. My life had been so different. Never had I experienced what these children were living. Will my whiteness get in the way, not only with the campers, but with the staff? My role was to be part of a team of counselors to day camp kids. I found myself leading a group of fifth and sixth grades girls. When all the children were assembled I found there was too much lecturing, too many rules and regulations. Boys and girls needed activity, action and fun. I always liked to get to know the kids, show an interest in them while sharing something about myself. This worked for me as my style of discipline came out of love and respect not hollering and threatening.

There were weekly trips as part of the program and the first one was to a market place in China Town. We had spent only a day or two with our group when we were sent off on public transportation to our destination. I wasn't even sure of everyone in my group and here we were riding on buses to an unfamiliar place. Fortunately we never lost anyone.

Our trip to Knott's Berry Farm, we had a charter bus. As we disembarked, when people saw me they assumed I was the leader. After all, I was the only white and I suppose my age was a factor. This assumption was also true when we walked the kids daily to a park and a swimming pool, where they had bag lunches to eat. I would always defer to the person in charge. The park was a place where lots of druggies hung out. Fortunately it seemed they seemed to fade from the scene when we made our appearance.

On one of those days, I had to leave early and the head of the day camp walked with my group, back to the center. She engaged one of my girls in conversation and was told that she didn't think she was going to like me, but she did. Her reason was not racial it was because I had been a school teacher. Obviously and thankfully the kids didn't see color.

A person I was forever impressed by was a tall, slender, elegant lady who ran the whole operation. She and her husband made a handsome couple. He was in charge of the landscaping and lovingly oversaw the care of the grounds and building. Grace had a presence that you felt when she entered a room. What a powerful role she played in soliciting support for the organization.

While in LA, I was able to take in the sights. What a time I had going to Disneyland. My hostess dropped me off at a hotel where I hopped a special bus. I had never been before and was thrilled. Being alone was no problem, people in that setting are very quick to chat and it feels like no one is a stranger. After taking in the sights, I tuned into all the special music that dotted the landscape. I was excited to see Duke Ellington perform.

On a weekend, I rented a car and did some exploring driving south to spend a few hours in San Diego. Surprisingly while strolling along the harbor, I was invited to take an evening harbor cruise with a church group. One of those, "being at the right place at the right time" happenings. I was strolling along the sidewalk where the boat was docked when a man in charge invited me to join the group, there was room. Our God is a God of surprises. The next day, I drove north up the coast to Solvang and spent the night in a motel in a rundown area in a ground level room. The window was right on the street and would have made easy access for anyone. It certainly was not a good place to be but I'm thankful for the Lord's protection.

There was no way I could be in Los Angeles and not go to a baseball game. Once again my hostess was more that willing to get me to one. She knew of a Dodger bus that people can pick up in a certain section of the city. Inez dropped me off at the bus stop and told me she would listen to the game and time her meeting me at the same stop. The bus was a blast with folks arrayed in Dodger paraphernalia. One senior lady was dressed in a satin outfit of Dodger blue. She could name all the players and it seemed she knew most of the folks on the bus.

It was great to see Orel Hershiser pitch and see my team win. I wove my way through the crowd and boarded the packed bus. When we approached the bus stop the driver was concerned and didn't want to let me off there. I had no choice because that was my predesignated "pick up" spot. A few people got off with me and proceeded hurriedly to their destinations, while I walked purposely behind them until they turned down a street. What had been a non-threatening place in the afternoon now was deserted. What a relief as I nervously paced when I spotted the car. Inez pulled along side the curb and threw open the door. Relieved I jumped into the seat and sat on something very hard. It was her weapon of choice, a hammer just in case. She was always willing to take me and bring me home anytime, anywhere. My adventures were stretching and always rewarding.

Growing up, I always had a special sensitivity for Blacks. Martin Luther King is one of my heroes. I've had the privilege of conducting Bible Clubs in a project in Danbury. I used to take turns bringing some of the kids home for supper. Boston was next and now this time in L.A. I'm thankful for those opportunities and that the Lord used me to bring his love and joy to this part of the family of God.

After my busy year followed by the month in LA, I was more than eager to spend the month of August back East. It felt good to make the usual rounds of family and friends. It was also a time of renewal preparing me for my second year. The school board surprisingly granted a second year leave of absence, keeping my position on hold another year.

my second year...

Upon my returned to Mount Lake Terrace, it felt comfortable slipping back into my role at the church after enjoying a second weekend at Tall Timbers. Dick had recently gone to a Sequim on a retreat for the current leaders of the Presbytery. He enthusiastically told me about the folks that hosted the group. Bob had taken early retirement and he and his wife, Ruth had moved to the Olympic Peninsula. They built a lovely dome-shaped house with a spacious kitchen open to the dining area. The entire west side was glass providing a spectacular view of the Olympic Mountains. They also built two guest cottages, each with a small living room complete with a motel size frig and a two burner stove, along with four bedrooms and two baths. They had shared their story with Dick how they felt God called them to develop a hospitality ministry where groups or individuals could come and stay for a variety of reasons, meetings retreats, study R&R etc. Delicious home-made meals were served in the Dome and everyone shared in the feast around the massive table.

This sounded to me like it would be an ideal place to combine a time in Sequim while accepting an invitation to go to Port Townsend to give a short talk on my volunteering experiences in the Sunday Worship. The two places were about forty-five minutes from each other. Dick encouraged me to take a few days off and enjoy a four day weekend. What a treat meeting the Barnes. Both Bob and Ruth were good listeners and loving people. They were keenly interested in what I was doing and I sensed a start to a new friendship.

While the busy weeks progressed toward Christmas, the realization that a major decision about my future would have to be made. But first I had a wedding to attend. Jim, my middle son was getting married in Salt Lake City and of course I was looking forward to that. It was a great introduction to Denise's family as her parents had me stay in their home. I really didn't know my new daughter-in-law but I picked up sweet insights as I observed her interaction with the multiple family members present. Her dad, a gracious host, took me up to see a ski lodge in the mountains and later to tour the extensive Mormon complex.

Tough time, back at Mount Lake Terrace, since the new year began with me wondering about my future. On one of my visits with Wes, my "personal pastor" I had shared a concern as to how I would know when it was the right time to leave. His reply was that God would give me a release. If I was honest with myself there was a sense of that. It was time to go and step out into the unknown and struggle through the wanting to stay. I had sent off several applications with no responses. Nothing was happening. Dick was involved in calling some of the places I had applied to with no success. All this tension had me wondering if I was supposed to go home to Connecticut and return to teaching. That thought was quickly rejected as I knew that didn't fit anymore. I couldn't be "normal" again. My friends when sharing this with them retorted "Ruth, when were you normal?" With friends like that...

My ministry continued while these decisions were processed. This year I started up an evening group of men and women. There were sixteen of us. Also, Dick and I working together planned and with the support and energy of an enthusiastic committee held an intergenerational church retreat. It was a Saturday event complete with a candlelight dinner and concluded with the Sunday morning service with communion. Many responded with positives comments and felt enriched. More "togetherness" was manifested.

Folks at the church, were urging me not to go.. we need you here. While I struggled with my decision I was impressed with the following thoughts. Staying on would only create dependency in the church. My calling was to stimulate involvement and equip people to step up, assume responsibilities, carry on the programs they were enthused about. There must be other churches that needed an infusion of energy. The Lord was calling me on. But where?? I had sent out my offers to serve but still had received no responses.

In March, a small group of us went out to Sequim for a women's retreat. This was a special time of being together in the warmth of the Barnes and a precious time of spiritual growth. After the retreat was over, a few of us stayed an extra night and at breakfast Bob asked what were my plans for the future. I shared they were unknown at the time. He asked if I would be open in coming to Sequim and with no hesitation, a big YES came out of my mouth.

After breakfast my friends and I headed to take a last walk at the Spit. When we returned, Bob came bounding out of the Dome telling me, as we climbed out of the car, that he had talked to the pastor and he was very interested. Of course, all those closed doors now made sense. This was where God wanted me.

How little did I realize how incredibly special this place would become for me.

the leaving process...

And now I was heavy into the leaving. Striving to prepare leaders I guided people into positions, sharing the responsibilities and then backing off letting them step up and assume the challenge. I felt this was essential for them and the church as a whole.

During this stretch, I soon realized that when leaving I would not lose what I had received from these people and this experience. This now was an everlasting part of me. Wherever God called me, he would provide for my every need. There would be more intimate connections, tender moments, love and hugs. He would provide the nourishment. He would have more challenges, new avenues that would cause personal growth.

During my two years at Terrace View I kept in touch with my church back in Connecticut via the U.S. Mail. Invariably it seemed the body of the letter would be directed to the general audience and then I would before closing include some tag-alongs. Tell so and so or hello to--. It dawned on me that the Apostle Paul had done the same thing at the end of some of his epistles... his comments were under the heading of personal greetings. I also noted how much Paul's writing came alive to me in new ways. I could sense how painful it was to move on after investing himself in a particular church. I picked up on hints of loneliness that were meaningful to me. I had never particularly been a Paul lover due in part I'm sure to the teaching I had pertaining to his stance on women. I was beginning to see more and more how his words were taken out of context. I also appreciated his challenges, his steady and inspiring love for the Lord, his willingness to be wherever God put him. Yes, he became a hero !

One of my last homes was with a family with two small boys.

After I moved in, at church the next Sunday the two of them were standing in the sanctuary and as I approached they came up to me, took my hand and led me to where the family was seated. After all I "belonged" to them now. When I reflected on this I appreciated even more the unique calling to live with people. The whole experience proved to be incredibly rewarding and deeply satisfying. I had been called to leave my own family, but God had given me new families where I was cherished... more than enough to nourish my heart.

The final days were busy, packing up and making decisions about what needed to be discarded and what to take. I had arrived at a decision that when leaving, I would not add to my gear. Sorting through my books, I gave away some to the church library and some I dropped at the door of another church. Books are tough to let go of.

Dick and I privately reflected on my two years and later with the Session, shared how much I appreciated working with him. His openness, his desire for personal growth as well as his capacity for caring for the flock and his sensitivity for my needs. It was thrilling to observe the growing vitality in the church. People were blossoming and eager to serve in new and various ways. There was a noticeable deepening of relationships coupled with a willingness to make new connections.

When I looked back at my ministry I marveled at the way God had blessed and used me. There were baby steps, learning how delightful it is to visit, to sit down with someone I didn't know and carry on a conversation. Leading retreats was another bold step that I'm so thankful I took. Playing my guitar while leading a variety of groups was a new venture. Never would I have expected to take a giant step to be in the pulpit, children's message...yes but giving a sermon? I had been stretched, didn't make me taller, but It filled me to overflowing... with joy and an eagerness for more.

The church gave me an unforgettable send off. A secret committee had set up the sanctuary with small tables and engaged caterers who prepared a lovely buffet. When I was led into the crowded room I was overwhelmed. I hardly touched the food as I bounced from table to table expressing my love and appreciation.

In my farewell talk, I listed a few comments about my time with them. Teasing, I said that I was considering giving tours of the various homes I had stayed in and make comments about that experience. Of course if anyone desired to not be on that list, bribes would be accepted. A hearty laughter spread around the room. Then I read a list of memories.

> *My homes.... a place where the light switch is in the hallway*
> *and not inside the room.*
> *a dryer that needed cranking to rev it up*
> *cats, one that wasn't as spooky as advertised. one that took ten*
> *days before it settled in on my lap*
> *Philip singing Solitaire for me and putting up a Christmas*
> *tree that refused to remain standing.*
> *the "quiet serene, leisurely meals" with the Gibsons*
> *my Rabbit with the awkward seat belts.*
> *Dick with his fleet of cars after much earlier sermon on not*
> *needing more than one*
> *getting smoked out of the house when Don would start a fire*
> *long conversations with Jamie as we stood on the stairs*
> *Ti and Tux routine, one would jump the fence while the other*
> *chose to dig under it*
> *Bill talking about his sweetheart, June and playing the*
> *piano*
> *So many more...*

Also shared something I had written......

You Called Me

When I was a little child you called me
>*while sitting in the pew of my small church.*
>*I heard your voice, I felt that desire.*

Deep down in the tender soil of my heart
I listened eagerly to those missionary stories
I sang those hymns, "I'll Go where You Want Me to Go, dear
>*Lord"*
I responded to the call in the scriptures..

I do not sense that I strayed on the path I followed
>*a Christian marriage, precious sons, a teaching career*
>*various ministries in the local church*
>*they were all along the path you called me to travel.*

Oh how beautiful this place at Terrace View.
>*I talk about the excitement, the fun, the freedom, the awesome beauty*
>*But we know, you and me Lord, that the bottom line is the ministry you've blessed me with, the answer to my prayers in time of brokenness my heart's cry "Lord, use this tragedy, all this pain for your honor and glory." Now dear God you have fulfilled that prayer, that heart cry. Love, affirmation, unlimited opportunities to grow and develop in new ways.*

Such JOY,
>*I am unable to list all the treasures you have given me*
>*dear folks who have shared their deepest hurts, sorrows, pain and treasures*
>*dear ones who are opening themselves in new ways to you*
>*And now you are calling me to take the new step*
>*please help me to be certain of your voice*
>*help me to let go, to trust you to lead me to*
>*new people that I can be there for and I can be with.*

Forgive my fears, my reluctance to go, my wanting to hang onto
what is not mine. Cleanse me from my desire to be possessive.
Lord God, I love you more than Terrace View, more than the affirmation, the fulfillment, the adventure, the being loved.
Help me to let go. You are my reason for everything. You are my God and I am your servant.
Keep calling, I will listen. Keep calling I will go!
To love at all is to be vulnerable. Love anything and your heart will certainly be wrung and possibly broken...the only place outside of Heaven where you can be perfectly safe from all dangers and perturbations of love is Hell.

3

Sequim '85

*Vulnerability..requires integrity and strength.. indeed the
power to risk enormous pain......It demands the stamina to open
ourselves to be touched with our own fragility... a willingness
to lose ourselves in the hope of finding our true self.*
C. S. Lewis

My summer back home with family and friends all helped
in the transitioning. I needed time to reflect and grieve,
to let go of my first church enabling me to shift gears and be
prepared for the new. Making the rounds of visits with loved
ones was rejuvenating. Dad always lit up when I came to visit
and spend some time with him. My darling granddaughter,
Kristen was now a precious almost three year old.

One highlight of the summer was the arrival of two friends
from Terrace View. What a great time we had as Georgie, Linda
and I touring New England. The three of us were walking in
Edmonds in the spring when I asked, "Hey, you know, how about
coming to see me this summer and we'll do some exploring?"
We stopped dead in our tracks, they dug out their schedules and
practically shouted "Yes, we can do it".

I rented a car, picked them up at the airport and brought them
to Connecticut. Folks from my home church had welcomed me
for the summer and were willing for my guests to share their

home. The family was scattered that part of the summer and the house was ours to use. I showed them around Connecticut, "my turf where I had lived first, before taking off on our tour that included Newport News, Cape Cod, Plymouth, Boston and a little of Vermont and New Hampshire. They were impressed with the quaintness and charm.

Linda loved to paint especially with oils and when she spotted something she liked as we drove around she'd yell from the back seat STOP! She'd jump out of the car, snap a picture of a door on a house or a barn or who knows what so that when she got home she might want to make a painting of her photo. It enhanced our pleasure as we took in the sights. I found myself observing details, savoring their uniqueness. Our last night on the road we enjoyed sitting on the lawn under the stars listening to the Boston Symphony perform at Tanglewood, a lovely facility that provides for concerts and a rich variety of summer classes for people in the classical music world, located in Lenox Massachusetts. It was very rewarding to me to be able to show them my part of the country. We joked that I could certainly qualify as a topnotch tour guide. They had both done so much for me it felt good to be able to give something back to them.

Our return to Kennedy Airport was on a Sunday and I took a risk, hoping the traffic wouldn't be a problem and proceeded south driving through the heart of Manhattan into Brooklyn and onto the airport. We made a stop along the Hudson near the Verrazano Narrows Bridge. We strolled along the river enjoying spectacular views of the busy harbor, the Statue of Liberty and the skyline. What a happy trio we were and what a fitting climax to our shared adventure..

My vacation evaporated and once again I was faced with multiple tender goodbyes. As that date drew near I was finding myself "getting into" my new assignment. This would be a new beginning, a new place of serving. What will I find here? What will my ministry be all about?

Lynn and Denny, friends from Terrace View, picked me up at Sea Tac Airport and took me to their home to spend the the night with them in Mount Lake Terrace. When morning arrived I was ready to begin this new adventure. It was time to head for Sequim. We loaded up Lynn's car with my footlocker, two monstrous suitcases, a few boxes of books and my guitar and caught the Edmond's ferry and then proceeded along an already familiar route that still gives me goose bumps of delight just thinking about it. When we crossed the Hood Canal on the floating bridge, I drank in the beauty while observing how the mountains formed an impressive backdrop, seeming to beckon you to travel westward onto the Olympic Peninsula. The mountains continued on the south and on our north the wide expanse of the water and islands created a road of wonder.

This transition was easier than the first because I had been out to Sequim on several occasions already. I had stayed at the Barnes and even met a few faithful "prayers" that met regularly at the Dome.

My first home was with Bob and Ruth. I moved into the guest bedroom on the first floor in the Dome. They were on a family reunion/vacation at Lake Chelan, the other side of the Cascades. I was welcomed by Patty and Ray, a couple who were presently living in one of the guest houses. They had been camping out, homeless and jobless when the Lord intervened and connected them to the Barnes where they found both needs met.

Staying at the King's Dome, so named as a takeoff on the Seattle sports' arena known as the Kingdome, was very interesting as I was able to view the ebb and flow of their hospitality ministry. Frequent groups would come and spend a few days on the campus holding retreats, meetings, whatever. Ruth would spend hours in the kitchen creating wonderful home made meals to the delight of all who came. She loved her huge garden and never wearied of working in it. The garden was very productive and I thoroughly indulged in the raspberries that were in great abundance even though while picking them many found their way into my mouth. I remember writing to my Dad that I thought maybe I had died and was now in "berry heaven".

Bob kept the property in A plus condition, the lawns were lush and well tended. The two guest houses always had an ample supply of wood stacked at their door ready to be used in the wood burning stoves. He presented me with their Datsun station wagon to be mine to use while I was in Sequim. After lovingly cleaning and washing the car and filling the gas tank, he handed me the keys. I certainly appreciated their generosity as well as the freedom the car provided.

Next morning it was time to go to church and get settled into my new challenge. Upon my arrival I quickly discovered a more complex situation than I had anticipated. On staff was an "unofficial associate pastor, in addition to Bill, the senior pastor who had experienced some difficult emotional trauma as part of his depression. The two men did not make for a good combo since neither appeared to have much drive and energy. Sunday Services were well done, but the other avenues of the ministry left much to be desired.

Gordon, the associate, was charged with leading the Christian Education area. That became an immediate frustration as he operated in a most lackadaisical fashion. His rare meetings were aimless and seemingly unplanned, hence nonproductive. He was a pleasant person both kind and affirming to me. The Session had appointed a search committee to seek a permanent associate and Gordon was hoping and expecting to be chosen.

The church was on Washington Street, the main street in town. The building was an odd one, unattractive from the outside but warm and inviting on the inside. The offices were located upstairs and Helen, the secretary showed me my space. She was very supportive and helpful, a person I could rely on. The children's Sunday School area was on the same level which made it very convenient for me.

Sequim is very unique. The area lies on a flat prairie and blessed with a mild climate. Lying in the rain shadow of the mountains, it typically has about twenty inches or less of rain per year. This provides a huge contrast to the Seattle area and the coast. It has been dubbed along with the San Juans, islands that lie to the north as the "banana belt". These factors create a most desirable retirement location. People living there came from all over the country and from a wide variety of careers. I never knew who I might be chatting with both in town as well as in the church. The church had a large percentage of seniors in the congregation and both the church and the community were endowed with warm and loving people.

The Dungeness Spit is located to the north of Sequim and is the longest spit in the U.S. extending about five and a half miles into the Strait. It is a national bird sanctuary and visitors are only allowed on the northern side to walk so they do not disturb nesting birds. A lighthouse sits out on the end and is a worthy enticement to hike out to. I soon learned that it was best to make that jaunt when the tides were right and the beach full of stones. That end of the Spit one would always be treated to seeing many seals swimming about.

Before moving I had become well acquainted on previous visits and taken many walks. Often I would see a lone seal that would fortuitously pop his head up and follow me at times while I walked. Dubbed him Smitty and wove a tale that he always knew where I was, following me even when I traveled to the Edmonds beach or across the Strait to Victoria, BC.

The beach, kept totally natural, is lined with countless dead trees that get stacked in various ways due to tidal changes and storms. I like to say that the "furniture" was always getting rearranged. What a great place for kids and families as they delighted in moving the logs about creating their own fort or house.

I always got a thrill walking that half mile trek through the forest, eager to catch your first glimpses of the Strait before you descend the steep path to the water. When you walk out on the Spit you are treated to views of Canada as well as Mount Baker. When you turn around on your return stretch, the Olympic Mountains form a backdrop for the rolling waves. That never ceased to bless me. On the East Coast one doesn't see ocean and mountains in one picture frame.

An added interest was watching the container ships and a variety of other boats making their way to the Puget Sound. On two occasions, I had close up views of whales that had strayed off course. Another thrill while walking early one morning I passed an eagle perched on a log. About ten minutes later on my return he was still there . This was most unusual as they usually fly off when seeing a person that close.

Many times I went to the Spit, my refuge. It was a great place to sort things out and get in touch with my thoughts and feelings. While I savored the intimacy with the Lord knowing he was listening, I received comfort and reassurance that his guiding hand upon me. Often I went with a snack, a book and a blanket enjoying a few hours of R&R.

There were two services on Sunday with Sunday School sandwiched in between. Immediately I became involved with the children and youth as they were in dire need. I had already met the pastor and taken out to lunch by him and his wife. He had shared many of his concerns about those needs. I've always said if I had ever doubted there really is a Santa Claus after meeting Bill I knew better. He is a big man with a beautiful face and a smile that warms you through and through. There's a twinkle in the eye and an aura of love that engulfs you. Pastor Bill was coming out of a dark time in his life. The depression made it difficult to focus and he had experienced losing his train of thought while in the pulpit that had totally freaked him out. He had been beaten down with much criticism and harsh judgment, but hadn't lost his swagger. His not wanting to conform to the usual expectations of a minister drove his secretary crazy. Often he was unwilling to keep her informed of his whereabouts.

In many of our conversations he shared deep hurts and feelings, many from childhood, which sent me fleeing to the Spit, my place where I could process it all and rest in the arms of my Lord. Another source of comfort and help for me were the prayers of Ruth and Bob. She was a woman of deep faith and prayer. Upon arising each morning she would go down into the basement to a large closet where there were some blankets on the floor and spend time in prayer before starting her busy day. One of my continuing prayer requests was for "buckets of wisdom."

Okay Lord, I'm here where you want me. I wonder just what this place will be all about. How would my ministry here open up, unfold. I began with some visiting, once again listening to people's stories. It didn't take long to realize that I needed to get connected in other ways due to the size of the congregation and there was no way I could find the time to visit all the members. This church had a few hundred people. I attended committee meetings and Session of course and used those times to interact with folks.

Again I was given the privilege of being in the pulpit. I referred to it as "sharing" and both pastors told me, "you were preaching, girl." I remember one of my Sundays being so nervous and Bill giving me one of his bear hugs and saying how surprised he was because he didn't think I was ever nervous. When I shared my fear was, I wouldn't have enough to say, he chuckled and told me, "Gal, they'll never mind if you're too short, they'll love you." I found myself in the ensuing years remembering those words, helping me to smile and relax a little when approaching the pulpit.

The church was right next to the Oak Table, a local institution that people lined up willing to wait if necessary to indulge in a great breakfast or lunch. We joked that it was the church annex. The original eating place was small and cozy with knotty pine walls and wooden booths as well as tables and chairs. Upon entering you immediately inhaled the wonderful aromas of coffee and pancakes. It reminded me of New England and I loved going there on many different occasions with different people.

As I had done in Mount Lake Terrace, I continued to live with folks from the church. My first move was from the Dome and while carrying my gear out to the car I found myself crying, not wanting to leave. One of the Barnes' daughters just happened to be coming into to the Dome and stopped, asking me if I was all right. Between sobs, I said, " Yes, but this is so hard, the leaving. You'd think I'd be used to it by now." Her reply was she didn't think it was supposed to get easier. That counsel has stayed with me all these years and brought a measure of comfort on many occasions.

Chuckles is born...

Clowning was something I just happened to stumble on. I had been asked to dress as a clown and make a surprise announcement in church about an upcoming Fall Festival event. That tickled me. I had always been intrigued with clowns, especially Emmett Kelly. I popped into the church during the announcements, dressed in costume and white face through an outside door by the choir. That both shocked and unnerved the pastor. His outward demeanor was calm and controlled and he immediately dubbed me Chuckles, but I received quite a scolding the next day when he told me how fragile he still was.

The people received me with great delight and that sparked an interest. I began to find books on clowning ministry and the more exploring I did, the more I felt drawn to it sensing the great potential.

I was treated to a conference in Edmonds and later an unbelievable week in Berkley, California to participate in a Creative Worship Conference that absolutely stimulated me. I was eager to learn more and explore the possibilities of this ministry.

While learning more about clowning, I found myself thinking and praying about what Chuckles would be all about. I began to think about my dress and decided it needed to be simple, something that would not cost me anything. Bill provided me with a pink shirt and Greek sailor's cap. I asked for colored scarfs from the men in the congregation and received quite a collection. I wore old pants, colored socks and my old sneakers. Later while in Sitka I added a gift of a custom-made pink vest with a jazzy lining. Pink is one of my colors. Feeling that my white hair is such an integral part of who I am, I decided not to wear a wig. Later, I realized that keeping my natural hair made me less frightening to children.

Reading about the make-up, I was deeply touched by the symbolism. Putting on the white face made a statement that I was dying to self and as I put the color on it signified a coming alive in Christ. That was taken from a life verse I had chosen while in my twenties found in

> Galatians 2:20 *"I have been crucified with Christ and I no longer live, but Christ lives in me. The life I now live in the body, I live by faith in the Son of God, who loved me and gave himself for me."*

Every time I put on my face with reverence and reflection, it became a sacred time, both humbling and inspiring.

Clown ministry is all about bringing joy and serving others. The clown needed to be sensitive to a person's reaction to you and not inflict yourself on him. If you saw a positive response you opened up more to that person. Some folks don't like clowns and lots of little ones are frightened. It is essential that you are sensitive to them and respect their wishes.

A new ministry opened before me. I invited the youth to join me in clown workshops. We had a delightful time preparing a skit to present for the children's message during the Sunday services. Right at the start I established that we would all put on our clown face together and then share a quiet time of prayer before we went out to minister. This was a time of commitment to our purpose to give ourselves to others, to bring them a smile, a laugh, a chuckle.

I established with all my clowning groups that no one was to show up in a store-bought or even a traditional homemade costume.

I wanted them to use their imagination in making their selection. They were to look around at home to find what they would wear, creating their own look and character. Bill had named me Chuckles and I resonated with that label and kept it. It was up to them to think about who they were and choose their own name. It tickled me to see their creativity come alive in their choices of how they did their face, what their outfit would be and what name they would use. I wanted them to experience the joy of giving yourself away and not needing to use money to enhance the experience.

new homes- new family...

My homes in November, December and January were with three widows. I was the first person in their home to stay after the death of their spouse. This presented a challenge getting them to realize I wasn't going to eat as much as their husbands had. When I shared this with Dick he couldn't resist saying "don't they have any "normal" people there?"

I had already spent some time with Bernice, my January hostess. When I moved in, on our first night she talked almost nonstop for hours. She was thrilled to have company and in desperate need to have someone listen and have someone to love. We found many common threads. Her husband was from Connecticut. They met at Moody Bible Institute in Chicago. I had enjoyed a deep friendship as a young adult with a person who had gone there. Also, her son had been a missionary and had gone through a painful divorce while serving in Laos about the same time I had gone through my divorce.

Bernice loved God's Word and an excellent Bible teacher. She was basically a positive person with an enthusiasm that was inexhaustible. She loved surprises and never lost her spontaneity. Our friendship developed into a beautiful thing and we shared many meals, trips, adventures through the years. We actually adopted each other. I became her daughter and she, my second mom. We filled a void in each other's lives in the beginning, but the relationship became much deeper than that and endured until she died. We shared our hopes and fears. We shared our hearts. Of course our deep love for our Lord was a precious bond.

My relationship with the Barnes, especially Ruth was growing. Her deep love for the Lord was evident as was her vibrant faith. She was the real thing, totally natural, upfront with a sense of humor and a keen interest in many things. It's obvious that she has opened herself totally to God. Bob and I hit it off, right from the beginning, indulging in lots of good teasing. He loved to sit up in the loft that overlooks the living room area while reading a book. Ruth and I would be talking when we would hear this authoritative voice inject a comment in regards to our conversation. The acoustics in the Dome were exceptional. We soon learned to simply comment, look at each other and say "that must be God speaking to us." Lots of fun.

Before I had left Terrace View I had received a phone call from someone in Sequim inviting me to lunch. She had been told of my coming in August to be on staff and was eager to get together. My schedule was full. I told her I could meet, but would need to leave at a certain time to play tennis. She still laughs about that, it confirmed her first impression was that I was real and vital. It didn't take a rocket scientist to realize that Agnes was a most special person. We talked Christian Ed and family that first time and very soon after I arrived she invited me out to her home on Three Crabs Road.

The house sat right on the beach. It was lovely with the kitchen facing the mountains and the big dining room table and living room facing the water blessed with views of the lighthouse at the end of the Spit and on a clear day, MT. Baker. The refrigerator had a magnet on it that stated "This is not Burger King you may not have it your way."

Dwight, her husband was a delightful person, warm, loving, full of fun. What an attractive couple they were and what a great family, all ten of them. All were loaded with musical talent with the exception of Agnes. As a consolation prize she had been given a " gut bucket" that was her instrument to play. Dwight played a "mean" harmonica. It was great fun to be a part of family gatherings and soak up the music. The big baby grand piano responded to the gifted musicians and the blending of the marvelous voices filled me with joy. I not only got to stay with them but also house-sat both years when they went to Arizona.

The guest bedrooms were all down one hallway with my room on the water side. In warmer weather I would leave the sliding door open, listening to the gentle waves lapping at the shore.

Among her many talents Agnes was a great cook and I was treated to lots of crab, clams and delicious seafood through the years. Her Manhattan clam chowder was to die for. Her wisdom and insights and gentle listening were a treasure even though she was also a no nonsense person. She resonated with the Nike sportswear line that says, "Just do it".

finding my place...

My first months were full of questions about what God was calling me to. It seemed much of my energy was invested with Bill, the senior pastor. He had gone through such a troubled time and our conversations were deep and difficult. He stirred up in me the need and longings for a mate. I spent time praying that the Lord would protect both of us from any physical attraction. Counseling I knew, can be very intimate and I knew I was vulnerable. Bill shared that when he looked at me he was aware of the presence of the Lord standing between us. His statement was both a blessing and a reassurance.

The kids' area needed sprucing up and I quickly found myself pouring lots of energy there. Two women who had struggled for years to keep the Sunday School going and appreciated my labors and input worked with me. Together we weeded out stuff and scrubbed down some walls. The fun happened when I put up new displays on tired bulletin boards and added some new posters. I tried some creative things with the children's opening time on Sunday mornings. My guitar became a hit even though my talent was very limited.

I was missing the friendships that had developed at Terrace View. At that church I felt like everyone's big sister. Here I was a daughter or the kid sister. Quite a shift, but I found both roles had their advantages and I readily slipped into either one, getting a kick out of both.

Being located on the peninsula, I was less that two hours away from Mount Lake Terrace. When Georgie's daughter was diagnosed with cancer I was able to get away and visit her and the family during her long stay in the hospital. It was a scary and painful time as Tina lost most of her stomach. It also kept me in touch with others. Dick was available and always provided a morale boost.

Before Christmas I was asked to write an article for the annual report. I tucked away that document and when rereading them find my words intriguing and revealing.

I hear so many intriguing explanations about how this volunteer has come to mysteriously be in your midst. Actually the tale is simple. I was in the application process, the testing time of looking to see what the Lord's plans for me were. While "innocently " retreating at the Barnes' with a group of women from Terrace View, I mentioned to Bob how great it would be to come to Sequim Presbyterian some day as a volunteer. Need I say more?

What am I doing? Certainly is a valid question and one I often ask myself. I feel a call to a ministry to local churches; a ministry to come and be a part of you for a while. A person who is not a member, has a fresh perspective, is not clergy and not a lay person either. This certainly puts me in an interesting position and a most free one.

Churches are not buildings or steeples but live organisms, people, Family. I've come to be a listener, a person who listens with both ears and with my heart. Each of you has your own story and it is precious to me when you open up yourselves to me. Like most families these include celebrations, traditions, disappointments, expectations and hopes and dreams for the future. In the listening I am often called to be a bridge, a connector between people. Sometimes I am more a mirror, one who reflects back so you can discern more clearly who you are and who you want to be. So, if you notice me poking around in places I don't really belong, there's a purpose in it.

I haven't come to do your work for you but actually hope to provoke or stimulate you to risk and grow in new ways, working diligently in the service of our Lord. Remember the scriptures that teach us, "whoever sows sparingly will also reap sparingly, and whoever sows generously will also reap generously."

What do I get out of all of this? God has promised that I will be made rich in every way. He is always faithful in keeping his promises. How richly he has blessed me with new experiences, new opportunity for growth, new relationships. How I praise him for the love and grace he blesses me with.

Christmas came and went and although it was tough not to be with my family, I anticipated a visit in March. Dan was winding down his studies at the seminary and would be responsible for planning, rehearsing and then conducting a choral group. This was a major requirement for his Master's degree. I would be there on that occasion. In addition to that, my trip would coordinate perfectly with the expected birth of my second grandchild. How's that... perfect timing! I would be there, participating in both of these important events.

During those first months I had wondered whether this place of ministry might be only a year in length. But now those thoughts were fading as I connected with folks, did some teaching and initiated groups. My involvement in church school both with the teachers and the kids all were instrumental in making me feel at home. I was also experiencing people's respect and appreciation while witnessing some positive changes. My love of this beautiful area, with both beaches and mountains to savor continued to grow. The walks on the Spit provided exercise for both mind and body. With Spring approaching I began to know there would be a second year. The healthy balance of meaningful ministry, availability of places to explore and significant loving relationships were blessing me.

quite a trio...

The search committee for an associate pastor had been at work through the winter months and now announced their decision. They, after much prayer and discussion, chose a young married man with a young family. There were some negative reactions, feelings that Gordon should have been picked, but Gerry quickly endeared himself, soon becoming everyone's son or grandson. He was bright and energetic with a passion for the Lord and the Word. Although only in his twenties he had experienced the illness and death of his mother which gave him a warmth, maturity and understanding that endeared him to this mostly senior congregation.

The three of us created a good balance and we bonded quickly. At staff meetings we kidded around as to who was able when preaching, to put the most people in the pews to sleep. One day we dubbed ourselves a trinity. Bill was the father, Gerry the son and me the spirit because they never knew what I was up to and where or when I might appear. Sense of humor I believe is one of God's gifts.

One sweet memory I cherish is Gerry sitting in his office,

that was open to mine, reading his Bible with tears streaming down his cheeks telling me how precious God's words are.

When Gerry was presented to Presbytery and undergoing questions from the floor he was asked how he expected to deal with conflict that might arise between Bill and himself. His response was "that's why Ruth is here". He and Bill both were apprehensive about conflict and tended to shy away from that, but I had learned that usually it needs to be dealt with and that conflict doesn't have to be negative. As if that wasn't enough for one day Dick, my previous pastor, after asking Gerry a question, commented that he hoped they would remember that he was the one who sent me to them. I was both humbled and flattered.

Still get a kick out of Pastor Bill's story about when he was completing his seminary studies and praying for a position back in Alaska, where he and his wife had lived before responding to God's call to the ministry. He shared that they were shocked to find a church that called them to Nebraska. His advice was when you pray be certain, Ruth, that you enunciate clearly. There were times he shared he had cried,"But Lord, I didn't say Nebraska, I asked for A-L-A-S-K-A!" Lots of lighthearted fun, what a special brother.

Another one of many perks in being on staff was a small group training event that was held in the Seattle area. What made it extra special was the featured speaker Lyman Coleman was one of the gurus. He was the head of Serendipity House that produced all sorts of studies as well as a very innovative Bible. He was just as creative and inspiring as his materials. He delivered a fascinating history of the small group movement that I found most interesting. Then he put us into small groups and demonstrated some principles. It was an effective hands-on experience. I had already tuned into small groups and that session injected even more enthusiasm.

Lots of the older folks in the congregation weren't into the concept, but in my second year I was able to launch a small group for the women out in the Mains Farm area. I had stayed with the choir director, a dear elegant lady, newly widowed who willingly opened her home to our meetings. One of the women had always worked outside the home and never really considered the Gospel. She became fascinated as we shared with each other how God had worked in personal ways in our lives. She was an eager participant and was comfortable enough to ask questions. It was thrilling to see her in the weeks to come open her heart to the Lord Jesus.

In this church as in other mainline churches I was finding "church going" people who were nominal Christians, not ever having been touched by the Holy Spirit. Many were open and seeking to learn what was missing, finding it at long last. I was told on more than one occasion that I stimulated a hunger for knowing God more intimately. People saw that in me and wanted more. I didn't have to be preachy, I just had to be real... be me.

one hundred beds...

On one of my many cross country flights to pass the time I began counting all the beds I had slept in. I had visited lots of people during the summer of '83 as I said my good-byes. Upon arriving in Mount Lake Terrace the bed count continued since I moved, usually monthly. In Sequim, this practice continued as the number grew closing in on the hundred mark. Bill used to kid that I should have stickers to mark the beds I had slept in. At another time he thought perhaps I could rate the beds ala Triple A.

In the spring of '86, another dream of mine was fulfilled. Dick loved to take groups to cities and give them a guided tour. This year his agenda was to gather a group and tour San Francisco. It turned out to be a small group of women from Terrace View and he graciously invited me to join them. What a blast that was. We all piled into Dick's station wagon and took off. We kidded him about his harem, that at times frustrated him. He would be dashing down the street and when looking back would discover that we had stopped to look at something, not on his agenda. He reluctantly learned to adapt and as always was a delightful guide. We covered all the sights, the waterfront, some churches and elite hotels.

We took the boat out to Alcatraz, touring the prison, a pretty grim experience. Of course we all hopped on and off the trolley cars squealing with delight. A highlight was Chinatown. Presbyterians from all over the country helped to sponsor the Cameron House, a mission there. Dick had arranged a tour. The grand old house was large and rambling with secret passageways and rooms that had been used to hide away young Chinese girls protecting them from the sex trade... quite a heritage. One of the Chinese staff persons took us out onto the streets and through back alleys showing us the inner workings of Chinatown. And of course she escorted us to a great restaurant where we all indulged in a superb meal. Most of us however weren't up to the challenge of using chopsticks.

On our return trip we spent a night in Oregon in the home of one of the older ladies in Dick's former church. When I woke the next morning I realized the one hundred bed milestone had been reached and I came bursting into the kitchen announcing my accomplishment. Imagine the look on my prim and proper hostess as I exclaimed I had now slept in one hundred beds. Needless to say there was a quick and necessary explanation given. The counting stopped after that, the game had gotten old.

In developing relationships with the many seniors, a reoccurring theme emerged, aging wasn't for sissies. The process of giving up one's independence is challenging. Driving skills begin to diminish and that demands adjustments. Usually folks find they need to eliminate highway travel first. A common complaint is everyone's driving too fast. The flatness of the town and the straight streets, in Sequim, helped to keep people driving longer than if they were in busier and more congested places... But selling one's home, moving into an assisted living facility... those decisions were tough. I was finding many lived with lots of pain and a terrible loneliness. I was witness to models of courage that inspire me as I face up to my own aging. Also it became apparent your health is much more significant than your age.

Bernice's and my relationship continued to grow. We both enjoyed going out to lunch together, as well as trips to the coast or the Spit. One day she opened up to me that her lack of friendships was a difficulty. While married, as a couple they had a circle of friends, but she had always sensed it was based on their love for Ed and she was just part of the package. My quick response was that certainly wasn't the basis of our relationship. I had never met Ed.

Her husband had been a quiet man, a well loved pastor and an excellent Bible teacher. Every story I heard from others about him made him sound almost perfect. I teased her that I didn't know what to think about him. I certainly had some questions about all the stuff he had stashed in his office. Even found some rocks from Connecticut he had saved. While cleaning out his office in the garage she was finding things that were designated as "throw aways" only to find he had put them into his office. We had some laughs over that.

Everyone in the church called Bernice by that name, but I had picked up from her that in other places she was known as Bee. She had an endless supply of colorful expressions. One of her favorites was "jiggers' when she got perturbed. I teased her that she was guilty of "Christian swearing". Of course she was horrified, but it led to me dubbing her with the pet name Bee Jiggers, for short BJ. I frequently used it in a most affectionate way and often in her correspondence to me, she would sign the message with her nickname.

During my two years in Sequim I was treated to three great visits. Dan, my youngest flew out for a quickie only to realize he had to make more time on his next visit. My dear friend Susan came and we stayed at the Masons. She developed a soft spot for Dwight as he stirred memories of her father. My eighty-seven year old dad visited staying at the Barnes. He was most excited with Lake Crescent and the Buchard Gardens in Victoria, taking countless pictures. He loved the fact that on the west coast he could watch the World Series in the early evening. It meant so much to both of us and as he told me, now he could visualize where I was.

Both of my years in Sequim I enjoyed housesitting at the Masons. They usually headed south to spent a few months in a warmer place. One of the years I enjoyed a front row seat on the stool by the counter facing the kitchen watching the frantic last minute gathering of their gear. The Masons were about to pull out with their trailer for sunny Arizona. Dwight kept going into the refrigerator snitching some tasty leftover venison in between loads. Finally the task was just about complete when he became totally frustrated, not knowing where in the world he had left his beloved pipe. All three of us started to search frantically. No way would he leave without it. He then reached in the frig to take one last snack and lo and behold there was the pipe. Whew! The day was saved and we waved goodbye. Still have a chuckle when I recall that incident.

While settling into "my" warm and inviting home I quickly found the stormy winter weather a delight. Being on the water and watching the storms blow in outside the living room window was fascinating. The staff soon learned that if the weather turned bad and the wind started blowing that sent me heading for my house on Three Crabs Road, eager to watch the show.

SEAVIMs...

The winter months progressed and I found myself thinking about my summer. What possible opportunity might be out there to latch on to. I figured being back East for two plus months was too long for I would be bouncing from one home to another. I had read in a Synod newsletter that help was needed in Juneau working with children, conducting Vacation Bible School. That certainly was right up my alley, so I wrote to the people in charge asking about the possibilities. The reply informed me that the position wasn't just for Juneau, but was an eight week commitment to travel as part of a team to various remote locations in Southeast Alaska. The living conditions varied, in some places even sleeping in the church on the floor. You had to carry your own gear. I felt both intrigued and challenged with the information I received. After bringing it to the Lord I was seeing green lights. I sent off my application, eager for a reply. Little did I realize that the director was very reluctant to have someone in her fifties be part of the group. The previous year an older woman had dominated the team and that wasn't what the experience was all about. This was one of Presbyterian USA premier leadership training programs that I had stumbled onto, geared for developing young adults. The acronym SEAVIM stood for south east Alaska Volunteer in Mission.

Obviously God was very much in this because when the director was sharing her concerns in the Juneau office and mentioned my name the interim pastor immediately spoke up and said he knew me from Puget Sound Presbytery. I would not interfere, but actually enhance the team. Wow, thank you Lord. Glad I'm in your hands!

As the summer approached I began planning about what I

needed to have with me as far as clothes etc. My hostess Jean, was a great help. She had done much camping, backpacking etc. She gave me a thin mattress that rolled up nicely and a duffel bag to stash my gear. It was a challenge to have enough personal stuff and to keep it light. There would be lots of carrying my own gear in my travels. I booked the flight to Juneau and made arrangements to return on the Alaskan ferry, thinking this might be my only opportunity to enjoy that experience.

The big day arrived and when getting on the plane I became aware of possible members of the team on board. Keeping a low profile it was intriguing as I observed them. I had been told by a pilot who flew for Alaska Airlines that landing at the Juneau Airport tests the pilot due to the location of the mountains. It was definitely goose bump time. The team was met at the airport, we picked up our gear and were loaded into vans.

The new adventure was unfolding. We all settled into Chapel on the Lake. There were eighteen of us most in their twenties, two still teens and me in my early fifties. The team spent some intense "getting to know each other" time. We were all strangers to each other, but it quickly became apparent that we were already beginning to bond and would become a caring team.

Everything about this program was top of the line. We were quickly exposed to several different people who instructed us about the culture and customs of the people we would be engaged with including both Anglo and Native. The area of southeast Alaska is home to three tribes, Tlingit, Haida, and Tsimsian. I had the good fortune of first hand experience with all three. Another topic discussed was what to do if you met a bear... don't run... do not look the bear in the eyes... and if all else fails assume a fetal position.

One of the instructors was a VIM who was serving near the North Pole. Her passion for Alaska as well as the Eskimos was apparent. She was from Appalachia and I was intrigued by her willingness to locate in a small community near the North Pole, such a contrast to her roots. Even Alaskans, most would have little desire to serve in such an isolated and harsh place. She shared that she loved the people and found many similarities. Both the mountain folk and the Eskimos tended to be positive, warm and friendly. They enjoyed simple pleasures knowing how to make the best in difficult situations.

The group was taken to a museum that provided great insight into the varied cultures we would be interacting with. Next we were turned loose to explore the downtown area. It was fun walking around and going into the shops checking out the native art and trinkets. Actually I purchased a lightweight backpack that turned out to be a wise decision. It's all faded now, but I still use it if I'm heading out to the woods to take a good walk. We were blessed with a bright sparkly day to visit the Mendenthal Glacier. It was unique to be walking on this mass of ice especially on a day I was wearing a sweatshirt and shorts. That was a first for most of us.

Chapel by the Lake is actually located in Auke Bay, adjacent to Juneau. The entire wall behind the chancel area is all glass. When sitting in the sanctuary you have a lovely view that often even includes an occasional eagle. While chatting with the former pastor I asked him if he found that distracting if people were not tuned into him. He shared that at first it was, but then he learned just to stop, turn around and enjoy the action.

On the property was the original small charming chapel blessed with a spectacular view of the lake. There was a long list of reservations for weddings as you might imagine. When "down" I loved going into both the sanctuary and the chapel for some space and quiet times with the Lord.

Our meals were brought in by members of the congregation and one unforgettable meal was a huge, freshly caught and baked halibut. It was smothered in cheese, what flavor... definitely a winner. We slept in the church on the floor. My mattress was put into immediate use. Showers were available. Churches in Alaska expect to host overnight guests. Meeting ferries in the middle of the night was routine. The Marine Highway was to become our way of travel. Southeast Alaska is basically a group of islands that can only be reached by boat or plane. The "highway" was a waterway.

Being an early riser works to one's advantage, especially when you are in a group of young folks. I never had any "waiting" time to take a shower. We were treated to lots of mouthwatering salmon and halibut. If in our travels our hosts served salad and even fresh vegetables, we were told that was a big treat they were laying out and we needed to acknowledge our appreciation. All greens were shipped or flown in due to lack of land to grow crops.

Our first teaching challenge was at the church in Juneau. The entire group worked together conducting Vacation Bible School. I used my guitar and was joined with a gal who was much more proficient than I. Music was lots of fun.

The director of the SEAVIM program, Bobbie had a gift of providing special treats that kept us refreshed and eager. One of the Sundays a very rainy and dark one, we were all transported up to a cozy home on a hill after church. When we entered the house we were drawn to a crackling fire to warm our hands. The smell of fresh baked muffins stimulated our appetites. The ingredients for omelets were spread out on a counter and we quickly lined up, choosing whatever we wanted our host to put into our individual custom made omelets. Generous plates of fruit were part of the feast.

Bobbie promised us before we left that every time we passed through Juneau she would meet the ferry and have our mail. This included middle of the night stops. Teams had been formed based on our input regarding who we would like to work with.

I was placed on a four member team. Steve, the youngest in the group came from a home schooling background and hadn't been accustomed to meeting many people, causing him some discomfort with his peers. His experiences with other teens had been very limited. Cindy was also a home schooler, but had been part of a variety of other activities and was very much at ease in any situation. Janet was definitely artistic and seemed troubled. She had put my name down as she was one of the older members and hoped to pick my brain on some issues.

The last night we were all together we had a picnic meal followed by a most special communion time at the waterfront and then a hike up the hillside where we gathered around a huge bonfire. As we held hands and prayed for each other and our ministry I remember looking around the circle of faces wondering what the next weeks had in store. One memorable evening it was. With our assignments, tickets and reservations we were ready to go in different directions. Our first stop would be Wrangell and that meant we would be on the Marine Highway via Alaskan Ferry.

All of us were pretty excited when we boarded the ferry. Toting my duffel bag and guitar, I lugged everything up to the deck. By the next trip I learned to put my bag on the luggage cart that stayed below and use my new backpack for personal items. I always kept my guitar with me. It was fun exploring the ferry and wondering what our first stop would be like.

The schedule had us arriving in the wee hours of the morning. We were met and transported up the hill to the church which would be our home that week. The church was attractive, but the town was rather shabby. It was Sunday and since our "bedrooms" were classrooms, we really couldn't settle in with our gear until afternoon. Vacation Bible School was set to start the next morning and we met with local people, all part of the team. Little thought had been given about our meals, but the church folks quickly remedied that. I gave a children's message in the church service. At the meeting I was teamed with a Salvation Army captain and assigned to the third graders for the week. We both found our kids delightful. Cindy and I led the music. She had a strong voice and put lots of energy into the motions making it fun for all.

During the week some men had caught a halibut and brought it to the pastor. Quite impressive, as they hung it on a hook after splitting it in two for all to admire. It seemed like the week flew by, our days had been full. We blended in with the many workers from the church and quickly affirmed each other.

Our second week found us back on the ferry, headed for Hydaberg, a native village of about three hundred people. The pastor was from Louisiana. His wife and kids were all home vacationing. He was a warm and caring host putting us up in his house and preparing tasty meals. He had a Cajun background and we all found his stories of his people intriguing. During the week we were invited into a woman's home who made beautiful baskets and jewelry. What a delight as we listened to her as she explained the demanding process. It was easy to understand why the baskets were expensive.

This had been a very comfortable week, being in a home and sleeping in our "own" beds. The last few weeks we had been sleeping on church floors. The children were great to work with. Having outsiders come was a big event and they soaked up our attention. My preschoolers were affectionate. I would miss their hugs.

Metlakatla was next on our schedule. This time we would be transported on a chartered seaplane. Our pilot had given us some concern when he commented while looking at our gear that he wished he had brought the larger plane. Lots of the village folks gathered at the dock to say good-bye. The kids were all jumping up and down waving at us. What excitement and sendoff as the plane taxied and turned before taking off, ascending into the sky.

The view from the tiny plane was superb as we flew between the mountains before landing on the water and pulling up to the dock in Metlakatla, home to the Tsmsian Tribe. This community had a population close to a thousand. They took pride in their salmon farm and a cannery that provided well paying jobs during the summer months. Preparing the giant fish is strenuous with the workers laboring around the clock. They were garbed in heavy rubber overalls and high boots that required additional strength and fortitude. Summer meant exhaustion, but it also put money in their pockets that helped to sustain them through the long dark winter.

Cindy and Janet were hosted in one house, Steve in another and I stayed with the interim pastor and his wife. They were a sweet retired couple that were filling in while the church was seeking its next pastor. They assumed that because of my age, I was in charge of the group. I quickly explained we were a team and any decisions were made by all.

Again the Bible school was enthusiastically attended. This was the only location that we stayed two weeks. Steve and I took several walks together and he shared a lot about his growing up and his faith. He was blossoming in multiple ways in this SEAVIM experience.

The next destination was Haines and this involved a long ferry ride. A team change was made at our stopover in Juneau. Steve was shifted to a group with another guy to pal with. I missed him but enjoyed our new teammate. Bobbie brought us our welcomed mail. She related that during the course of our travels different team members would give her some of their gear to store until our tour was over. What had seemed necessary to one's existence had become a burden. One very attractive gal had come complete with hair dryer, all sorts of make-up, dress-up clothes and was now shedding stuff, simplifying her load.

Haines is a beautiful town not far from Skagway. Rainbow Glacier is situated there and the mountains are awesome. The team was once again living in the church. We were well provided since this church was more comfortably fixed and experienced in hosting teams. We each chose our own spot to claim in the church as our turf that week.

One afternoon I had a special time of going along with the pastor on an errand. He showed me the Chilkat River which draws numerous eagles in the fall when the salmon are spawning. He was a Tlinglit Indian and had gone to Sheldon Jackson in Sitka, at that time a boarding high school. He was accused on many occasions of being an "apple". This was a derogatory label inferring he was red on the outside, but white on the in. I would have enjoyed more conversations with him. He had much depth to share.

Poor Janet was struggling with the constant challenge of adjusting to new places. Each place we went brought different problems and we never knew until we arrived what would be expected of us. Some churches had staff and plans in place and we would just blend in while other locations didn't seem to be even expecting us.

At each location the team would choose what ages they would work with that week. This kept anyone from being stuck in a given slot. In her frustration with the kids she questioned me as to how I always seemed to know which age group to pick wherever we went. They were always the easiest ones to be with. I don't know if she ever caught on that just maybe my experience had something to do with my success.

During our stay Cindy and I took the short ferry ride to Skagway and soaked up the atmosphere of the little frontier gold rush town complete with boardwalks instead of sidewalks and gambling halls. It was a fun evening and a great change of pace. Plus it was so Alaska.

Our next place was Gustavus and involved a charter plane that flew us over Rainbow Glacier to our last destination. It was a particularly gorgeous day and the pilot made our short flight a most memorable one. As our small plane climbed up to the top of the glacier we entered into an ethereal area complete with swirly clouds. The place had a mysterious aura and left me breathless, full of wonder. Then the pilot gently descended circling Glacier Bay. He told us this wasn't the designated flight pattern, but he wanted to treat us to these sights. We landed at Gustavus, an Anglo community of several hundred.

Lane and Amber met us and drove us to their home next to the church. We were warmly welcomed and settled in quickly. They were a delightful couple and very interested in each one of us. One morning our hostess had gone downstairs early and heard a noise at the front door. She flipped on the porch light and found herself face to face to a black bear. Fortunately, they both spooked each other and the bear ran off.

That week it was my turn to have the older kids. Fifth and sixth graders are a favorite age of mine and we gelled immediately enjoying a great week together.

One afternoon when we were relaxing we heard lots of shouting and saw people running down the street toward the dock. It was "the" barge pulling in and that meant an event equal to Christmas in creating excitement. While the crew unloaded the crates names were called out and people stepped up to get their long awaited orders, thrilled with their newest treasures.

The time flew by it seemed, and when we boarded a commercial plane to return to Juneau there wasn't a dry eye in the bunch.

We were back where our journey had begun at Chapel on the Lake and what bedlam as the group reassembled. Everyone hugging each other, all trying to talk at once, eager to share their experiences. There was visible evidence in our demeanor as well as in our words of a maturing that had occurred in each of us. The debriefing was insightful and provided closure. The team was asked to write something that we had experienced. These would be printed and given to us as a remembrance. My writing I called.....

Faces

My summer has been full of faces of all descriptions, young and old, Native and White. Some revealed shyness, some boredom. Some were closed while others were eager, open, responsive. Memories of these faces are treasures that have both challenged and enriched me. Precious are those who have shown they have been touched by our Lord in a special way and that the Holy spirit has chosen to use me in that process. Let me share a few with you.

With a slump of his shoulders, a solemn expression and a reputation as a troublemaker, Danny entered my VBS class. He had missed the first day and was an hour late on the second day. He chose a chair on the outer edge of the circle. Silent and withdrawn, he was quite a contrast to my lively, alert, vibrant group of third and fourth graders.

By Thursday he had more or less blended in but during the recreation time the entire group trooped back from the play area full of accusations. Danny was being singled out as the source and cause of the class losing its game time. I called him aside and we walked together upstairs to our classroom. Gradually some of his story came spilling out as he responded to my arm around his shoulder and my willingness to really listen to him. When we rejoined the group they were willing to acknowledge they had been a part of the upset and needed to put into practice the lesson of loving one another. I discerned a slight lifting of that sadness that always seemed to surround Danny and could detect a beginning of a smile, a look of hope that maybe he was all right, maybe it was true that God loved him.

Boyd was a big, burly, bored with a "go ahead, make my day, lady"

attitude. I sighed, thinking, "Oh boy, this group is going to be fun". We ground out our lesson and craft time, attempting to overcome the negative vibes. Finally it was time to go outside and play a game. A fast and hard keep-away began with me very much a part of the action. In the heat of the game Boyd's facade faded away exposing a big toothy grin and a warm look of acceptance and I knew this group would be a joy. Thank you Lord, that I never outgrew my tom -boyishness.

The theme for the day was trust and the kids were picking partners for the trust walk. Anna was a girl with some physical problems, but she was not about to sit this one out. She immediately picked Jamie to blindfold her and lead her around. I could see the look of panic in Jamie's eyes. She shrank back from the responsibility. What if Anna fell and hurt herself? I quickly reassured her she could do it, and I'd be there to assist her if needed.

Gently, tenderly Jamie led Anna across the deck down the few steps and out into the grassy yard. No mishaps, mission accomplished! Then they switched roles and Anna led Jamie.

Jamie returned with a quiet look of confidence. She had overcome her own personal handicap.

So many stories, so many treasures; thank you Lord for those times You showed me love and affirmation reflected in the faces of Your children. Thank You for love, for "Love does not delight in evil but rejoices with the truth. It always protects, always trusts, always hopes, always perseveres." 1 Corinthians 13:6,7

Before leaving we had one more challenge, a last VBS at the Auke Bay church. It was great to be together even though I experienced a restlessness, a readiness to get home to my "own" world. I was stressed with the clutter and messiness of the young group and found a secluded spot in an empty class room where I could savor some privacy and some order.

In spite of our weariness and wanting to go home we thoroughly enjoyed working together with a great group of kids. There seemed to be a sense of celebration and we all found an extra supply of energy. Chuckles the clown made her final appearance of the summer on the last day of VBS and delighted the crowd. It had been well worth the effort of carting my gear and treating the kids at each stop.

Our last night before leaving, we were treated to a great feast. My seat was next to Bob Palmer, the Presbytery Executive as well as the husband of Bobbie, the director of the program. He was inquiring about my reaction to the experience and he was pleased when I said, "I had a feeling I wasn't done with Alaska". Beaming, he told me he was hoping I would feel that way. My commitment at Sequim would be complete in another year and then I would be seeking a new challenge. Bob told me to call him in January and he would purse the possibility of my going to Sitka.

The team was flying home, but I was going back on the ferry. I boarded the boat in Juneau and set up my gear on a very crowded deck. All the lounge chairs were taken so laying out my mattress and sleeping bag helped to define my place. Later in the journey the crew brought more deck chairs out and I was able to grab one.

During my first night many people had boarded and even set up pup tents on deck. The next day I got a big kick when one of the men who had been below deck milking his goat, walked about offering milk to his fellow passengers. His family was moving back to the lower '48 to Montana. Listening to the many stories from the wide variety of people on board helped to pass the time. Different languages were heard for there were travelers, especially vacationing teachers from other lands.

When the ferry docked at Ketchikan I was primed to get off and enjoy a vigorous walk. This would be the last stop until we landed in Seattle. The trip takes a few days and it does get long. The morning of our arrival I was up, packed, eager to go and ready to drink in familiar sights as we sailed south along the coast of western Washington. As the ferry passed the San Juan Islands, including Widby, my excitement mounted. At last I spotted the familiar waterfront at Edmonds and then finally Seattle. Standing out on the deck, I could see dear Agnes waiting for me. She spotted me waving and later told me I reminded her of pictures of refugees coming into the harbor in NYC.

My Alaskan SEAVIM experience was complete and now it was time to go home to Connecticut. After a quick stop in Sequim to park my gear I was flying back East before returning to begin my second year. My eight week adventure had been totally satisfying, allowing me to see I was capable of maintaining a vigorous schedule, of adjusting to a wide variety of challenges while enjoying the energy of the young adults.

more Sequim...

Once again I was finding the second year in a place to be rich and rewarding. My ministry developed and deepened. I felt the trust and appreciation which cherished and fed my soul. God had promised me that...

> *He would both enlarge the harvest of my righteousness and I would be made rich in every way so I could be generous. 2 Corinthians 9:10b–11a.*

The above passage was being fulfilled in my life continually. I was privileged to be living it and was glad I had stayed.

The Presbyterian Women's organization had a vital ministry in the church. They held monthly Circle meetings that met in homes for a Bible study and a monthly Gathering with an inspirational talk that met in the church drawing all the women together in fellowship. I joined in and helped in a variety of ways.

Into my second year, I was asked if Chuckles could come to an upcoming Gathering for the women of the Presbytery. My answer was a happy "yes", welcoming a new challenge.

Coming along with me would be another invited guest, Bev, dressed as a "bag lady". She would just appear and attend the meetings and meals. She would remain visible while keeping a low profile. Chuckles' job was herding people into the meetings and entertaining the ladies as they gathered. I also did a pantomime at the closing. It was fascinating watching how the participants reacted to both of us. Mostly, the ladies found me a delight, but there were a few that felt I was a nuisance.

The bag lady, it seemed was a person to be avoided not to get involved with. When she had walked on the ferry en route to the meetings dressed in her "appropriate attire" she was approached by one of the ferry staff and ushered over to an area where she wouldn't be easily seen. Now at the Women's Gathering many shunned her. There were exceptions, a few who attempted to engage her. Jo, from the Sequim church was the head of the organization and had set up this whole scenario challenging us as Christian women in a powerful closing talk. I think all of us did some heart searching confronting our own fears, prejudices and reactions to people that push our comfort zones.

The next transition was unfolding and conversations were taking place. The wheels were in motion for me to go back to Alaska and serve in Sitka, a place I hadn't seen in my SEAVIM summer. Bob Palmer had told me the church was a healthy one with a young pastor and he sensed it would be a good match for me.

I had asked the Barnes if they would be praying for clear guidance on this and Ruth told me that would be tough. She hoped I would go to Okanogan and work with her oldest son, another Bill.

In some of my last conversations with Pastor Bill I shared how especially during the closing months, I sensed a disconnect.... a pain of not really belonging... not really being a part of the church. That had occurred when leaving Terrace View. Once again I found myself living with the realization that I would be moving on... feeling removed... like an onlooker watching the show. My commitment to this church was deep, making the thought of leaving, painful.

Gerry, one of those days, popped into my office and burst out with "I know who you are, you're Mary Poppins. You fly in from who knows where, fix things and then fly onto your next assignment." I was flattered and later when I watched that movie I sensed Mary's pain when making her goodbyes to the family.

Comments from varied sources were telling me I needed to write and/or I should become a minister. These were flattering, but I savored the freewheeling position I was in. As Bill and Gerry would say from time to time, "really, what leverage do we have with a volunteer, we certainly can't fire her."

Leaving was going to be tough. This giving of myself, creating deep caring relationships was painful. But I recalled an experience way back during those long waiting years when dear friends were moving away. Facing that dilemma I noted two choices. One I would choose to not get close to anyone, thus avoiding the pain. My other option was to continue to love deeply even though the cost was excruciating. Never have I regretted my decision, choosing to love even if it hurts.

Once again a lovely farewell celebration and of course the last Sunday worship services all complete with thoughtful cards, gifts as well as innumerable thank yous. A few of the teens sang with me as a farewell Michael W. Smith's song,

> *Friends are friends forever if the Lord's the Lord of them*
> *and a friend will not say never cause the welcome will not end*
> *Though it's time to let you go in the Father's hands we know*
> *But a lifetime's not to long to live as friends.*

Everytime I hear those words I get a lump in my throat and tears in my eyes.

4

Sitka '87

Botanists say that trees need the powerful March winds to flex their trunks and main branches so that the sap is drawn up to nourish the budding leaves. Perhaps we need gales in our lives in the same way.

Another summer... another huge transition... another challenge. Acknowledging that God had called me to this ministry and not knowing where this might lead and how long I would be serving in this capacity the realization had sunk in. I was foolishly wasting money keeping furnishings and other items in storage. Even if I did want to settle down, I had already fallen in love with the Pacific Northwest and the expense of bringing all my worldly goods cross country would be formidable.

A friend led me to a special man in New Fairfield, Connecticut, who along with his wife, managed yard sales, giving a portion of the money to missions. At that time in the Danbury area, there were many refugees from Cambodia that he was involved with. Now, home a short time I met and shared with him my problem explaining I had no place to hold a sale. He arranged for me to use his church's fellowship center. Men from his church had helped me before and once again were available. They emptied my storage place, trucked my belongings and even helped set up furniture. It was time to face the challenge of deciding again what I wanted to keep and what I was willing to let go of. I spent several hours by myself going through everything. When I had packed up my goods I had used every nook and cranny to tuck small items into so now the task required sorting through everything again.

The work began slowly, cautiously at first, I decided to make three piles. To go.. to keep... to reconsider. The task progressed, becoming easier as I began to relinquish my stuff while reminding myself how deeply satisfying my ministry was to me. The afternoon dwindled and now I was into books, lots of pictures, visual aids and teaching materials I had used through the years with kids. It was easy to create a few piles to leave to the Sunday School hoping they might be put to good use.

I found considering my books to be much more difficult and dove in, letting go of some cherished "friends". Book lovers understand what I mean. I was surprised to hear someone come in and when I looked up I realized it was the youth pastor. After a brief explanation of what was going on I offered him the opportunity to claim any books he would like to have. He was like a kid in a candy store, with a big smile on his face he enthusiastically grabbed book after book. That was fun providing a light moment in the midst of my arduous afternoon. Next I attacked the "keep" pile and moved most of it over to the "let go" one.

Finally after a long day, I walked out the door physically and emotionally exhausted with only a large plastic box of very personal items. As planned I then took off for some R&R at the Jersey shore. Walking the beach I worked on my grief.

Costly?... you bet. Regrets?... not really. I've always prayed, "Lord I want your best" and that usually requires some giving up, some letting go. Wondering again Lord, I know Sitka's next, but what will that be like and what comes after that. It was time to back off and remind myself that every journey requires taking steps, one at a time.

En route to Sitka I spent a short time in Sequim. I faced more goodbyes. It was wonderful to feel the love and know I would have much prayer support. John and Armenta, friends from the church, provided my transportation to the Alaskan Ferry, docked in Seattle. They picked me up at the Barnes. John loaded my gear, one footlocker, two large suitcases, my carryon and of course my guitar.

When we arrived at the dock the place was alive with activity. We noticed the familiar carts, where I needed to stash my gear. They appeared full. We hustled my stuff from the car and John rearranged luggage to successfully get my bags on the cart, actually putting my bags underneath the other ones as my stop would be at the end of the line.

With a huge sigh of relief and a thankful prayer we said our goodbyes. Their look of love, pride and concern warmed me. They had hoped I would be in Sequim longer and Armenta had even prayed I would find a mate and settle there. Our lives and decisions have effect on many people.

With a blast of the horn the journey began. The ferry pulled out of the harbor proceeding up the coast line while I easily identified well known places. I had secured a deck chair and arranged myself for the two night journey. Once again I was heading to a place I had never been to work with a person I had never met. This was my first trip north and I've often recommended that if you are only going one-way on the ferry, this is the way to go. The trip starts with multiple lovely scenes and as the boat carries you north the view progressively become more spectacular.

Little cardinal... sweet lady...
 are you ready for this new place...
  seems like it's terribly far away....

After a most needed stop at Ketchican where I was able to get off the ferry and spend a few hours walking around, it was definitely sinking in that my next adventure had begun. Those ever present questions resurfaced... Lord, what will this be like... what do you have for me here to give... what am I to learn and receive? When the ferry came around a bend my first views of Sitka appeared. The pastor had told me he would meet me at the dock and I would be staying with him and his family for a while. Land at last, my gear was loaded in his car and I was homeward bound. Dave and Holly had three sons that were most delightful. My room thoughtfully was in the basement providing privacy as well as darkness. This was helpful while adjusting to the very long summer days, aiding my sleep.

Dave was an extrovert and eager to fill me in on the church, its needs and where he saw me stepping in. Being in their home provided us with ample opportunity to talk.

The church was anticipating the September startup of a Logos program after some intensive training. I knew already from previous phone conversations that I was to play a major role in that after school, Bible based program. It was August and VBS time and that involved me immediately. Got a kick out of the kids not enjoying the sunny days. "It's was too bright", they complained. That was one I never had heard before.

Sitka, I'm convinced, is one of the most beautiful places on this earth. It is located on a natural horseshoe harbor on Baranoff Island that is enveloped with mountains on its three sides. There are small islands in the harbor. One houses the Coast Guard and the airport. Mount Edgecomb is on another. This is a volcano that resembles Mount Fuji in Japan. It's beauty is ever present. A great local story tells of how when Mc Donald's came to town their protocol is to position the fast food building so that the diners are facing the road, hence will eat faster. The proprietors begged for a change of policy and finally a big exec flew up to asses the situation. An exception was granted when he agreed it would have been a crime not to have the customers enjoy the full view of the Mount and picturesque harbor. The view was more than likely to attract customers rather than deter them. Many a time I stopped there just to savor my cup of coffee while reveling in the majesty of the volcano.

Sheldon Jackson College has a rich Presbyterian background. Named for the first missionary in Alaska, it had been a boarding high school. There were a few members in the church who had attended. Now that it was a college, students came from the lower forty-eight as well as from Alaska.

The city spread out along the waterfront, approximately eighteen miles from one end to the other. The summer I arrived the gravel roads were in the process of being blacktopped, a big event for the island. There were shorter roads climbing up the hillside and winding through some residential areas. So me, the one who loves to drive, when I had a car would go back and forth on the limited roads. If you drove south the road deadened at a lumber yard. The north end had a pleasant park I enjoyed walking the paths. In the early fall I spotted the salmon making their way to their spawning places.

A bridge linked the mainland to the island where there was a boarding high school, Mount Edgecomb. Students came from all over the state and it was fascinating observing the rich variety of Eskimo, Native Americans, and Caucasian in this small city. It was very cosmopolitan and made me think of a little New York City. There were all kinds of politics and power struggles going on below the radar.

The Russian Orthodox Church was largely made up of the Native American population. The other churches were essentially white with the exception being the Presbyterian Church. Due in part to the Sheldon Jackson connection, it reflected the demographic make-up of Sitka, forty per cent native, sixty per cent white. Many of the leaders in the church were from a variety of area tribes. A few of the men represented them, commuting to D.C. to speak for tribal concerns. This was a bonus, providing plenty of opportunity to enjoy their input and perspective since many were vitally engaged in the life of the church.

The Alaskan Ferry docked a few miles out of town, while the huge cruise ships would anchor in the harbor and transport their passengers to the dock right next to the community center. The tourists were ushered in to watch the lively Russian dancers, who were all women dressed as men with their high black boots and Russian garb. They gave a tremendous performance that captivated the audience. The tourists would then pour out of the center and rush up the street, past the Russian Orthodox Church and into the gifts shops and eating places. The shops were full of Native, Eskimo and Russians objects and paintings.

an almost tragedy...

The first weekend in town the pastor's wife and I attended the Russian Orthodox Church, knowing that once I officially began my work I would be too involved to squeeze in a visit. A young Tlingit boy around ten or eleven had hiked up with his older brother into the dense forest. He had been instructed by his brother to wait at a certain point because there was something higher up he wanted to check on.

Upon his return he discovered his brother had wandered off. After much calling and looking he hurried frantically down the trail to tell the family his brother was lost. Quickly men gathered and began searching until nightfall. No sign of him had been found. The next day a helicopter was summoned and combed the area equipped with sensors that detect warm spots indicating a person or a large animal. Word has quickly spread all over town and churches were united in praying for the boy and his family. Many joined in the search. Sunday morning came, two nights he had been missing in the woods. Fortunately the weather had stayed warm giving cause for hope and everywhere in town you went there was obvious concern. It permeated the entire population.

After we were in church for over an hour, a man hurried in proceeding up to the priest and interrupting the service. He whispered into his ear and then turned and exited rapidly. The priest stopped his recitation and announced the boy had been found. Everyone clapped when the family got up and slipped out while the priest immediately returned to the litany. Soon we heard church bells from all over town as the news spread. I had wondered why the boy hadn't just walked down the steep hillside, but was informed that the forest is very thick and full of multiple "ups and downs" making it extremely disorienting. The boy was cold, frightened and hungry but after a thorough checkup at the hospital returned to his home. Quite a way to launch my new year.

While settling into a new routine I was usually without a car. Occasionally one would be available if the owner was going "outside" to Seattle or south. That was a totally new concept for sure. Invariably it seemed whenever I had use of one car another was available at the same time. Often I would alternate, certainly didn't want either vehicle to be offended.

My part in having a loan of a car was to meet the owners at the airport to transport them home. I always got a kick out of watching the sky for the lone jet to circle the harbor before going to pick them up. It was fascinating and fun watching the unloading of the baggage because of the wide variety of items. People shopped when they went south, so along with duffle bags would be all kinds of packages. Remember spotting lampshades, ski and camping gear, fishing rods all coming down the baggage chute ready to be claimed.

When I started to visit and get acquainted I sensed a desire on the part of some of the young moms to get together for a Bible study. What a joy that became for me. They shared their struggles and concerns and our meetings were marked with laughter and tears. We grew close as we dug into God's Word and opened our hearts to him and to each other. In later months, I led another small group of women that was rewarding also, but they were in a different place in their lives with their own set of issues and concerns. This created a different dynamic.

While visiting in homes and engaging in conversations with folks, I began to pick up on the dangers these families lived with. Many tragedies occur when the men are fishing. Both loss of life and severe injuries happen. The loggers also face serious injuries that in a moment can change lives. Many jobs were seasonal, especially for the men, leaving long months, usually in winter, of idleness which led to drinking problems.

It became clear quickly that fishing and hunting were not considered sport but a serious venture to supply venison and seafood for the winter months. I enjoyed the best venison, both sweeter and more tender than I had ever tasted. My host explained to me that the flavor of deer is based on its diet and whether they had to run a lot to find food. In the dense forest the food was plentiful so they did not have to cover large distances to find more than an ample supply. I was receiving quite an education.

On another visit with a couple in their sixties, shared they had met each other at Sheldon Jackson when it was a boarding high school. Polly described what a significant time that had been. She was a Tlingit and found at the school both an education as well as her Christian faith. Listening intently, I remained quiet when she paused and then heard her BUT. "But, we were told that everything Indian was evil, our dances, our rituals, our language, even our totem poles." As the couple opened up even more I sensed the intense feeling of both love and hate for those high school years. Glad I learned to not be afraid of silences in conversations. They often lead to deeper things.

On a lighter note, Herb shared a fishing story. They were visiting his relatives in Minnesota and had been taken fishing on one of the many lakes. He kept reeling in fish but kept taking them off the hook and throwing them immediately back in the water. Finally his host asked him what he was doing? He explained they were all too small! He was quickly informed that this was not Alaska, he wasn't going to find any larger fish.

One of my first homes was with a family of five. The youngest was a little fellow close to two. I was blessed with a lower level apartment of my own, joining the family at meal times. The little guy, every chance he got, would make his way down the stairs and try to open my door. When he succeeded he would burst into the room and with a big grin say, "Ha Ha!" He became known as my Ha Ha boy.

Dale, the dad worked for the Coast Guard. Sue, his wife was Italian They had fun telling folks they were both Indian. He Tlingit, she was a "Sue".

My next home was with Garth and Evelyn, Dale's parents. Evelyn's brother was the pastor I had met in Haines. They had a lovely home and on the top floor they had set aside a comfortable place with a marvelous view, a special place where visiting ministers could stay. They called it their "Elisha room", naming it after the Old Testament prophet who was provided with a comfortable room on the roof whenever he was in the area. They were really sensitive and caring of my needs while in Sitka.

Living on an island was another learning experience. That kind of isolation was unique to me. The realization that you couldn't just pick up and go whenever you felt the need took some rethinking. I had to deal with those longings to go home in new ways. Watching the sky and seeing the lone plane departure of the day heading south was a poignant reminder that it took both planning and money to leave. I was identifying now with the need to go "outside" I had heard expressed by many. That common experience of feeling closed in, trapped, desperate to get to the lower forty-eight where choices, variety, loved ones, fresh stimulation could be found demanded adjusting to a different reality.

Christmas time...

Early December I found myself at the right place at the right time. Two whales had gotten off track and wandered into the harbor and then turned south where the water ends. Surprised and confused the huge mammals stayed a few days. On one of those days, I happened to have a car and had driven to the south end. I spotted a few cars parked at the pull out. "Hm, what's going on?" People were out of their vehicles and looking intently at the water. Quickly I parked and hurried over, rewarded with an unexpected sight. Two whales were cavorting close to shore. They were putting on a show doing all sorts of maneuvers and breaching right before our eyes. It appeared they were having a ball. We watched intently, totally enthralled. Overwhelmed, I was thankful for my early Christmas gift.

Another unique happening occurred when I was working in my upstairs office located in one of the classrooms. I had found a small artificial Christmas tree with a few decorations and had put that up so both the kids and I could enjoy it. I felt an odd sensation almost like the room had moved and happened to glance over in the direction of the tree and saw all the decorations were swaying. Hm, was that an earthquake. Quickly I ran downstairs to the church office and asked Jane, the secretary was that an earthquake? Yes, was her reply and in moments you'll hear sirens warning of a tidal wave and the children in the school will be marched up the hill to the high school where they would be safe just in case. Later when I heard the news on the TV, the report was that the earthquake occurred near Anchorage and was only a minor one.

A particularly precious time happened on the Sunday before Christmas in Worship. I was giving the children's message and invited the boys and girls to gather around the manger. While telling the story, I picked up the baby doll wrapped in swaddling clothes and went to each child showing them the babe. There was a moment of awe and reverence. Their eyes were all sparkly. I was reminded of those words in 2 Corinthians, "You will be made rich in every way....". Amen, I thought. God's promises repeatedly come to life for me.

Another Christmas treat was a trip to Sequim and Bernice for a holiday break. She had moved in October and now lived near the church. Bernice and her husband had lived in a module home in a rather isolated spot. Her son had encouraged her to move and now she was living in a small neighborhood across from the church. She realized how much safer she felt.

While visiting, I made phone calls to family and chatting with my Gretchen, daughter-in-law remember clearly her saying "You know Ruth, there are lots of churches around here that could use you." I sensed that my getting further and further away was a worry for my family. I suspect they were thinking where in the world will she go next? That gave me food for thought.

back to Sitka...

Logos Club is the after school program that the church started in the Fall. The elementary school was located right across the street so the kids could run over to the church to attend the club meetings. I was finding the lesson material to be wooden and dated, too much like school work. With my teaching background I had some success in making it more alive. My evaluation was not appreciated and was told the material was mandatory. The other teachers shared my analysis and frustration.

A strong point of the program was a sit-down meal was provided. Volunteer table moms and dads ate with the kids and guided the conversation while striving to develop good table manners. The program was demanding, especially on the volunteers who were responsible for the kitchen prep and cleanup. But there's lots to be said about the value that comes from sitting down and eating a meal together. It creates a closeness, a bond.

Another one of the strengths of Logos was its emphasis on service. Everyone was to be involved in serving in the church in some capacity. The usual way was to participate in the children's choir. After the new year we were able to inject into the program two electives, puppetry and clown ministry. Clowning was mine and proved to be a healthy outlet for my creative juices. The group was fun to work with and enjoyed the training and preparation. Sunday Worship was the culmination of the workshops and what excitement as they put on the white face. When we stood in a circle holding hands praying that God would bless our ministry, it was definitely a cherished moment. The clowns were thrilled and well rewarded with the response after their presentation. The feedback they received from the congregation was satisfying to all of us. The puppets were also well received and appreciated.

One of the Logos club nights a couple of the boys came up to me and asked me where did I live? When I named the home I was presently in they said "oh no, where do you really live?" This provoked a response to their question I put in the church newsletter.

A VIM View...Sitka
But where do you live, you know , where is your home? that's a question I've heard before and one, believe me I ask myself from time to time.
Perhaps part of the answer comes in asking, what is home? Is it simply a place to stash our

stuff, to take a shower, grab a bite to eat. Or is it something more than that?

Home to me is where I'm accepted where people care about what's going on inside of me and care enough to share what's going on inside of them .
When I think of the more than thirty homes I've been a part of these past four plus years I'm flooded with many precious memories.

What variety I have experienced. Small homes with a room where my suitcase became my dresser to large rooms where roller skates would be handy. Single beds, daybeds, couches to a king-sized bed I never needed to change the sheets. I simply moved a little each night.

My home have been with families with teenagers, families with small children. Grandparents who had almost a constant flow of children and grandchildren coming to visit. Houses of widows who needed to give and receive love.

I've shared homes with dogs, cats, birds, a white rat and a variety of fish

fortunately they all weren't in the same house.

"Home sitting" has been a joy along the way that provides a time to enjoy my own space. A time where I get the opportunity to dust, vacuum and take out the garbage just like an ordinary person.

Where is my home, where do I really live? Why, I live with you, the church family where I have been invited to be a part of you and you become a part of me as we share together in God's love and grace. You see, I live with my family!

Being without a home was challenging. Saying I was homeless

wasn't really accurate. If anything, I was "homeful". The constant moving and adapting to each situation wasn't natural, I can attest to that. I was keenly aware that the Lord had given me a gift and even as a child had been preparing me for this calling. Looking back at my childhood, it was evident that experiences I had were training me for this phase of my life. Lessons learned had formed and equipped me in multiple ways. Let me explain a little...

childhood memories...

My older sister came down with scarlet fever. I was three and a half and my baby brother almost one at the time, so when my aunt and uncle offered to take me home with them, my parents were relived to have me away from the contagious disease. This began years of my spending time with them.

While with them, I was a cherished only child. They bought clothes and dolls that stayed at their house when I returned home.

Still imprinted in my memory is the difficulty experienced when a child, I moved from home with my parents to my aunt and uncle and back again. This caused lots of guilt and confusion, strong feelings of being disloyal because I didn't want to leave, either home. The emotional swing from being the middle kid to being an only child was big. It was painful learning to be adaptable and flexible. Neither my mom nor my aunt seemed to be aware of this stress as I guess I was a born "stuffer" pushing down the feelings and thoughts so not to hurt anyone. Something I had to unlearn in my later years. Thankfully at an early age I learned to tell Jesus about my "stuff". Skippy, the family dog was another safe listener.

My relationship with my Uncle John, I will always treasure. He had been wounded in World War 1 and still had shrapnel in his leg. He was unable to bend the leg, but it never prevented him from functioning. His job was with the New Jersey State Park system and after spending a few years at Washington's Crossing he was transferred to Ringwood Manor when I was around five. He lived there until I was nine or ten.

The Hewitt family had given the property to the state to be used as a park. An impressive manor house that sat up on a knoll over looking some ponds below, lovely developed gardens complete with fountains as well as some wooded areas that made good picnic places all were part of the gift. My Aunt Daisey and Uncle John lived just a few steps from the manor house in a renovated building that had housed the laundry and servants' quarters.

To me, it was a fairy land. I could romp on the paths, visit the fountains delighting in the bullfrogs and was often even taken into the manor house. The cleaning lady was a friend of my aunt and she allowed me to wander around and even climb up on the beds as she worked. For a little girl with a big imagination, it was paradise.

After dinner, my uncle would head to his chair and turn on the radio. He'd sit down, light up his pipe and then invite me to sit on his lap as he listened to the world news. I felt like the well-known newscasters Lowell Thomas and Gabrielle Heater were old friends. How I loved that special time just sitting there and enjoying the togetherness. My relationship to my Heavenly Father was enhanced by that experience. I love to feel my Lord's arms around me as I sit quietly and peacefully on his lap. There's no need for words while I rest in his love.

My uncle and I would later walk down to the entrance of the park and close the gate, locking it for the night. On our return walk we would sing, " Hi ho, Hi ho it's home from work we go." Our next chore was an honor as I was allowed to take down the Americanflag and assist my uncle as we folded it properly. Quite an impressive ritual.

Both my aunt and uncle loved going to the beach and staying

in a hotel in Ocean Grove. They were rich or so it seemed to me, we ate all our meals out. We loved jumping the waves and playing on the beach and what fun in the evening, walking the boardwalk in Asbury Park and enjoying the merry-go-round as well as some other amusements. Watching the candy machine making the salt water taffy also intrigued me.

But there were times I longed to be home with my family and that made me sad and confused. How could I even think about leaving my aunt and uncle who were doing so much for me. I don't recall being stressed after the transition was made. It was the anticipation, the leaving that was painful.

Looking back at those experiences I marvel how God used that training ground to equip me for the volunteering lifestyle. Living in different homes, settling in and nesting only to be uprooted, going to someplace new. Of course on a larger scale the leaving churches that I had heavily invested myself in and going to a new one was even more costly. The "going to" wasn't a problem, perhaps a little scary but always stimulating.... but the leaving... oh my. I learned to "handle" it better but never could avoid the pain.

stresses...

The new year had come and the early weeks were passing quickly. I couldn't avoid the obvious question, am I to stay for a second year or am I to go? My body was talking to me with unusual aches and pains, even broke out in hives. In September, I had experienced weeks of diarrhea and now other signs of stress were manifesting themselves. All very strange happenings for me.

In my earlier experiences there had been an openness with the pastors I had served with. Even an expectation that I would be visible in morning services including an occasional sermon. To me it was a great joy to read scripture, offer a prayer as well as give the children's sermon. To be given the privilege of presenting a sermon was both thrilling and humbling. Dave seemed to have a great reluctance, until he finally allowed me to speak he expressed his surprise at my effectiveness.

I had always been a team player, that didn't seem to be part of his agenda. My reaction was one of feeling stifled, squashed. Being creative is a necessary piece of who I am and my body reacted before my heart and mind had acknowledged this situation wasn't a good fit for me. Inner turmoil manifesting itself in different ways alerted and caused me to face the hard facts. It also sent me to the Lord, my source of strength and wisdom. I did not want to get sucked into the negativity.

This was going to be a long stint. My health as a volunteer demanded a delicate balance or I found myself seriously hurting. My needs for love, affirmation, ministry that was appreciated and significant were all crucial to my being able to handle not having my own home and being away from family and friends. When relationships and meaningful ministry are lacking the emptiness becomes overwhelming, the scales are tipped and I find myself hanging on for dear life. Our relationship was painful.

Thankfully however, as I searched my heart wondering whether I had misread the Lord's leading I felt God's reassuring peace. Many times he calls us to difficult uncomfortable places for he has his own purposes that we are unable to discern. Once again I appreciated my Master's hand in leading and placing me in a chosen sequence. Each church was unique and in each one I was growing and stretching. Terrace View and Dick had freed me to "be me" and not get hung up with a fear of failing. "So what if you goof.. just pick yourself up , dust yourself off and start all over again." Remember that old song?

In retrospect, I was battling some depression. The people were great but I felt somewhat guilty about my lack of energy, lack of vision. It was difficult to not let my frustrations spill out. I was fearful I was holding back not giving myself fully to others. Was that from a sense down deep in my gut this would be a one year commitment? Had I made a mistake in coming to this church? Those questions always sent me to my knees. The situation was difficult, but I was right where God wanted me to be. The question remained, would it only be for one year and if so, what's next Lord? I knew that the Barnes especially Ruth, wanted me to spend some time with their son Bill in Okanogan. But Lord, central Washington, high dessert, no water?! Are you really sure?

After much prayer I put out a feeler and contacted Bill Barnes in Okanogan. I asked if he and the church would still be interested in my coming. In my Bible reading in the book of Acts I read the part about Paul changing his plans when he sensed a call from Macedonia. That resonated with me. There was that sense of a call, a familiar Holy Spirit nudge I had experienced before.

In February I was blessed with another special happening. Bob and Eme, a most precious couple from Sequim, were part of an elder hostel group traveling on the ferry and would be arriving in Sitka. It was great to see them and I relished their warm hugs and keen interest in my welfare. Their visit coincided with my trip to Presbytery in Petersburg. I was able to travel with them to Ketchican and then board a different ferry to take me to my meeting.

Going to a presbytery meeting in southeast Alaska is a really big event. No one drives there, it involves an overnight on the ferry or air flight. Traveling in the off season on the ferries had a different flavor from my previous trips due to lack of tourists. Most passengers are Alaskans, a good mix of Native and White and the atmosphere was relaxed.

Petersburg was a pretty little spot with a strong Scandinavian flavor. It was good to be with the various pastors and their wives, most of whom served in isolated villages. All were thankful for the diversion. The church put out a traditional smorgasbord rich with lots of seafood and sweet treats. After the meetings were completed, most of us stayed to attend Sunday Worship. We had been instructed to bring our luggage to church and they would be checked and loaded on the plane for us. Before the service was dismissed, those of us flying out were instructed to stand and leave. Cars were lined up, ready to drive us to the plane. We boarded through the rear of the waiting jet. How's that for VIP treatment! I felt like a celebrity.

A short while later Bill,the pastor in Okanogan called to say that I had an open door. I then shared with Dave that I would be leaving the end of the school year. The whole process of leaving and difficult goodbyes began. As I reflected on my experiences I wrote for myself the following.......

Special delights. from one of the most beautiful places.

sounds of sitka
the cry of the raven
    the quiet lapping of the gentle waves on the shore
the drone of the float plane as it struggles to take off
    the roar and thunder of the jet heading for home
the somber chanting , Lord have mercy on me
    the joyous music and stomping of the dancers' boots
the haunting beating of the tom toms
all unique..all calling to me to return..

sights of sitka
the yellow tour buses
    the luxurious cruise ships in the harbor
        the rush of tourists as they blanket the town

the kayaks moving silently in the water
   the ever present eagle high in the trees or swooping
      down for a catch
   the jumble of houses some garbed in gaudy colors
      the ever present fishing boats
the mountains that encircle the harbor

         smells of sitka
the salty air
   the engine smell of the boats and float planes
the smell of the coffee in the coffee express
the aroma of freshly caught salmon and halibut cooking on
the grill..

In the spring the Young Moms had a good ole girl slumber party. The laughter and the tears were memorable. We all went home the next morning aglow. To celebrate our year a week or two later we enjoyed a salmon feast with the husbands. One of the men cooked the fish on the grill and it was declared the greatest. His secret weapon was a little brown sugar. Needless to say goodbyes were tough.

I attended a Tlingit funeral and was impressed with the lack of their concern with the length of the proceedings. Everyone sat around in a large circle after the structured service sharing a story or two about the deceased. There was such a honoring. Often feel we in our culture don't know how to grieve. Too much of a hurry to be alone depriving ourselves of the comfort and healing the community can bring.

last events...

Rainbow Glacier Camp was to be my last piece of ministry before leaving. The camp is located just outside Haines on an absolutely gorgeous spot facing the glacier. My duties would be to serve as a counselor for the week and then escort the campers from Sitka home on the ferry.

I was blessed with a cabin of ten to twelve year old girls. Getting up early to enjoy my coffee and a "quiet time" before the campers were roused, worked well for me. The day was full. I soon discovered that when the kids were on the beach in the afternoon my presence wasn't needed. After checking with the leaders, I would slip away to my cabin, stretch out on my cot, relishing the quiet enabling me to keep up with the camp routine. The women in the kitchen and office had wondered how I would bear up and at the end of the week were most complimentary regarding my service.

Once again I was able to do some clowning, involving the campers. Our skit and songs were a big hit and well worth the effort. The trip home was a melancholy one, knowing it was my last time on the Alaskan ferry. I'd soon be flying south and would miss the Marine Highway I had so enjoyed.

Sitka had been a hard and challenging place for me. I'm thankful that in spite of it all, the Lord had given me a peaceful heart realizing I was right where he wanted me to be. Following him as he leads, doesn't mean my path will be easy. I was learning anew that the Lord chooses at times, to put us in difficult places that bless others while stretching us, deepening our commitment and trust.

Now a new opportunity in a new place was soon to begin. I was thankful for my fascinating year and will always cherish the sweet memories of dear folks.... the awesome beauty I was engulfed in.... the ever present eagles that I never tired of.... the fascinating multicultural environment that was reflected in the church ... and even more important the ever present comfort of my Lord and Savior, Jesus Christ. Yes, Father, you do things well!

In reading the Gospels and tuning in to Jesus' words, I

appreciated some of the anguish he faced leaving his disciples. I was touched when reading his last words teaching them, opening them up to deeper treasures right to his last breath. Sure he was more than ready and eager to be with his Father. But how painful the leaving must have been. They had spent so many intimate times those three years together. He had invested himself in their lives. Those goodbyes were not easy, they came at a great price.

5

Okanogan '88

*Help me to discover the gifts you have given me and how
to use those gifts in a way that is worthy of the giver.
Help me to discover something of who I am from the
things I write whether those things are a letter or a journal
entry, a poem or a play, a novel or a note to a friend.*
Ken Gire

The flight home was awesome. The crystal clear sky
created great visibility. When the plane approached the
Seattle area it was easy to spot the San Juans and the Olympic
Peninsula stretching out from end to end. Identifying Neah Bay,
Port Angeles and the Dungeness Spit all heightened my eager
anticipation to be in this place again.

Bernice was there to meet me. The next few weeks being in
Sequim and Mount Lake Terrace were priceless. All those hugs
and precious conversations with dear folks fed my soul. Bernice
was enjoying her new house. It became a home for me in the
coming years. The cherished friendships with Pastor Bill, Agnes,
BJ, Barnes and others were telling me deep down within, that
Sequim would always be a special place, a "home" I would always
both want and need to return to. An added bonus was that I
also was able to have some time with my Terrace View friends.

After my short respite it now was time to say farewell and fly back to Connecticut. House-siting had be arranged in a lovely old home in Easton complete with the use of a pickup truck. What fun! The charming house dated back to early eighteen hundreds. Several deer grazed in my yard late afternoons adding to my delight. I found myself savoring the quaintness and prettiness of New England.

Time with family was a top priority and I relished the time with John, Gretchen and my little girls. Kristen was four and a half and Lindsay, now two. Kristen came to me with open arms while "Lins" held back with a questioning look. She sensed that there was something about me that she recognized and yet she didn't quite know who I was. That was tough on this grandma although it was not a problem since she quickly warmed up to me. I was able to have special times with the girls, especially Kristen.

Dan was now serving in a church in Pennsylvania. This location provided the opportunity to spend time with him. Connecting with Susan, Barb and of course Chuvalas was a must on my list. Visiting my "home" church in Brookfield and seeing the new building, in addition to spending time in conversation with Jim were a delight. Even more hearing him preach that Sunday, blessed me as always.

Visits with Dad, my sister and her family, and then with my brother and his family were fitted into my busy agenda. All these times with loved ones filled me up. I wished there was some way of packaging them and carrying them with me. And now it was time to head back to Washington.

onto Okanogan...

Why in the world are you going to Okanogan? That was a repeated question and one I was asking myself. My usual quip was "I'm heading east to dry out", (from western Washington). I found myself wondering what is this part of the country like?

Guess I could still hear my dad talking about wanting to see this country.

This place would be totally different than any I had ever been exposed to. This time I had met the pastor I would be working with although we hadn't engaged in conversation. I knew Bill Barnes was Bob and Ruth's beloved eldest child. My expectations were that he would be a man of the Bible and a man of prayer. His mom had shared her perspective and sensed his need for encouragement and a prevailing loneliness. I expected he would desire my input and would be seeking personal growth. It was time to go and the Barnes would take me "over the hill" to my new home and church.

There were many goodbyes to dear ones, the peninsula, the ferry and now the North Cascade Highway. Remembering my first trip I was eagerly anticipating this one. The ride is spectacular and inspiring. After descending from the mountains we drove through Winthrop, a tourist spot that is a living replica of an old wild west town. Boardwalks, hitching posts, shops with cowboy regalia and eating holes line the streets, all encouraging visitors to stop and spend some money. There are scheduled gun fights to add to the scene.

Now we were on the east side of the Cascades and after a short distance south, we turned east and traveled over another mountain.

The terrain was such a contrast to the lush green western side of the Cascades. This was high dessert and as I peered out my rear sit window I began to notice both ranches and orchards. At the bottom of the long hill we took a sharp right and turned into the Barnes' driveway.

The family was all there to greet us since this was still August and summer vacation. Bill showed me proudly around the house that he was remodeling and expanding, pouring much effort and labor into creating a most attractive home. The kids, Carrie,

Heather and David enthusiastically welcomed me as did Jan, Bill's wife.

This was my home during this first month. Their trailer parked outside the house and next to the pasture gave me my own space which provided me with a comfortable nesting place. There was plenty of company with the busy family, enjoying meal times and hearing about their activities. Jan had horses and I got a kick out of this new experience. The pasture was right out my window and it was delightful watching them move about. They always became frisky, kicking up their heels while galloping around if a storm was approaching.

Davey, the youngest child, taught me about dry thunderstorms, when the sky would darken and a sudden fierce wind accompanied with loud claps of thunder and bolts of lightning appeared but there was no rain. Storms like that often cause fires. This hot and dry climate was brand new for me. Once the sun began to drop lower in the sky, the temperatures would quickly cool. By nightfall I loved snuggling in my bed and needing to pull the covers up.

Jan thoughtfully took me with her my first morning while she tended to errands. We drove into Okanogan and continued on into Omak. The two towns run right into each other. This is high desert. To the east were plateaus that were reminiscent of Cowboy and Indian movies. I wouldn't have been surprised to see a group swoop down and attack the settlement.

We stopped at folks, the Martins, from the church and they reminded me of my friends the Merchants in Sequim. Wineva greeted me with a freshly picked peach that was the size of a grapefruit. When I reached for it the peach was oozing juice. What an unforgettable treat that was.

I spent time the next few days getting familiar with the church and working on my office. I appreciated help from Jan and Colleen, one of the ladies in the church I would later stay with. We made a good team as we threw away lots of stuff providing room for my books etc. and scrubbed down some walls. My office space had been significant to me in each church as it becomes my constant and dependable space. Hanging up a few posters and putting some other items around gave me a "home".

My childhood church had been small and simple in decor and my sense when entering this small church was a feeling of comfort. This feels familiar. Seems to me God must have a special place in his heart for small churches for there sure are lots of them. The building was attractive and I loved the way the windows lined both sides of the sanctuary. Sitting in the pews you could observe the road coming down from the plateau. During the harvesting of the apples, loaded trucks would rumble down the hill.

The choir, although small was blessed with some outstanding voices and were an asset in Worship. It was a treat singing some well known hymns and songs and to hear a Bible based message. The choir director had a lovely voice, was attractive, energetic and personable, but most often late. I spent a month with Colleen and her husband and was amused as I observed his way of coping with her tardiness. They were going to a wedding one Saturday when I was there and I noticed he was just relaxing as the hour drew near. He explained he had learned to wait until she reached a certain point and then he knew it was time for him to get ready.

On my first official Sunday we decided to introduce Chuckles to the church. While I pranced about there were two intense reactions, one of shock and disgust, the other... "oh, how delightful".

The Barnes and I had spent the previous weekend attending Family Camp at Tall Timbers. Such a joy for me to be there again and to share the weekend with folks from Terrace View as well as getting the opportunity to be introduced to some of the families from Okanogan.

the county fair...

This was followed with a week at the Fair. Bill always brought the camper to the fairgrounds and that became home for the week. The Barnes' kids were 4Hers. They had their rabbits and horses with them ready to show. Many from the church participated in a variety of activities. This was a great way to meet folks in this setting. I loved waking up at the fairgrounds, hearing the early morning sounds while wandering about observing all the activity as the animals were fed and groomed.

The early weeks brought a flood of migrant workers that swept through the orchards picking the apples. Trucks could be seen and heard from the church rumbling down the hillside with the produce. There was a sizable Mexican population that remained in the area since they had been able to find work year round.

Meetings with Bill were positive. He began to share his heart as a pastor. Often I was finding a pervasive loneliness exists especially in isolated areas and solo pastorates. Quickly, we developed a bond of trust that was mutually beneficial. I felt we were partners, a team and that was both necessary and nourishing.

A pastor in a small church is expected to be involved in all aspects of the ministry and I felt as a teammate that same challenge. I had learned in my other churches that attending committee meetings, Bible studies and small groups was an efficient and insightful way of getting connected with people. This combined with visiting in their homes, helps you to begin to sense what the temperature of the congregation is. Bill and I talked about some of the difficulties and that led me to do some trouble- shooting.

The entrance way and down along the halls had bulletin boards. The old school teacher in me took over since they all appeared too old and faded. Within a few days, I began sprucing things up, changing the bulletin boards and getting rid of clutter. This produced an immediate positive response. The fresh look was appreciated.

I started an after school time for kids interested in clown ministry. It was enthusiastically supported. My group included a range of ages from kindergarten to high school. When you are in a small church you find that there aren't many kids. The children are accustomed to being together and enjoy each other and don't get hung up with what their grade was. We all experienced lots of laughter while engaging in some serious learning. They listened intently while I shared the significance of the white face and explained that clown ministers give themselves away to bring joy to others. After several weeks of meeting together and practicing a skit we presented it to the congregation in a Sunday Service. The troupe felt rewarded with the response.

In October, I led a Saturday Retreat for the women at the church. My teaching was taken from the beginning chapters of Exodus and focused on the early years of Moses' life. This portion is a favorite of mine where Moses hears God tell him to take off his sandals for he's standing on holy ground. How much we deprive ourselves of the intimacy our Lord wants us to experience because we're too preoccupied to take our sandals off and soak up the moment.

Slowly, I was adjusting to this very different place even though I confess to feeling somewhat "shellshocked". The high desert is barren, full of tumbleweed and rocks of all sizes and shapes. Many familiar passages in the Psalms especially, now took on more meaning. I could understand David's reference to God my rock... my refuge... my hiding place. Without the large rocks a person would be totally unprotected.

Irrigation transforms the valley making its orchards productive. Both the northeast and the northwest are very green with lots of trees and I needed time to adjust to this new barren land. I quipped that in Sitka there wasn't very far that you could go in a car and that now I was in central Washington, I could drive forever and still not be anywhere.

new places...

In my wandering around, I began to realize that the enormous landscape was nourishing my soul in some way, reminiscent of being at the beach and looking out at the wide expanses of the ocean. An awe and reverence for God's creation coupled with a humbling of how I'm just a speck in the universe and yet the Lord doesn't just know my name he knows me through and through and cares about every detail of my life.

My explorations were reaping rewards as I discovered some lovely places. Driving south, I found the stretch of road between OKanogan and Brewster interesting. The changes in the terrain, the valley full of orchards, the river you caught glimpses of and driving up the hills to the flats. I quickly noted the landscape changed colors as the day progresses. Continuing south, I came to the little town of Paternos where I could sit on the banks of the Columbia River watching the water and at times, some wind surfers.

Continuing along the river I discovered Lake Chelan was about an hour away... a gorgeous lake that always seemed to have a sparkle. Wenatchee was available if I needed a "big city" complete with a modest mall. Leavenworth, nestled in the mountains was always charming, especially Christmas time with its Bavarian atmosphere. It was a delight to hear the oom- pah sounds and see the cuckoo clocks in the stores as well as a wide variety of nutcrackers. One of my must stops was a store stocked with many wooden toys. Upon entering the charming shop my attention was drawn up toward the ceiling where I spotted a train running on a track, that circled the store. In addition, my German heritage occasionally needed a sauerkraut and sausage fix and was more than satisfied until the next time.

Early in my stay I needed to go to Spokane for personal business reasons and was impressed and pleased with the drive noting the changes in the landscape. The ride started out with a steep climb up to the higher plateaus, through Indian country and then descending around the Grand Coulee Dam area, an awesome sight. Continuing east you find yourself in rolling wheat country that covered miles before arriving in the city.

In case you hadn't noticed this little female cardinal was out exploring again.

homes...

My homes were varied, some with couples, one a recent widow, some with families with children of a variety of ages. My next home was with a young couple who lived on a small ranch up on the hill. Bill towed the trailer to their ranch and that continued to be my private quarters. I was warmly welcomed into their home and quickly assimilated into the family. Their two kids, Billy was just starting kindergarten and Ginny, a delightful four year old provided me with lots of good "snuggle time." They were raising turkeys, in addition to keeping horses and some other animals. I was treated to a turkey feast of the freshest bird I will ever have. Stacey slaughtered it and then cooked it ever so slowly on the charcoal grill. What a flavor !

Across the road the cattle from another ranch were gradually being moved down the mountainside to be nearer the homestead during the winter months. Occasionally, they would wander onto the road much to the consternation of truck drivers accelerating up the steep incline. Some even wandered into our yard and I was given instruction how to take a pot and wooden spoon and go out banging to chase them back. That's out of my comfort zone, but I got quite adept at it and took some pride in my success.

Shortly after my moving on, Stacy lost his job at the orchard due to downsizing. This couple, that loved their home and ranch struggled to find a place and a new job to prevent them from having to leave the area. They did have to move but settled north of town in Conconully, a place that I enjoyed driving to as well as walking along the reservoir. They purchased and ran a tavern. When visiting, I found myself perched on a bar stool chatting with the both of them, a most unlikely place to find me. I know God has a marvelous sense of humor.

Another young couple provided me with a very warm and cozy nest. They had one child who was three and oozed energy. Impulsive, difficult to manage, he manifested all the classic signs of hyperactivity. Poor mom needed lots of reassurance that his behavior wasn't her fault. I loved being in that home. Brent filled a void in me, created by being totally apart from my sons. There was a caring, a sweetness about him that reminded me of my "boys".

One night I was relaxing on the couch when Darin burst in complete with coonskin hat and rifle and handed me another gun. He told me he had to go and kill the Indians and if they came running into the living room I should shoot them. "But Darin", I told him, " I can't shoot Indians I've lived with them. They are my friends". Perturbed with my statements, he quickly answered me by saying with hands on his hips. "Okay, you be nice to your friends and I'll just shoot the bad ones."

My homes in Okanogan continued to be very special but there was one that touched me deeply. God gave us a deep special bond. Tollie was loved by everyone. She was thoughtful, loving and giving, a beautiful example of what a Christian should be. Woody was a gnarly guy. He was known to be gruff and hard to get along with on occasions, but we just hit it off and developed a special bond. He shared with me, telling about events from World War II that he had never talked about. He, in his early twenties had to order younger men to fly missions into France, many who never returned. He and his squadron participated in the invasion of Normandy.

Some early mornings, when I would get up to use the bathroom I would see them sitting on their bed talking and laughing together. It seemed like their laughter flowed back and forth between them. Tollie told me that their relationship had gone through many testy times but I sensed it was more than sweet now and she agreed.

Woody had trouble sleeping due to back pain and would often be up early sitting in his chair. Usually, when I got up he would serve me a cup of coffee whenever I made my appearance and sit down near me and chat a while.

Just before I was leaving to go back east, I had made a trip over the "hill" to Sequim and Terrace View to say my goodbyes. After my long beautiful ride back, I pulled into their driveway and bag in hand, walked up to the door only to find a note telling me there was no room available. I could hear giggling behind the door and Tollie telling Woody to let me in. We all laughed together over that one.

When returning in the following years to visit, their home was always open to me.

Lots of relationships were deepening. A mutual respect existed. Another one of the younger families in the church, when they discovered I hadn't been home for Christmas the last few years, solicited donations totally surprising me with a generous gift of money enabling me to fly home as well as purchase some family gifts. This small church had a most generous heart. What a joyous Christmas morning that was as I delighted in the excitement of my little ones in North Carolina.

challenges...

Upon my return, Bill picked me up at the airport in Wenatchee, and said he had been worried that I might not return. He was relieved and happy to see me. My response was that I had left my gear behind and he told me he wasn't impressed with the importance I placed on my possessions.

Working with Bill was refreshing and rewarding and especially appreciated after my difficult year in Sitka. As the months went by, we planned and taught jointly... a Lenten Series... a confirmation class.. as well as sharing the Easter message.

I met a couple, going through a rough time in their marriage robbing them of joy, energy, enthusiasm. We began to meet together and immediately felt I was in over my head but also knew the Lord would give me the tools to help them. I found myself needing those "buckets of wisdom" again. Often I would find myself amazed as the Lord would provide me with just the right words to say.

Central Washington is full of orchards and I found myself intrigued while observing the wide variety of pruning methods used by the different orchards. Also, it became obvious that there is lots of work done in the winter months tending to the apple, peaches, pear and cherry trees. I found it fascinating noting the variety of techniques in pruning.

Early February and into April a rancher had to stick close to home keeping a check on his pregnant animals. The birthing season had no schedule since each new birth occurred at random. Ken, a rancher might have to miss teaching his high school class at church if a newborn decided his time had come.

He was a bachelor who eagerly committed himself to working with the teens even though that did not come naturally to him. He saw a void in the church and stepped up, filling that need. Not only was he their teacher, but a friend who was always available to them.

Often he would share how tough it was and the stress he felt. Interestingly though, he also shared how much he loved to visit folks in the nursing home and when he came away from those visits, he was energized. This was a perfect illustration of how in ministry, if we are placed in an area of our giftedness, we thrive, but when we struggle in other areas, we are depleted. Unfortunately in a small church, sometimes we are needed in areas that don't match our giftedness.

Come February the Session discussed the possibility of my staying for a second year. Bill with tears in his eyes, shared he was surprised I had come to their remote area in the first place. Of course I surprised myself and only God's calling, combined with his mother's earnest prayers brought that about. The group most enthusiastically urged me to stay. My heart was already confirming what the Lord was telling me. Much energy goes into developing relationships and implementing new ways of thinking and doing in the first year that allow the ministry to intensify in the second year. There is momentum that continues to build as people's trust and appreciation increase. The decision to stay was not a difficult one.

In early spring a few of us attended a conference in Spokane that was terrific. I enjoyed the city and some of the eating places I was treated to. Our group had a great time laughing and learning. The speakers were inspiring, but my biggest treat was hearing Max Lucado. He already was a favorite author of mine and I responded to his low key manner. His love for his wife, his children and his Lord reminded me of my friends Gary and Gale, back home.

Another highlight for me and the kids was the Vacation Bible School, we had before I took my summer break. There was a park up the hill from town actually near Ken's ranch. We met at the church and then transported kids to our camp site. Bill brought the trailer up and that became the craft center. We had created our own curriculum based on the adventures of Paul. Each day we had a different storyteller. The most unique one was Ken, who rode over from his nearby ranch on his horse and did his teaching. The kids loved it and all the folks involved felt it was well worth the effort.

I always said to Bill that this church was unusually blessed with outstanding people. If these same folks were placed in a large church they would like cream rise up to the top. Doris was one of many and was an encourager and inspiration to many. Both winters I was blessed with spending a few months when she and her husband went south. Those housesitting opportunities provided great breathing places for me.

an eventful summer...

It was summer and time to go home for a while. The anticipation of seeing all of my family and cherished friends was building. Little did I realize what this would involve, what major life changing events would unfold.

My son, John and his wife, Gretchen had found a most delightful charming old house dating back to the mid-1800's. There was a lovely spacious yard that made you feel like you were in your own private park. Discussions with banks and real estate agents were happening and before I returned to Washington the transaction was underway.

My middle son, Jim and his wife, Denise had bought and moved into a new house in Concord, North Carolina. Jim unfortunately had broken the lowest vertebra in his back. I had previously booked a flight and now was doubly glad to be able to spend time with Jim while he was recuperating. Denise and I had fun as we discussed redecorating plans. I loved having the time being with both of them. My return flight to Connecticut was a beauty. When we approached La Guardia Airport the sun was setting. The plane flew low over New York Harbor creating great views of the Statue of Liberty, lower Manhattan and the Empire State building.

My pastor of my home church in Connecticut was leaving after several years. He had been the organizing pastor and seen the fledging church through the construction of the building. His stimulating sermons and conversations we had shared were a vital part of my decision to volunteer. He was both a pastor and a friend and his absence would leave a gaping hole for me.

The church gave him a delightful farewell and we all had fun with various skits and readings. When Jim delivered his sermons he would pace while he talked. Four or five of us sat up in the front pew. One of the men imitated Jim walking back and forth and as he spoke we all shifted back and forth from one seat to the next while he paced, moving with him. Everyone was cracking up at our portrayal. His new church had a raised pulpit in it and I asked him if he was going to have a seat belt to anchor him.

He and I had so enjoyed our mutual passion for the Dodgers and that led to my tribute to my Dodger fan buddy......

Down in the valley we all listened to the man
Who told story after story of how the world began
He told of Sandy Koufax, Orel and La Sorda
He raved of Dodger blue and said everybody oughta
Give the Dodgers a hand, join the Dodger band, be a Dodger
  fan
Down in the valley this man of devotion
A leader and a friend to folks in commotion
But when championship and Series times rolled around
All meetings had to cease for by the TV he was found
Oh the chills and the thrills, oh the pain and the tears that
  lives in every Dodger fan down through the years
But when your blood turns completely to Dodger blue
Whether you win or lose your heart stays true.

My connection with my home church evaporated slowly after Jim left.

But the most shocking and difficult happening that summer was the tragic death of my dear friends, Gary and Gale's daughter. They had lived in Danbury and Gary had been pastor of the church I attended. We had shared many sweet times together and I had the little girls over to my house so Mom and Dad could enjoy some solo time. Marcia crashed her car on a rainy slippery evening, a few days prior to her high school graduation and her upcoming eighteenth birthday. Her sister was with her and had been thrown from the car, resulting in a concussion and a broken leg.

In the days to follow there was a flow of teenagers, who knocked on their door desperately needing to sit down and talk. Much ministry came out of this tragedy as both Gary and Gale was "there for them". Gale was given a passage of scripture that brought some comfort:

> *Isaiah 57:1&2 "The righteous pass away; the godly die before their time. And no one seems to care or wonder why. No one seems to understand that God is protecting them from the evil to come. For the godly will rest in peace who die."*

Dear friends in Vermont, Susan and Geoff also were experiencing pain. One of their sons was put in jail for a short time.

In the midst of all this stress I was deeply blessed with a visit from Dan my youngest son, visits to my aging dad and the joy of spending a few days on my beloved Long Beach Island. I stayed for a few days at Harvey Cedars Bible Conference where I had been blessed many times attending services as well as one of my summers working with the children at a Family Conference. When reaching to pay for my room, Al, the director told me it had already been "paid" for. Remembered that verse of mine in Isaiah,

> *"come buy wine and milk without money and without cost,*
> *you will be made rich in every way".*

Leaving my family and my grandkids seemed to be getting increasingly difficult. My son asked about the church in New Jersey I had some conversation with and I was sensing he and the family were hoping I would come home. The East coast was drawing me although I knew my time in central Washington was not complete. I found myself wondering what things would be like this second year.

After all these intense happenings all packed into that summer I "hit the wall" emotionally. I had returned to Washington to spend a little time in Sequim before returning to my duties in Okanogan. My reactions caught me by surprise because Sequim was truly one of my favorite places to be, rich in relationships and rich in awesome places for me to walk and reflect. The traumatic and intense events of the summer coupled with much listening to folks deep hurt, now produced a need to acknowledge, I was hurting. It seemed "nobody" had tuned into that. Then dear Bernice picked up that something was wrong, she shared her concern and asked me if I was all right. That opened the flood gates and I broke down and let it all pour out.

Satan has a huge advantage when we bottle things up. My bottling tendencies still existed and I found myself doing the "poor me" routine. Another factor I realized, I was dreading hearing all of the stuff I knew would be forthcoming when I returned to Okanogan and sat down with my troubled couple. It was essential that I first dealt with my own grief and pain.

an awesome trip…

My plans were falling into place for me to take a trip to visit Montana, Yellowstone and Glacier before cranking up my ministry in Okanogan. Jan's Dart would be available and the Bergs, a couple from church would be happy for me to stay with them in Yellowstone. The timing of this trip was perfect and I jumped at the opportunity I was handed.

After a few days in Okanogan my adventure began. I was somewhat apprehensive, but the excitement overcame that. Up early, I drove all the way to Yellowstone. Bergs, my hosts were surprised as they were in the habit of stopping overnight en route. Leonard had worked the last two summers at the park as a consultant for the road construction. They treated me to dinner and I tasted my first buffalo entree. I wasn't impressed. We chatted at home and I shared my desire to not only see the park but to also go to Jackson Hole and take in the Tetons. Many folks had urged me to do that. Barb said she would love to take me as she had not been there. That was perfect for me after a full day of driving.

Refreshed from a good night's sleep I was eager for this new chapter. Our route took us for a short stretch through Yellowstone, continuing south to Jackson Hole. Barb stopped so I could see some elk grazing off the road and then a quickie to show me Old Faithful.

What an awesome day. The splendor of the Tetons made me hope that I would be able to return and experience more of their beauty some day. On our return we stopped at the lodge in Yellowstone. There was a huge fire in the fireplace and a man playing the piano. We both enjoyed the atmosphere and the music. I had told Barb I had no difficulty in exploring Yellowstone on my own. She was relieved to hear that since her summer had been full of guests she had shown around.

Yellowstone is huge with such variety of terrain and

geographical sights to behold. It was Labor Day weekend and there were lots of sightseers. I stumbled into a place where there were a few other cars stopped in the midst of a herd buffaloes... intimidating... and fascinating.

Geysers... Old Faithful... the canyon ... the impressive falls... Jenny Lake complete with waves lapping at the shore..elk.. buffalo..moose... much to see and experience.

After bidding farewell to my hosts, I headed north to Glacier National Park. It was now Labor Day and here I was experiencing new places instead of preparing myself to begin a new school year. Finding a pleasant motel that faced the park entrance was no problem. I loved my view of the mountains while sitting on my bed sipping my coffee. In the park I found an inviting restaurant that suited me. At breakfast I devoured a bowl of hearty oatmeal with fresh blackberries. The water was crystal clear and delicious to drink I had some guilty feelings it was so good, thought I ought to pay for it.

Exploring Glacier, I located some lakes and lodges. There was a pleasant sprinkling of visitors enough to feel safe, but few enough to feel like there was plenty of space for all of us.

The second day I drove the Highway to the Sky. The road was a huge engineering success and the Dart did all right handling the hairpin turns, as I climbed and climbed some more. Up at the top the weather abruptly changed. Clouds moved in and dropped rain while thunder rolled around the parking lot. As if that hadn't been impressive enough I was pelted with hailstones. My devotions were in Revelation that morning and I had been reading the eleventh chapter that mentions a hailstorm. I still think the Lord was overdoing the "special effects".

Next I drove down the other side of the mountain and into the eastern part of the state and stumbled upon a very fascinating Native American Museum. These tribes were very different from the northwest ones... much more colorful in dress and headpieces.

Their clothing was made from elk, moose and bison. The Plains Indians lived in teepees that were moveable while they roamed the landscape in search of their food supply.

The time in Glacier will always hold a special place in my heart for the Lord tenderly drew me ever close to him, strengthening me in preparation once again for the ministry he had called me to.

> *Phil 4:13 "I can do all things through him who strengthened me."*

He knows I cherish the solitude and the awesome beauty...
His precious presence reminding me that, I am loved...
His gift of filling me up with thankfulness and appreciation... after an unbelievable summer.

The trip back to Okanogan was lovely. I made two significant stops after enjoying the drive along Flathead Lake. First one was at St. Ignaus where Pastor Bill, from Sequim had spent his sabbatical year. My second stop was at Cour D'Alene where I took the time to enjoy a boat ride on that gorgeous lake.

my second year...

I arrived home to a dark and empty house. It was Fair week and per usual, the family was there. The next day I entered into the activities watching Davey, on his horse Ginger and the kids from the church showing their animals. The Barnes' girls had raised sheep for the year to fulfill their 4H project. At the fair they paraded their prize sheep around the pen as bids were made to purchase them. Carrie, the oldest sister complained that Heather, who was both younger and small for her age got better offers. The biggest factor in the higher bids was that she sobbed while parading her sheep around the pen.

Also I found it exciting seeing a rodeo in its proper setting.

As a child my parents had taken us into NYC Madison Square Garden. We sat up in the nosebleed section thrilled to see Gene Autry and then another year, Roy Rogers. This was a new experience to see one outside in real cowboy country.

We had a lovable elderly couple in the church. Bill and I went to visit them as Mary was about to celebrate her 90th. The family had big plans to celebrate it at the church. Her husband quipped "I don't know why everyone's making such a fuss I would have been ninety by now if my father hadn't been so shy". He was 89 and still driving an old pickup. Bill warned me that if I heard his truck coming to quickly get out of his way.

A significant event happene when attending a Full Gospel meeting with some of the church members. I went forward wanting prayer. " What was I seeking?" was the question the preacher asked me. My reply was that I longed for a special anointing on my teaching. When he put his hand on my head and began to pray a warm glow came over me. I was keenly aware the Holy Spirit was touching me. When I look back I can see that my prayer was answered many many times and I'm thankful for his touch.

upcoming transition...

It was time once again to begin the process of seeking a new challenge as the calendar marked a new year. When I was home at Thanksgiving I went to talk with Roy, the pastor, about the possibility of serving in New Fairfield at the Methodist Church. I enjoyed some connections there since friends of mine had been members and we had shared prayer concerns through the years. A brief time, before beginning my volunteering, I had attended the services but felt drawn to go elsewhere. I recommended the church to my neighbors and it was the right fit for them. This was where my yard sale had taken place.

My meeting with the pastor was very encouraging and his

interest was keen. He could see possibilities when I shared what I had been doing as a volunteer staff person. He told me he would bring my proposal to the board and would keep in touch as to the reaction and progress. I couldn't help getting excited at the prospect of coming not only back home to Connecticut, but being in the same community as my oldest son and family.

Increasingly, I was hearing in quiet ways that all of my family were wanting more of me. Those desires and those longings were intensifying. And so slowly, because that how churches work, the pastor did make the contacts and the prospects were encouraging. By the first of March it was official after we made some two way adjustments. I wasn't hesitant to speak up about what I was offering. The board seemed to be approaching my position as an employee since that was their corporation mindset. They had experienced a "full-time" volunteer before that hadn't been accountable of their schedule. That had created problems.

Those months, "back at the ranch" were difficult but very rewarding. Bill said he was hoping I would stay forever although he was happy and understanding of my need to be close to family again.

There was a restlessness I was sensing in the church. Sadly it became apparent that many folks were verbalizing dissatisfaction with Bill. He had been their pastor a long time and even his avid supporters wanted/needed him to realize it was time for him to leave. They identified their personal need of a change and felt that it would be mutually beneficial. There was some resistance to his ministry. A few husbands had stopped coming over the years due to his style. His demeanor was a weary one and he was perceived as one who was unyielding and unwilling to change. There were other negative vibes I was picking up.

I brought some of this to Bill and we both spent significant time in prayer. He began to consider the steps that he would need to take to facilitate a move. Of course a dossier would be essential and that proved to be a huge stumbling block for him, personally. That was not a part of his comfort zone.

The counseling sessions with my troubled couple continued and were costly to me emotionally. Lord, these missions were painful. Sitka had been tough and now Okanogan was in different ways. Bill blessed me with his concern about my needs. Listening to two people you are deeply invested in and allowing them to pour out their deepest hurts about each other was excruciating. I was not a professional counselor and still the middle child that typically tends to see both sides of an issue. I keenly felt pain for both parties.

The Lord always provided serendipities that nourished my soul and gave me a fresh supply of courage and strength. I often enjoyed a particular walk up to the flats that overlook the area. The route began down in town and wound up the hill past homes and a stretch of orchards after reaching the top. At the end of the road was a lovely cemetery with great vistas. This particular morning there had been a few inches of snow and I remember how special it was making fresh tracks while I walked the quiet paths among the gravestones.

I initiated some small group Bible studies in Philippians, one of Serendipity studies. Happily some folks got involved that hadn't been used to going to such offerings. Bill had made a comment to me that I cherish when we talked about the study. He told me, I knew how to ask rifle questions that hit the target cleanly. Shotguns can make such a mess.

In my reading, I came across a deep and moving book on marriage and forgiveness written by one of my favorites Walter Wangerin. While reading it, I wept at the beauty of the intimacy our Lord wants us to have with him and also with our marriage partner. It was painful for me because it exposed once again, all that I was missing and longing for.

The farewell was warm and affirming. A meal followed the

morning worship, accolades by individuals followed and then the kids surprised me when they came running out garbed in their clown outfits. One of them had a white wig on and was burdened down with guitar and suitcase. The humor provided us with a good laugh.

Okanogan! I'm so glad I've spent these two years there. I learned to appreciate the beauty of the area... thrived with the warmth and kindness of the people... left aching for Bill and Jan... left aching for this special little band of believers that will always have a place in my heart.

Colleen sang her own words to the tune of an old song Red River Valley...

From this valley you say you are going,
We will miss your helpful ways and cheerful smile
So whenever you get the urge to do some traveling
Don't forget to come this way once in a while.

Though we don't have an ocean at our doorstep
With its tasty seafood and its pounding surf
You must admit we have rocks, sagebrush and blues skies
For variety and a different kind of turf.

We've been thinking of the two years you've been with us
Of the work, the fun, retreats and clowning, too
We will miss the happy times we have shared here
And we're glad we've had the gift of knowing you.

We all know your new VIM job will be special
Spending time with family and friends you love.
So we pray for God's protection and guidance
And showers of blessing from above.

May your future be all that you hope for
May you enjoy good health and find contentment too.

Just remember the Okanogan Valley
And the friends who all wish the best for you.

I made my goodbyes to dear ones in Mount Lake Terrace and Sequim. Bernice and I had talked about this move and we already were planning a trip to see me. Leaving the Okanogan Valley I knew there would be more visits in the future.

6

New Fairfield '90

*We may leave home but home never leaves us. Deep
inside all of us is something that draws us back.*
Kierkegard

After all those heavy duty farewells to dear folks in Okanogan as well as Terrace View and Sequim, I was now back East at home. I experienced pain leaving the northwest not just because of the deep personal relationships but also my connection with the natural beauty, the rugged mountains and beaches. My heart and mind were at peace, thankfully as I knew God had called me back to my roots, significant events and precious family times would unfold.

Almost immediately was the need to see my dad. It was time to empty his apartment at my brother's since he now needed full time assistance that only the nursing home could provide. He was in a private room, which made it so much more comfortable when visiting him. Dad was about to be ninety and there were a few health issues.

Fortunately, it wasn't difficult deciding what to do with his possessions. My other siblings had well established homes and my sister was now able to provide storage so I was the recipient of some furniture and kitchen items that would be of great help when I would settle into my own home. This gal had some possessions again.

It was good to be able to visit Dad. He was experiencing some confusion and kept expecting he could go back home now as the 'principal' had promoted him. This was a challenging, but fascinating because as he struggled with his choice of words his somewhat amusing substitute word usually made some sense. He was referring to a person who would have the authority to discharge him from the hospital.

When visiting I would push him in a wheelchair around outside which we both enjoyed. Dad, as hard as it was for him to see me leave, always was gracious in letting me go and appreciative of the time we had spent together. I hope I will remember to do the same, some day.

I made the rounds visiting family and friends. It was August now and a new challenge was beginning. My first home was with a couple who lived in a charming Victorian house on a lovely tree lined street in Danbury. I was surprised to find my new place even had an elevator that was most helpful as my son and friend Ruth helped me move in. Dan had come for a short visit that included a great evening at Tanglewood listening to the Boston Symphony while we sat out on the lawn under the stars. We had done this so often when he was still in high school and college.

My granddaughters were a delight. Kristen was almost eight and Lindsay was four and a half. How fabulous how the Lord had orchestrated my being with them at these precious ages. Come September 22nd, Jessi made her appearance. She was my third grandchild and firstborn to Jim and Denise. What a delight to make a trip to North Carolina early October to enjoy this little one.

New Fairfield was now happening. The new challenge was unfolding and little did I know what would be involved. I was back home, but in a different community. It used to be made up of modest homes and many summer cottages sprinkled around Lake Candlewood. There had been a real population shift and now had been transformed into an upscale bedroom community. Many of the leaders in the church worked for corporations resulting in continual losses as families were frequently transferred.

The level of commitment was impressive. I witnessed on many occasions a person coming in from a long day or even returning from a business trip hurrying into a meeting with a hamburger in one hand while the other hand was engaged in removing his tie.

The church facility was lovely. The decision to keep the old typical New England structure and add a large spacious worship area worked beautifully. This creative blend of tradition and contemporary was both functional and ascetically satisfying.

The staff consisted of the pastor, a youth pastor charged with some additional duties, a full time secretary and part time music choir director and an outstanding pianist who worked with the adult and children's bell choir. Roy, the pastor had been there for several years and was very comfortable in his position. He was warm and friendly although he seemed to prefer operating as a loner. I had known Liz the secretary, since she had been in her teens. Always had a soft spot for her and greatly respected her mother. This was an added plus to have lots of contact with her.

My office space was in a classroom. Once again I built my nest, as I settled in. The room was on the lower level and convenient to many of the activities I would be involved in. An added treat was an old Datsun station wagon similar to the one I had used in Sequim . It had been donated to the church and the pastor told me it was to be mine. Wow, that's a first.

Before arriving I had been contacted by a young man, John who was most eager and enthusiastic about my coming. He was eager to start up a new program, an Adventure Club aimed at fifth and sixth graders. He was not only hoping, but expecting me to be part of a three person team who would run this program. We met weekly beginning about five with games, followed by a meal. Some lively choruses and teaching came next, finishing with a small group time. Most of the two years the team worked well together. Creativity flowed. We were blessed with a few dedicated moms who handled the kitchen duty. Sitting down together, kids and staff sharing a meal developed relationships.

Younger kids were banging on the doors wanting to be a part of the club and later fourth graders were included. My reluctance to do this was well founded as the age span was too great. Typically sixth graders are in the beginning stages of adolescence and felt displaced by the influx of the younger children.

Another area for me was an attempt to inject some energy into the children's department openings in the Sunday School. I met unfortunately with minimal success in that area. I enjoyed livening up the blank walls with pictures and posters etc.

It was with great surprise and pleasure when I dug into the Sunday School files, to discover the children's material I had donated to the church when I had that yard sale. Eagerly I put them to use. Also, I was able to borrow back a few books from Scott, the Youth Pastor. He looked a little worried when I asked about them, but was reassured when I told him it was only temporary he would get them back.

Women's ministry was limited to a weekly morning Bible study ably led and occasional Saturday morning brunches with lay woman sharing their story. A new ministry was launched dubbed "Gimme a Break". I was part of a lively committee who put lots of creativity and energy into that program. A wide variety of activities drawing upon some 'in house' abilities and talents were utilized. I was responsible weekly to give a short devotional. One of the hopes and expectations for the program was our gals would invite friends and neighbors. Of course, refreshments were a part enhancing the connections that took place.

Once again, part of my challenge was to participate in meetings and interact with the staff as well as the church leaders. I experienced some frustration in finding out just where and how I was to be involved. This was the biggest church I had been in so far, and that creates a different dynamic. Also, it was a Methodist church. My other experiences had been strictly Presbyterian.

While settling in I was finding many closed doors, but one that stood wide open was clown ministry and Chuckles came to life again in a Sunday School Rally Day event. The forming of a clown ministry troupe began, creating my first intergenerational one. Always found myself invigorated when an intermingling of ages occurs, it was always particularly delightful and rewarding. My clown troupe ran the gamut from my little four year old Lindsay, elementary kids, teens and even included an adult. After several sessions of training we presented a clown skit in church much to the delight of the congregation.

Christmas is always a special time and I was informed at a staff meeting, that the Christmas Eve services were so well attended they held three services. One was a Family Service at five O'clock. The second was always packed and was the traditional one at seven. The last was at eleven. The pastor had nothing positive to say about the early service, describing it as chaotic. All the kids were either crying or running around they were so hyper over Christmas. We were told candle lighting was never allowed in that service due to the fear of fire with many little ones. Scott, the youth pastor was relieved when I offered to take the responsibility for that service.

My plan involved families in reading the scripture, musical numbers and ushering. I think it gives an spoken message first to the children, that they are important and valued and to the congregation, the beauty and significance of family. I spontaneously went to folks seated in the pews "volunteering " them to come up front and portray Mary, Joseph and the shepherds. The few simple costumes helped make the tableau come to life. I had asked Kristen, my oldest granddaughter to bring one of her baby dolls wrapped in a blanket. At a certain part in the service I had her bring to me the baby Jesus. With the babe in her arms she came and placed him tenderly in the manger. Her face was radiant with a look of wonder. Such a gift my Savior gave me.

Next two of my Adventure Club girls stepped up and lit the candles on the table. A flute and guitar played "Silent Night" as the lights were dimmed. In a room full of families with young children there was an unforgettable hush and a reverence. The young woman I asked to play the part of Mary told me afterwards that that had been a life changing experience and had opened her up to the Lord.

After that service, I went home with my family and enjoyed a festive meal. I returned to the eleven o'clock service assisting Roy. At that late hour there was an unique quietness.... a hush.... a sense of the holy... that was very moving and memorable to me. So simple... so pure.

Small groups were well established in the church with several effective groups meeting on a regular basis. I added to the mix and led a small "Edge Of Adventure" group of people who weren't a part of any existing groups. There was noticeable spiritual growth that occurred during the twelve week series that rewarded me. While there, I also taught some other short term studies.

I teamed up with another woman and we led a teacher workshop. I was finding my way in spite of "closed" doors. My relationship with the pastor was slow to develop. He was always pleasant, but our conversations were lacking depth. As the weeks turned into months, I began to hope for more opportunities particularly in the Sunday services. I had shared how much it had meant to me to participate in Worship in various capacities and on an occasional basis have the opportunity to give the sermon. The visibility also enhanced my ministry as people in the pews felt they knew me better.

The door began to crack open a little and in January I was asked to give a sermon. I was blessed with many positive comments as well as second hand ones the pastors had heard. A few months later Roy shared that he was hearing complaints re... a women in the pulpit and/or even up front in any capacity. That stirred me up and as I processed that it like life drained out of me. Feelings of not really belonging surfaced again, even though I was committed to a second year.

Reoccurring questions surfaced... thoughts of returning to Sequim, would that be possible Lord ... what is my ministry here... how am I to satisfy my need to be creative... my need to be stretched and develop...was I to deny that part of me? The deepest pain was being attacked because I was a woman and/or because I was divorced. I strongly believed that God was redeeming and restoring my brokeness, using it for his glory, answering my heart's cry when my marriage broke dissolved. My prayer had been... Lord, somehow use this for your glory and now it felt like I was being told you can't... you're a second class citizen... your ministry is not valid. Perhaps I'm to finish the year and then leave. Maybe write? Maybe do retreats? In addition to my own personal dilemma there were other undercurrents in the congregation.

a variety of homes...

In spite of the limitations I experienced my homes were a plus... all warm, lovely, and most comfortable in every way. I have often marveled how God has orchestrated the folks that opened their home and their hearts to me. One of my first in New Fairfield was with a warm, loving young couple with a young child, who were only marginally connected with the church. It's been a joy to watch them through the years get more involved in the church and grow in their faith.

A couple who lived in NYC and spent summers on the lake offered me their home for December. I was and still am thrilled. What fun to have my own Christmas tree and have my girls over to make and decorate cookies and to have my family over for a meal.

Such a cozy cottage, how I loved sitting on the couch looking down the hill at the ever changing lake. Little did I know I was going to be able to enjoy many more times in my special house.

On one occasion when I moved into another lovely home, the couple, when we sat down to dinner, explained that this was a rare occasion. They welcomed me into their home, but they didn't usually sit down to meals. Each person helped themselves and usually ate while watching the evening news. They chuckled a little as they shared they had realized that there would be no way they could sustain perfect behavior for an entire month so they decided to be up front from the beginning. Got a big kick out of that one.

Later I was approached by a couple asking if I would be willing to house -sit for two or three months. The husband was suffering with cancer and they had heard of hopeful treatments being used in Houston and wanted to try them as a last resort. The house was huge with five baths. My only responsibility was to flush the toilets on a regular basis. I handled that by using designated bathrooms on certain days of the week. There was a balcony in the family room area and when the girls came over they would play office. Lindsay loved to float memos down from the upstairs. Great precious times we shared, enjoying some of "grandma's houses". We built lots of sweet memories that even today we reminiscence about.

After two months, living extravagantly, my next home was a modest one complete with three little boys, one was still in the crib and only one bathroom. I have always known God had a way of keeping me humble.

I stayed with lots of families, which I enjoyed and even did some "teenage sitting". One week I moved in with three girls who were eager to be independent, but the parents wisely knew they wanted an adult presence in the home. I had gone over to the house in the morning and was shown around and given the key and garage door opener. That particular day was an Adventure Club day and I didn't get home until 9:00. It was a heavy rain and windy evening and when I pulled into their driveway was glad I had the garage door opener and wouldn't have to get out in the rain. I clicked the opener several times with no results. Disturbed, I frantically clicked again. Finally it dawned on me, oh no, I was in the wrong driveway. Quickly I backed out and into the proper one. Of course one click was all it took for the door to open. When I knocked on the kitchen door, the youngest daughter was greatly relieved to see me. She was the only person home and she blurted out, "this is such a scary night with the rain and wind and then my garage door kept going up and down and up and down." I couldn't contain my laughter and immediately told her my part of the story. Another adventure!

There were many great places to walk, Ball Pond, Put Lake and Squantz Pond. How I enjoyed many vigorous walks along the water. My rides up to Sherman and Kent were refreshing and renewing. Whenever I visit in Connecticut, making that ride is a high priority.

Another positive was being able to spend time with all three of my sons as well as seeing my siblings and my dad. Such a joy. In the spring, Bernice came and stayed a few days with me at "my" lake cottage. I took her to New Jersey to visit cousins she hadn't seen in years. Believe me, it was a painful leaving when we had to separate. I remember returning to my house after taking her to the airport, walking in to my empty housing, still feeling her presence. What a precious week we had shared. She was a delight. Her sense of humor, sense of adventure and most of all her love for me and for the Lord were treasures, I relished.

Memories of another leaving came to mind. When my husband left, it had taken hard work to change "our" home to "my home"... to not being a couple to being whole as a single. Often I would wonder if there ever would be someone special, a second husband to love and be loved. At those times, often "crying out" times, it helped to reflect on what God had chosen and called me to as well as the comfort of his rich intimate presence. I'm also thankful the gift of freedom that he has given, enabling all of us to be candid and open expressing our deepest longings and not feeling we have to bottle these thought up and keep them silent within us. The Lord understood these needs and desires. When talking with others, married couples and singles it's obvious we humans all cope with a loneliness, a restlessness that will exist until we are made complete in the Lord. We won't ever be truly home until we're with him.

The church had a traditional Mother- Daughter Banquet. The head of the committee was a difficult person for me. She bustled around and made elaborate plans for this event. I happened to go to my office to find all my personal things had been taken down and stuffed in a cabinet. Even the posters on the walls I had put up for the kids were considered a distraction. I was stunned, shocked and felt deeply wounded. As I arrived at my home sobbing, I couldn't quite figure out why I was so distraught until I realized it brought back a painful memory I thought had been dealt with.

My family was attending church regularly. My granddaughters

expressed a desire to be baptized. How awesome this was for me. When Roy sprinkled the water on Lindsay she giggled with glee and I felt keenly the Lord's hand upon her. After this when visiting the family I often found Lindsay playing church. She was the pastor and her dolls were baptized repeatedly.

summer visits...

July first, I was treated to a visit with the Barnes family. Bill, Jan and kids had come cross-country in their van pulling the camper. What fun showing them around in my world and treating them to "real pizza". I LOVE the Pacific Northwest but there are a few things the northeast does better. After tasting the pizza they all agreed. Jan and I rode around some of the many winding narrow roads and she tickled me no end with her comment," why don't they straighten these roads". Growing up in the wide open spaces they all were experiencing some claustrophobia.

The family was interested in seeing New York City. I became the navigator while Bill drove into Manhattan along the West Side Highway into Brooklyn. We all enjoyed a stroll along the river near the Verazano Narrows Bridge. We were thrilled to see the Statue of Liberty and the skyscrapers.

I preceded them to Massachusetts attending a stimulating conference at Gordon Conwell Theological Seminary. They followed a few days later. Bill attended a seminar there to fulfill part of his study leave requirements. The family and I met, spending an afternoon at the beach. The next day I played "tour guide" again, escorting them around Boston taking in the sights. Old Ironsides was by far everyone's favorite. We parted ways after that as I went north to friends and they headed south on their journey.

August found me traveling west with my first stop in Sequim. In my journal, I described the folks as

> people who have dignity with a twinkle
>   and a formality with a grin.

How sweet to spend time with dear dear folks. Many of their words blessed me. It's nice to hear, "we want you back". One lady, a former school teacher told me she saw so much growth in my speaking. I had given a short talk at the Presbyterian Women's picnic. I remembered Ruth Barnes' words when I was leaving that she knew God would bring me back again to be on staff.

After a few long years not having their own building, the structure was in the finishing stages thanks to the many people who gave countless hours of work in many capacities to complete the new church. It was spacious, welcoming, soft and light. It really captured the essence of the congregation. Pastor Bill on my first Sunday there gave me his patented hug and had me assist him serving Communion.

Next my travels took me "over the hill" to Okanogan, where I had been invited to lead a women's retreat. While getting reacquainted with this "strange" land my thoughts quickly centered on the spirit, the psyche, the real affection that I had developed for the beautiful people that lived in this valley. Again, I was filled with thankfulness for this place, these people and the way God had blessed my ministry there.

There was a scheduled Session meeting that night. Jan felt very apprehensive about it. Bill didn't get home until after ten and as he entered the house it was obvious he was troubled and unsettled. He shared it had been a difficult, tense meeting. Several of the leaders seemed disturbed and discontented and he wondered during his time away had folks been overwhelmed with all the responsibilities.

The next morning I was approached by a few of the strategic people in need of a trusted listener. They, too were troubled as they had tried to tell Bill, they needed him to leave. He had been there for a long time and their perspective was ... everyone needed a change, including him. I asked if they wanted me to talk to him before the next go around and they were relieved. Once again I sensed God's having me in the right place and time.

Bill and I talked about the situation. He had been caught totally off guard. On their cross country road trip with the family, he had been eager to come back to the church with new energy. Jan understandable reacted with anger. She was hurt, frightened and wounded. We talked and prayed and then hugged before leaving to go to the church. When we arrived, people were tearfully hugging Bill. The three of us talked and I was thankful I could help to ease the pain for everyone.

After a nap and shower we left for the retreat. The Lord blessed me with a calmness and gave me the words to say and needed wisdom. In spite of everything I was blessed with their love. The worship time we shared together uplifted us all. My God will supply ALL your need in Christ Jesus.

Some more visits and then the return ride, this time a planned stop to Terrace View. I stayed with Dick and Christine and was told my sister- in- law had called. It was much too late to call her back due to the three hour difference When I woke early next morning I dialed her number. She shared the shocking news my dad had died. He had returned to his room at the nursing home and while talking to the attendant slipped to the floor and was gone. Probably he even had had his beloved ice cream. What a peaceful way to go to be with his Savior.

These events demanded a quick change of plans. Lynn, my ever-ready Terrace View friend took me back to Bernice's for a quick good-bye and to pick up my luggage. My flight was rescheduled and the next day I was homeward bound to be with my family.

vacation is over...

September, back in New Fairfield, we had a family retreat.

It was held in nearby facility and was well attended. I played a vital part on the planning committee and also was a part of a trio who played guitars and led the singing.

One Sunday, we presented the Adventure Club to the congregation in Worship. In our club meetings I used the Victory Chant, "Hail Jesus You're My King" at the close of our meal as a gathering call. I would sing out a line and they would echo it while coming into their seats. In the church service we deliberately had the kids sit at random with their families throughout the sanctuary. When I stood up in front and started the chant they all stood up and came forward as they echoed my lines. Still get goose bumps thinking about it. They sang another song or two then John, one of the team talked about the club.

I was blessed deeply with leading more women's retreats, first with my sister-in-law, Judi in New Jersey. Our gathering took place in a charming home that resembled a barn. There was a large open area downstairs where we gathered for our sessions. Circling this space were balconies ringing the outside walls creating bedrooms on the upper level. The retreat started with the evening meal. This caused some logistical problems confronting the kitchen crew with the job of making room in the refrigerator to handle the left overs. Also the kitchen crew was tied up with chores. I learned a valuable lesson. It worked best to have the women come after they had eaten at home with their families. Desserts was an easier way to handle Friday nights.

Jim, Denise and little Jessi came the second Thanksgiving to visit me in "my" cottage on the lake. I thoroughly enjoyed making a big turkey dinner for everyone. It was great to have the three granddaughters playing together. The 'big' girls got such a kick out of their baby cousin.

Christmas soon followed, and Diane the choir director asked me to develop some drama that would fit in with the music that was being presented. Yes, another outlet for some creativity.

While listening to the various choral pieces I visualized working in a liturgical dance. My girls from Adventure Club were willing performers. I enlisted the boys and dads as shepherds and wise men. It all worked beautifully, the kids loved every bit of the preparation as well as the presentation.

My second Christmas Eve I involved families again. Giving gifts was my theme. Needed a clown to pantomime as I read the story and Mark was my choice. He was the youngest in a family of high achievers and he was wired a little differently with a creative streak I noted and loved. He threw himself into the role and gave a top notch portrayal. A few years later his mom told me how much that had meant to him. The honor of being selected and the affirmation of many stayed with him. The children's bell choir performed, then putting down their bells picked up the candles and standing in the front facing the people as the lights were lowered, their candles were lit. There was a holy hush and we all sang Silent Night. Both years hold a special spot in my memory book.

One of my most treasured ministry occurred during my second year. I was asked to lead an adult Sunday School class based on Richard Foster's "Celebration of Discipline." The book was a favorite of mine having felt it spoke to me each time I read it. Undertaking the charge with a certain amount of fear and trembling I recognized that this church was blessed with some gifted male teachers. But I learned over and over again when the Lord leads you to a task and you obey, through the Holy Spirit all parties will be richly blessed. And we were for the class was alive and we all felt challenged working through the text together. This was another time I was glad I said yes and didn't let my apprehension rob me of great joy.

The second retreat was for the church gals and it was held in one of my homes in February of '92. Meals were simplified with our lunch, a variety of crockpot meals. The worship, the teaching, the bonding due to the sharing were such a blessing to me personally and to those who attended. The Moms really appreciated getting up Saturday morning and having breakfast served to them. Retreats are definitely a favorite area of ministry.

There were stirrings again in my heart entering the new year. Lord, what's next? Wasn't at all sure I was done here. I knew it would be difficult to leave family and home again. I had initiated overtures in the mountains of North Carolina, but what was offered didn't appear to be the right fit. The assignments were either too short, a three month stint or another offer that involved lots of traveling, working with three small congregations. That didn't work either, I wouldn't be able to cultivate any deep relationships. Knowing myself, I knew my need to have warm connections with people and a home base would not be satisfied.

What's next was becoming a huge question. Perhaps I should consider staying another five months. I made an offer to stay until Christmas not realizing what the undercurrents were all about and that talk was underway of letting go both the Youth Pastor and me while seeking an associate pastor to ease Roy's load.

Scott was asked to step down and my proposal was denied. There was some turmoil with the changes. Some church members as well as myself, felt that a much smoother and effective transition would have happened if I had remained for that additional stretch while the two pastors adjusted to their roles and each other.

Once again I was given a gracious farewell with generous gifts. My family came and joined the party. This leaving was VERY different because this time I didn't have a place to go.

another interlude...

It was summer and even though my future was unknown, I took off on my usual rounds of seeing friends. First stop had me driving north to visit Susan and Geoff in Vermont. They lived near the Canadian border and I had decided it was about time to go check out a northeastern province. I had heard nothing but great things about Quebec City and that became my agenda. This would be another solo trip since no one could go with me. My motel was just outside the old city making it most convenient to be able to walk to all the sights. What a picturesque setting Old Quebec has, situated high on a bluff overlooking the St. Lawrence River. I investigated some museums, enjoyed watching The Changing of the Guard and ate in some charming places. The city is bilingual, French and English signs are posted everywhere with restaurants providing a choice of two menus in either language.

When I went for a tour in the Parliament Building, there were two guides, one for the French speaking tourists and one for the English. I was the only one needing an English speaking guide so I had a new young gal all to myself. She was most anxious to pick up some American ways of expressing herself. We had a most delightful time together as she took me on the tour. she was eager to learn some American ways saying things. Later in the day, I indulged in a delightful river cruise.

On my return to Vermont, I had a scary experience with my car. The motor stopped running forcing me to pull over, off the road. After popping my hood and tying a white hanky on my door I found no one was stopping to assist me. What a sinking feeling I had when car after car, enroute back to the states, passed me by. Finally a car from the area pulled over parking behind me. The young couple, who hardly spoke any English, offered to assist me. We both experienced some language difficulty but I understood enough as they told me they were from the area and would take me to a garage. I climbed into their back seat wondering and praying this would all work out. They drove me to the closest exit and the promised repair shop. Next step was climbing into a tow truck and returning to my car. My alternator had stopped functioning so they charged my battery informing me, I should be able to could get back to the States. You can imagine how relieved I was, thankful that once again God provided and protected me.

Summer continued to unfold. Once again I was westward bound to Washington. I found myself immersed in the love of precious folks. It was difficult to share what was happening in my life since I didn't know what my next mission would be. This was a new experience, definitely hugely challenging.

On one of my Sundays in Sequim, I sat next to Mary Jensen, a lovely lady in her late nineties. She was a person I loved to visit since she maintained a keen interest in world affairs and in other people. Even though she now lived in a nursing home, she was not self- absorbed. We reached the point in the Worship Service when everyone recites the Lord's Prayer in unison. Every word Mary spoke was laced with reverence and were deeply felt. I became aware of tears welling up in my eyes, sensing a strength and a hope she possessed as she honored her Lord. What an inspiration!

There were many visits and once again it felt like I never left. The trust and the bonds never weakened making me "rich in every way". Of course the "comings" followed with the "goings" were emotionally taxing. This whole experience was a stretching one, but again I was blessed with a keen awareness of being engulfed in my Lord's love and not forgotten.

My next stop was Okanogan and how sweet that was. Bernice traveled with me soaking up the beauty while we drove over the North Cascade Highway. A warm greeting awaited us at Tollie and Woody's. He grabbed and hugged me while he said he thought I would never get there. They wanted us to stay with them and told me they were moving out of "my" room, so I could enjoy it.

On our return trip we drove south along the 'Mighty' Columbia and bought peaches in Entiat. Of course we stopped to eat in Leavenworth and then went onto Tall Timbers. Eric, on the camp staff was a teenager from Okanogan. It was worth the extra time and miles to see his look of surprise when he spotted me and to receive a big hug telling me how thrilled he was to see me again. Bernice had never seen the camp and agreed with me regarding the spectacular setting it occupied in the Cascades.

Upon our return to Sequim I enjoyed more good times at the Spit and even at Beach Two in La Push. Bernice made the trek through the forest with me and then down the steep bluff and even scrambled over the logs on the beach. What a trooper. Of course the return was even more taxing. Her face was radiant at the Presbyterian Women's picnic as I bragged about her escapade.

My days were quickly evaporating as September was approaching. Bernice's joy of the good times we had shared all summer delighted me. She was very talkative and into everything we had done. I sensed how alone she felt when I was not there. Happily, I was able to squeeze in a few days at the Masons and once again savor the sounds of the gentle lapping of the waves out my sliding door and enjoy the time with them.

One morning when walking the Spit I found myself engulfed in a thick fog. While I kept on walking, I had to focus on my feet as the visibility was nil. While asking the Lord for an affirmation that I was to stay back East I spotted, there in the sand, the name RODGER. The name was even spelled with the D my brother has in his name. He lived in North Carolina. The experience aroused my curiosity and made me curious about where I was to be.

family sabbatical year...

Returning to Connecticut I noted subtle changes, the early stages of another Fall, my favorite season. I contacted the folks who owned the cottage at the lake and explained my predicament. Once again they made the generous offer that I would be free to use the house starting in November and could stay until things opened up for me. During September and October, the Chuvalas and another family in the church provided homes for me.

Fall retreats opened up. First one was in New Jersey with the women from my sister-in-law's church. Next one, a friend had arranged for me to lead a group from her church. The third retreat was with the gals from New Fairfield. I relished each challenge, noting subtle differences in the groups as the women were from an Assembly of God Church, a Baptist Church and my own Methodist group. Blessed with all three! They certainly helped to fill the void I was experiencing.

In the meantime, I was engaged in making contact with the Presbytery Office in Fayetteville, North Carolina. I connected with Lewis, the Presbytery executive and found him to be very interested in what I had been doing. Although busy with multiple responsibilities, he generously promised he would send out "feelers" and see if there were possibilities. After several weeks it was obvious nothing was brewing in North Carolina. Both of us were disappointed. This certainly found myself wondering what in the world God's plans were for me. Sitting around wasn't satisfying at all and I was dealing with feelings of confusion.

And then some momentous phone calls. My son Jim called to tell me Denise was pregnant with twins and the doctor wanted her off her feet in January in the hopes of avoiding an early delivery. I inquired how were they going to manage with Jessi, a very active two and half year old. He reassured me that their friends would all help out. When we hung up, memories of my third pregnancy surfaced. That whole experience, when

I was put down, requiring bed rest with an almost five year old and a three year old. It didn't take me long to recognize that most interestingly I was available, actually the only time in my life that I was free to make my offer. I had no other commitments. Reaching for the phone my question was..."How about if I come in January and move in until the babies are born.... talk it over and let me know what's best for you." It took about five minutes at the most for my phone to ring and tell me, COME!

Now it was clear, the Lord had it all under control. This was settled and then I received another call that caused me to stop look and listen. The voice at the other end said, "This is God calling and I want you to go to Sequim." It was Pastor Bill offering me an opportunity to come and be on staff again. The Lord, in his wisdom and grace, clearly showed that this was not to be.

A couple of special treats awaited me before taking off. My first one... I invited Dolores and her daughter over for Thanksgiving. We had connected toward the end of my two years in New Fairfield when we were escorts for an Adventure Club outing to a waterslide park. The two of us engaged in a deep discussion about personal matters. Her husband had left her and she was struggling with her two teenagers attempting to adjust to the new situation. This forged a friendship. The three of us had a great time celebrating Turkey Day, in my cozy lake house.

A week or so later, we shared an overnight to Mystic Seaport, in Connecticut, a replica of an 1800's whaling village, complete with its own ship. We participated in the annual Lantern Event. Part of a small group of ten, we were escorted first to the ship and led down below the deck where the captain sat next to a small potbellied stove, smoking his pipe. He warmly greeted us and asked had we heard the news of the early arrival of the baby. The young parents named her Holly. The news had spread all over the village, creating great excitement. Our group quickly realized we were part of the story and not spectators. It was Christmas Eve and there was a bustle of activity. We were led around the village using lanterns that shed some light on the dark paths. Our group was blessed with a eight year old lad that was enthusiastic about the entire experience. Our guide allowed him to lead our group while carrying the lantern. His eyes sparkled and his smile extended from ear to ear. We arrived at a house that was alive with music. A party was going on and some of us joined into a square dance while others sipped a mug of warm spicy cider.

While walking down another path the guide asked us to be quiet as we approached a house. Standing behind a picket fence we spotted Santa busily laying out the gifts in the family's living room. When he spotted us he put a finger to his lips to warn us to be silent. It was a magical night, I would love to do it again someday.

During the Fall months, no longer on staff I had attended frequently, a church in nearby Sherman. I was richly blessed with the quiet worship and preaching. After a month or more I made a request to come and serve as a volunteer. The pastor was interested but my offer was turned down. Meanwhile nothing much was happening in NC. Couldn't help but wonder about September '93. Was my volunteering coming to a close?

January '93

I arrived a few days after New Year's in Concord. Poor Denise was having difficulty staying off her feet. Jim had opened up the couch so she could spend time in the living room. Jessi could climb up and cuddle with mom. This little very active, independent, two and a half year old was adorable. We established a routine of preschool, two days a week, going shopping and playing outside. I still have a vivid picture in my mind of her telling me emphatically, "ME do it myself" over some issue I don't recall.

Thoughtfully I was told to take a break from the routine on weekends. As the days passed my son continually told me how much he appreciated my being there and how they could not have done it alone.

Beginning in February I visited a new Presbyterian Church located in a growing area of Concord. The pastor and I met and he expressed an interest, but when he spoke about it with his leaders they didn't feel it was the right fit for them at that time.

The babies were born in February. After three granddaughters I had reminded the Lord that I like boys too, and now I had two. Denise had gone in for a routine checkup and was sent immediately to the hospital after he determined she was dilating. The doctors were able to slow down everything and ran tests to see if the boys' lungs were developed enough to be born. It was determined they were and when she was taken off the meds, she immediately went into labor.

February 13th was the big day. When I arrived with big sister at the hospital the proud papa greeted us with both new borns in his arms. She was wide-eyed and eager to hold them. When the three adults looked at the three little ones, we all took a deep breath acknowledging their was no turning back now. The original plan had been for Denise's dad and step mom to come when the boys were born but we decided it was best for me to stay a few more weeks. It would be beneficial to keep things steady and calm as possible, not to make more changes, helping Jessi to adapt.

Denise nursed the babies. While they were in the hospital a few extra days, she pumped her milk and brought it to the hospital to be used for the feedings when she wasn't there. Jessi cracked us all up when she was found in on her mom's bed trying to put on the breast pumps.

When the little ones came home, mommy quickly began to feed the boys at the same time. I soon took over one of the night feedings and found I could also manage the two of them. Denise's dad had made an oversized cradle and it was precious to see them close together wrapped in their blankets. Busy, busy time! We all looked like walking zombies for a while.

Reinforcements came, Pa Pete and Grandma Sally freeing me to drive to Connecticut to take a break. When I returned to my lake cottage I found Kris, from church, had moved in. Our standards of housekeeping differed and she seemed to feel resentful of my presence. Fortunately, our schedules didn't provide much togetherness.

I returned to the family after three weeks. This time I took some side trips so mom and dad could see if they would be all right on their own. I enjoyed exploring Charleston South Carolina and my ride north up the coast. Those beaches and sea breezes were not hard to take.

After returning to enjoy a few more days with the family I found Jessi was comfortable with me again. She had pulled away from me. I think she had been fearful that if she was with me, Mommy might disappear again. It was time to head for home.

... ...

March had come and when I returned to my cottage I was treated to several days of snow that created a winter wonderland. I kept as snug as a bug in a rug in my cozy cottage venturing out occasionally on foot to tramp about.

Time was quickly passing. I knocked on every possible door. Doors were closing and I was learning to be a step back when knocking in case the door slammed on my nose. My year was winding down and even though I had not been in my customary volunteer mode it certainly had been a memorable one. I had tested out the mountains, made overtures locally while Lewis, in

Fayetteville had been looking for a placement. But all was much too quiet...

Then a phone call from Lewis inviting me to come spend the night with him and his wife and the next day he would take me to a new church on the coast for an interview. Maybe at last, this would be the answer... When we arrived at our meeting place, we were treated to a great seafood lunch followed by what appeared to be a positive conversation. I enjoyed their hospitality and was optimistic about our appointment. Lewis called a few days later to tell me how stunned and disappointed he was that they turned done my offer. He found out later that the committee felt people would not be open to having me stay in their homes. That would be an invasion of their privacy. I never had heard that one before. There always had been enough folks ready to open their homes and their hearts. Was this typical East coast or a southern mindset?

In my Family Sabbatical year, that sounded so much better than the year I was unemployed, homes as well as financial provisions were more than ample. I was living the Lord's promise that he would supply my every need. I had loved leading the three retreats in the Fall. The Basketts, folks who I had previously lived with, during my sabbatical year on many occasions had me housesit and care for the dogs, always paying me generously. I had also been richly blessed with my special cottage on the lake, a treasure. Yes, Lord... thank you.. but what's next? All is so quiet and I'm feeling lost, confused and hopeless. Those contacts I had to acknowledge were really remote. I found saying to myself "get real girl". Lord , I'm so glad that you have limitless resources.... glad I'm in your hands... glad I'm your problem. I certainly acknowledge... I have no answers.

what an opportunity...

Spring came, the snow long gone when I received a call from

Lewis telling me he would be moving to another position in another Presbytery, but he at his last meeting, would make one final announcement about my availability.

More quiet... more not knowing ... what should I be dreaming... how was I to handle all this. Thank you Lord that I know whatever my next steps you will be there and will be in them. I had just returned to my cottage from a most blessed worship service when my phone began to ring. It was a pastor from Little Chapel on the Boardwalk in Wrightsville Beach. He was responding to Lewis' announcement at the Presbytery meeting and told me he and the leaders were very interested in meeting with me to purse the possibility of my coming. They had recognized the pastor needed help and had hired an intern for the summer, but realized it was time to add to the staff. I certainly didn't need to mull that possibility over and told Huw, " yes, I'm interested". The next step was an interview. Before making a decision they would fly me down and put me up for a weekend in July.

My flight required a short stop in Charlotte and my family came to see me at the airport. We all talked excited about the possibility of me being located at Wrightsville Beach. When my small plane landed in Wilmington it was easy for both the pastor and myself to solve the puzzle as to our identity. He graciously drove me around in Wilmington and then treated me to a lovely waterside restaurant on the Cape Fear River.

At last we headed out to the island, crossing the draw bridge over the Inter coastal Water Way. After a few quick turns we arrived at the church, Little Chapel on the Boardwalk. When Huw took me inside I responded to the ambiance. The stained glass windows and the open beamed ceiling made a most inviting and lovely sanctuary.

Next stop was his home on the channel where I met Huw's wife. Rachel was gracious, making me feel immediately comfortable. She explained that folks from that looked out on the Personnel Committee and the Session would be coming for dinner. The evening was pleasant and there were good vibes. Folks felt comfortable with me and that feeling was mutual. I took some teasing from one of the men about my accent. After all, I was a Yankee among southerners.

After people left, Rachel and I had a chance to relax on their porch that looked out at the channel and began to get more acquainted. Huw came home from his meeting about eleven and we talked details. Car, food allowance, job description... they envisioned me as a pastoral assistant. I resonated with that challenge. My emphasis would be in Christian Education, Congregational Life and Women's Ministry.

Sunday was full. First an early service followed by Church School and then with a second service. I attended both services and was shown around to the various groups during the Sunday School time. I was treated again to a lunch, this time at the Oceanic, a great restaurant on the pier, overlooking the ocean and beach. The choir director, secretary, Huw and Rachel made up the party.

Huw has a presence in the pulpit. He's from Wales and his vibrant and rich voice was a delight. After we got to know each other I teased him that we really didn't care what he said, we just enjoyed listening to his voice. The congregation was lively, warm and loving.

Right next to the church sat the house that was mine available to live in. It was only used Sunday mornings for a class. At first I felt some reluctance as I wouldn't have the connections that happen when you live in homes, but ... wow I'd be on the beach ! When I checked out the place I found it equipped even with a washer and dryer. The possibilities of making a delightful nest for myself were evident.

While waiting an answer from Little Chapel, I spent a brief

time at home and then took off to Sequim. Quickly, I made my way to the Spit saturating myself in the beauty and solitude. Huw called me with an enthusiastic yes. How great it was to have everything settled and to land in such an awesome and unexpected place. Friends and family on both coasts remarked and wondered at my new location. This beach bum was getting to live out her dreams. The year off didn't mean God was absent, he had just been busy orchestrating my path.

The Pacific Northwest as always, was rich and full of great dinners and precious time with people. I covered all the bases with Sequim, Okanogan and Terrace View. While at Dick's I received a phone call from Mickey, a close friend of Bernice, telling me she had been in a terrible accident and was in the hospital in Port Townsend. What stunning news. We had spent an interesting morning together in Port Angeles to obtain information about hearing aids.

We then enjoyed a relaxing lunch before I drove to Kingston to hop on the ferry to spend a few days with friends there. Bernice had been alert and feeling fine when we said our goodbyes and she slipped into the driver's seat. I enjoyed my ferry ride and Dick met me on the Edmonds side. I was looking forward to sweet visits with dear friends. Once again, ironically while I was at Gibsons the phone rang asking for me. What a shock when I heard Mickey's voice telling me that Bernice had been in a horrendous accident on her return trip. She was in serious condition in Port Townsend Hospital. Bernice had told Mickey not to call me, it would upset my time with Terrace View friends. Glad she didn't listen but contacted me the next morning. Dick loaned me an extra car. Unfortunately, it was a summer Saturday morning and that meant a long wait at the ferry. There weren't any options but to sit there in line, working on patience for a l-o-n-g few hours. Finally I arrived at the hospital. When I entered her room, Bernice spotted me and gave me a smile in spite of her pain. Her son and daughter-in- law were there and filled me in on the painful events.

Bernice had either blacked out or fallen asleep while driving. She crossed the center line and smashed into the side of a camper. Her car was demolished and anyone who saw it wouldn't have believed the driver survived. God had more good years for her.

Paul, Jo and I stayed at Bernice's. It provided us time to get to know each other. Their immediate reaction was to move their mom over near them, but I intervened reminding them that their mom had always said she would want to stay in Sequim. There were lots of caring people who would be there for her. A constant flow of cards, visits and phone calls helped to convince them.

Unfortunately, I only had a few days to spend time with her while she was in the hospital before my scheduled flight home. She was improving, but oh was it painful to have to leave her in this difficult time.

What mixed emotions I felt, while flying back to Connecticut. Thankfully I returned to my cottage on the lake to spend a few weeks before I would be driving to North Carolina. I was grateful I had some space to process my thoughts and feelings.

Everyone was ecstatic with what was on my horizon. I enjoyed throwing a party at my 'own' house. The weather was delightful and a treat to be able to sit out on the deck as we shared a meal together. Viewing the action on the lake the boats and water skiers added to the festivities. The goodbyes were enriched by the promise of the next adventure. I was once again shifting gears and able to acknowledge that my cup was full and running over. A new volunteer challenge awaited me. Plus I would be living on the beach and only three hours away from my little ones. When heading south, I was full of anticipation...more than ready for new beginnings.

7

North Carolina '93

God has a way of tickling ourselves in the places we are least expecting it...

After all the wondering and waiting, here I was with a car packed full of my gear, crossing the draw bridge over the inter coastal way and driving straight ahead to the beach. Oh Lord, you are too much. How can I ever say thank you enough. I easily found Little Chapel, my new home. Two ladies were in the office and greeted me warmly with hugs. The pastor arrived and we all went over to my house with everyone helping me carry my stuff up the stairs and into my living room. The Discovers Class, that used the house for their Sunday classes had stepped in and fixed up my place giving it a homey look. Upstairs on my double bed sat the softest Teddy Bear I had ever seen. He was most welcome. Huw then took me out to lunch and thoughtfully drove me around the local area helping me locate groceries stores etc. Back to church, he showed me the classroom that would become my office. Once again I enjoyed the nesting process, fixing up my space to reflect my personality. In addition to my office, I now would be settled in my own home. What a really big change that would be.

The first days and weeks were busy as I eagerly jumped right into the action. I attended committee meetings and being a skilled listener picked up many insights. Harriet, one of the church elders, asked me to participate in the Caring Evangelism Program. What an excellent study this was with its emphasis on the need to cultivate relationships and allow discussions of faith to flow naturally rather than "force feeding" people. The program had built-in times of requiring lots of interaction within the group. I thrived on this as it provided opportunity to share and in the sharing get to know each other. This study was a highlight and wherever I went after that experience, I led groups that were equally appreciative.

Huw immediately used me in Worship and asked me if I would like to take over a service in October since he would be away. It felt like doors were wide open. Once again I regularly gave the children's sermon. Many compliments and affirmations came my way that enhanced my confidence and buoyed up my spirit.

In contrast to some of my other pastors, Huw was a conscientious visitor and quickly included me in on his rounds that enabled me to get acquainted with shut-ins. Two senior ladies, in particular occupied much of my visiting time. They were absolutely delightful, each in their own unique way.

Ready to both exercise and check out the territory, my first two walks, I did the "loop". This is a popular walk that the local people use as well as the many college students that rent on the beach when summer is over and school is in session. I decided that wasn't for me with the beach just down the street, that would become my tramping ground. The church is located just about in the middle of the island and gave me a choice of walking north or south. Usually, I headed into the wind so on my return, the wind would be at my back. Never have decided which direction I liked the best, they were both satisfying.

Bernice was very much in my thoughts and heart. My concern for her recovery, kept me wondering how she was doing after the accident. Also, I needed to be replenished after all the goodbyes on both the east and west coasts. Having the ocean practically on my doorstep, the Lord had handed me a perfect place to heal. While I walked and prayed, his presence was a comfort.

Wrightsville Beach is on a barrier island off the Atlanta Ocean. One has to travel through Wilmington, a charming Southern city to reach the beach. It is endowed with lots of lovely tree lined streets, homes that sit back from the road and an abundance of delightful flowers and shrubbery.

The original Little Chapel had been located in the dunes and sat on a boardwalk. The congregation, when the new church was built, wanted to maintain that unique and cherished name. The area, now a mecca for retirees, attracted many people who relocated from the northeast and midwest. The congregation still included many local residents that had family roots, creating an interesting blend. The people were generally warm and friendly. The Carolina blue skies combined with comfortable weather provided the many golfers in the area and the church with the ability to play most of the year.

Some church members lived on the beach, but many more lived in Wilmington. When scheduling meetings you learned that if someone didn't appear at the expected time the drawbridge that crossed the Coastal Interway probably had been "up".

The church had its own set of unique features. Monthly breakfasts were held after the first service and were very popular. The food was excellent for the church not only had skilled cooks, but in addition, professional ones. These meals developed my appreciation for a southern tradition, "grits". People enjoyed the aromas when entering the church and loved the chatter and warmth that permeated the fellowship hall.

Another ministry was a dynamic weekly commitment to Meals on Wheels. On both Thanksgiving and Christmas there were volunteers that spent part of their holiday cooking dinners that would then be delivered that day. The slogan, "Little Chapel With A Big Heart" really was a mantle that fit.

Music was another highlight. The Bell choir was top notch with several very skilled ringers. Young Michol, the pastor's son was in high school at that time, was superb and even gave a few solo concerts with piano accompaniment.

My involvement in many of the areas of the church included stints of teaching an adult class and assisting with many Youth activities teamed with a person who's still working with the Middle School kids. Mila and still maintain a special bond.

From my other church experiences I had found it worthwhile to spend time delving into the different areas of the church, noting my first impressions. Little Chapel had identified the need to attract young families. While surveying the preschool area, I was appalled at how dated and dingy it appeared. I even shook some of the cribs and was shocked at how unstable and unsafe they appeared to be. In sharing this with Huw, he wanted me to present this input at the next Elder meeting. Even though it's difficult to be critical, I felt this was an important function. Coming in with both fresh and experienced eyes, these problems were apparent to me.

My background as a teacher, a parent and a grandparent made my input even more valued. When sharing with the leaders, they were shocked. I challenged them to walk through those rooms and see. Most of them had not gone back into that area. The sanctuary, narthex and fellowship hall as well as the adult rooms were lovely, but much needed doing back in the children's area.

Beryl, who now was on the Christian Education Committee, enjoyed coming in on a weekday morning, helping to haul off some of the stuff and also doing multiple minor repairs. Two women, when they heard of my observations, responded to the needs and really jumped in and began not only cleaning and clearing, but did some painting. Both were artistic and created some delightful murals. Quite a transformation was happening.

Shortly after that, a wonderful Mothers Morning Out program was started, led by Linda, a very capable lady with a passion for preschoolers and their moms. It has been a strictly volunteer ministry that keeps expanding. The church has picked up some families as a result of the program. My contribution was to have the little ones come into the sanctuary and sit on the floor with me as I told them a short story about Jesus. Next we would stand up together and sing a song or two. They were fascinated with my guitar. I anticipated that special time each week.

Marian, one of the adult teachers asked me if I might be interested in an after- school program that met in a church in Wilmington. She had volunteered and thought I, with my teaching background, would enjoy joining her. I felt drawn and quickly made a commitment. My assignment was a little guy, a third grader. He always had a big smile and usually was motivated as we focused on his homework first and then some reading and math skills. Twice a week we met and mutually enjoyed the experience.

While getting acquainted with people I realized there were several widows and single women. Now that I had my own place I decided in early December to have a tea. It was such a to be a hostess and enjoy a delightful time.

Next was a sweet visit from my sister and her husband, on their was south to winter in Florida. Lil and I went to the Festival of Trees held every Christmas season at the Holiday Inn on the Cape Fear River in Wilmington. A wide variety of church, civic and other groups each commit to decorate a tree. Nautical themes were prevalent. School and church groups also signed up to perform, adding to the festivities. It's a great fund raiser for cancer. Another annual holiday event is held on the channel a little after Thanksgiving. The boats all are decorated and line up, parading up and down the waterfront. This is followed with fireworks.

Christmas I was anxious to visit Bernice to see for myself how she was progressing from the horrendous accident. Thankfully her recovery was positive and while visiting we began to plot an April visit to Wrightsville Beach.

Every few weeks I was able to go visit Jim and his family and enjoy my little ones. It was both fascinating and fun to watch the growing process.

problems...

Two roadblocks stopped me short. The first one happened in my early months. While attending a Christian Education meeting there was a big discussion about the need to make some changes in the nursery during church service. The ongoing custom had been that our teenage girls were paid to care for the babies during the morning service. What message were we sending the girls, regarding the importance of attending Worship. After much input, a consensus was reached that a change was needed and the committee voted in the affirmative. It was concluded my some that the decision had been mine, alone. What turmoil and repercussions ensued. How dare I come in and make changes that caused disruptions. No one ever came to me, all the complaining was taken to Huw and was rather nasty. Huw dealt with them while supporting me. It took quite a while to blow over, but eventually it did.

It was questioning time again as the new year began. Am I to stay a second year? I was wanting to, but needed to make sure that this was the Lord's leading. I certainly wasn't looking for a change. The combination of the ocean, being near my family as well as having my own place was precious. It had been terrific to have open doors and opportunities in my ministry. Yes, there were a few scrapes and bruises, but they were minimal in the big picture. The Session okayed with enthusiasm a second year.

My second mishap happened in March. Huw, in one of our meetings, showed me an article about using a clown in the service. Of course, I jumped in and offered Chuckles. He was pleased with that and respected the training I had pertaining to clown ministry. The Sunday arrived and we had a great time as the clown "played" with the Worship. Chuckles was full of curiosity, checking out the candles, sharing her large glasses with the pastor, assisting with the ushers collecting the offering and joining with the children as they came forward for their children's message.

What a hornet's nest I stirred up. Two woman were totally turned off, vehement that the clown disrupted the service and was totally out of place. Interestingly another lady, actually a recent widow had the opposite reaction to Chuckles. She expressed how good it was for her to smile and laugh a little. Worship should be joyous. The prayer group that week invited me to share my explanation. I remember that morning walking down the long hallway, wondering whether I was walking into the lion's den. A quick Lord, I need you and your words, I entered the room. and was able to share more about clowns in ministry. There was a keen interest on the part of some of the group as they listened intently, gaining an understanding.

Huw still was badgered and in the next week's bulletin he wrote an affirming article about the clown and why he had asked me to do it. I certainly appreciated his support and loyalty. I, too wrote an article for the newsletter talking about clowns.

Clowning, a Stretching Experience

Recently I had the delightful experience of participating in a Clown, Mime and Storytelling Workshop in Edmonds. How fascinating to listen and to learn how every culture down through the ages has had a clown figure. He has been the one who has taken the traditions, played with them, provoking the people to look at their solemn ceremonies. The concept of a clown in ministry excites me. When he puts on the white face he is in essence dying to self. As the color is applied he is coming alive in the newness of life that is in Christ Jesus. In the dying process he is saying with David "I am willing to act like a fool in order to show my Joy in the Lord." 2 Samuel 6:21.

Clowning in Worship does indeed stretch us. After all everyone knows clowns belong in the circus. Wrong! Like giraffes and elephants we've put them there, domesticating them and rendering them harmless by limiting them to entertainment. Clowns should be and are much more than that. They expose our human pretensions, they liberate us from the tedium of daily routines. They hold mirrors before us, not of glass but of actions, parading our often preposterous poses and posturing.

What a JOY that Sunday was for me. I will never forget your faces, alive with surprise, delight and glee. I hope you were able to detect with me the divine laughter as we joyfully worshipped our God together, celebrating his church and celebrating the playful part of our God given personalities. As Chuckles invited you to help blow up his balloon , to share your breath, the breath God has given you may we all continue to come together and truly be one in his Spirit and be known by our love. If we are to be holy people, we must make room for the clowns.

Working with Huw and listening to his resonant voice I began to savor my words, especially when reading the scripture. Every time I heard myself speaking a vivid memory surfaced. I had been told as a child that I talked funny. It was a lisp that no one knew what to do with since this predated speech therapists in the schools. When applying to Jersey State Teachers College, as a prospective teacher I was told that if the lisp was corrected by my Junior year I could complete my studies. Fortunately the drama teacher directed my mom and me to a Speech Hospital in New York City. During my first semester I'd jump on the ferry and go over to Manhattan, plus I was thrilled. Finally I had found someone who knew how to help me. By Christmas, the lisp was gone That day, when my therapy was completed, saw me ecstatically running and leaping down the Manhattan street on my way to the subway. The whole experience had set me free to speak. Now I'm often complimented on my speech and once again I'm thankful. Amazing how the Lord's hand had always guided and shaped my life and now I was experiencing the joy of bringing his sacred words to others.

a sweet visit...

My old Datsun was rusting away, giving me trouble opening the passenger side front door. One time when taking Mila, my buddy to a meeting she had to enter the car from the back seat and climb over to get into the front seat. She was young and agile. Bernice was amazing, but there was no way she could handle that maneuver. BJ was coming in a few weeks and something had to give. One of the men in the church worked at the Ford dealership and in no time at all he called to say he had a Tercel that was in good condition and thought I should take a look at it. After having my son Jim give it a look, I bought the car. When Bernice arrived we had reliable wheels.

It was April 6th when I picked her up at the airport. It was amazing to see how well she was recovering from the accident. She had to climb the stairs to get into my house and then another flight when going to bed. As the week progressed her strength improved. Our time together was a source of joy as always. She went with me out to the senior residence where I taught a weekly and of course fit right in. She loved the church and appreciated the lovely fuss Huw paid her.

Especially due to her upcoming birthday I planned a

sightseeing trip. We w headed west to the mountains, but first spent an overnight with my family. Bernice enjoyed watching me play with my three little ones. The next morning we headed for Montreat, a Presbyterian Church conference center she had always wished to see. From there we turned south to Charleston. It happened to be her 82nd birthday. With some help, she climbed up into the horse drawn carriage to tour the city streets and hear the stories of its fascinating past. This trip was my gift to her, but what a gift she was to me.

After Bernice returned to Sequim, I certainly took advantage of spending time on the beach when my schedule permitted. Actually it became a second office, I found it a great place to study and do some prep. The water temps were great for this 'ole Yankee, making May an optimum time before the water warmed to the nineties and the sun intensified.

It was also strawberry picking time. The farm was on the same road Michael Jordan lived as a kid. I heard tales of people who moved into the house after the family had left and how they were puzzled to find frequent cars slowing down as they passed the house. Some even pulled in the driveway, checking out the old basketball hoop that was still there. Jordan visited the area and often took time to visit his old high school. The students were given new footwear and even more important he spent time talking with the kids..

summer ...

Soon June rolled around and found me heading north to New Fairfield. I was asked to stay in my friends' house to take care of their dog, while they traveled. This had been one of my homes, so I was well familiar with everything and more than comfortable with the dog. It seemed strange to be in their empty house that always was full of warmth and TLC. When I stopped by the church, Roy invited me to lunch and shared he would be leaving to go to another pastorate. We both enjoyed the time together.

Another trip to Sequim and this time Bernice had something very special for us to share. We hopped the boat in Port Angeles over to Victoria to spend the night. The next morning we took the bus to visit the lovely Butchard Gardens. On our return to the city a serendipity occurred. While the bus traveled down the highway, we kept noticing people with lawn chairs setting themselves up along the sides of the road and on the overpasses. Many were waving UK flags. The bus driver told us that Queen Elizabeth and Prince Philip were due to arrive momentarily and would be traveling this very highway. We were comfortably ahead of their trip from the airport. The driver let us off near the street that faces the harbor and is in front of the famous Empress Hotel so we would be positioned to see the motorcade.

The Queen was there to open the Commonwealth Games, a track and field event, causing much excitement. We had a great viewing spot and when their car slowly passed us we could plainly see them both. Couldn't resist teasing Bernice that Philip had winked at her. We then walked over to the Parliament Grounds where the Queen addressed the hushed crowd. It was fascinating to observe how much and how important she was to the Canadian people. After a brief ceremony that included a presentation of a totem pole in honor of this occasion, the royal couple was escorted to the harbor, boarded a sea plane and flew to a private island.

The next morning Bernice's friend met us and took us to her home on Salt Springs. We enjoyed the ferry ride to the charming island. Anne proved to be a great tour guide as well as hostess. On the last morning there, I was able to leave the old friends providing them with some time alone. This freed me to roam around the lovely property filled with flowers. I enjoyed scrambling on the rocks and found a comfortable perch, high on the bluff overlooking the water. My eyes spotted seals in the water splashing playfully below, putting on a show just for me. Also, several eagles swooped down, plucking fish from the water, reminding me of a favorite verse in Isaiah that promises us that.... but those who hope in the Lord will renew their strength. They will soar on wings like eagles.... How I love that verse I surely would love to soar like that and I know some day I will.

There was a wide variety of birds of all sizes and shapes. I savored some alone time with my Lord. On my walk back to the house, I discovered some blackberries and must confess to eating a few.

Returning to Sequim, I enjoyed doing some chores around the house. Always felt a sense of belonging in BJ's home. In many ways, it filled an emotional gap, a need for home. In addition to that need, she was my "second" mom and I, the daughter she never had.

heading east...

Time to fly East. I could hear the family calling, tugging on my heartstrings. After some good visits it was time to prepare to begin my second year and settle into my beach home. Upon my arrival, I was surprised to find, the summer intern had taken down many things, rearranged furniture and removed the rugs. Once again I felt dishonored. It was difficult to figure why he hadn't at least attempted to return things the way he had found them. He also hadn't fulfilled his part of a bargain we had made.

Huw was eager, always looking for ways to stimulate growth, willing to step out of his comfort zone even though that was difficult. He encouraged the flock to spend some serious time in thinking about and looking together at possible changes in order to strengthen the ministry of Little Chapel. The church in many ways had already made a step by having me come on board. They had survived my coming and rattling their cage.

The leadership of the church engaged a church growth consultant. He was excellent in his analysis, after conducting a most extensive exploration to determine where the church was at and helping us to identify what we were hoping to achieve. I have a keen interest in this process and have done some serious reading written by church gurus. Gary, a dear buddy had received a Doctorate of Ministry in this area that has piqued my interest years ago. The consultant was most affirming of my presence. He also reenforced many of the things I had identified.

One of his recommendations was to activate the Capital Improvement Committee. At their request I became a vital member. There were numerous meetings. Decisions needed to be made both about the future of the manse, which needed immediate attention as well as the need for church expansion. Included in the mix was consideration whether "my house" should be demolished to create more parking space. The committee was well chosen as it was composed of people with strong personalities and insights. Bonds of support and respect for one another developed. The chairman fell into a habit of calling on me to close our long sessions with prayer and at times when our meeting had been extra long one of the committee would ask when will Ruth to pray? This caused some teasing that added humor to the mix.

My former husband and his wife had relocated to Concord from California in order to help Jim and Denise with the children. Living with three little ones was a continuing challenge. Having them on the scene was a shift for me and I had to acknowledge that it stirred up some jealousy and insecurities as it felt like my territory was being invaded. Every time we were together I experienced hurt and a deep wounding. Thankfully, this wasn't due to unforgiveness or bitterness. The Lord had taken care of that years ago.

The second year I jumped into an adult literacy training and was assigned to a woman who was struggling to get her GED. I quickly learned to appreciate how daunting that is. Her area of major difficulty was in the Social Science/History area. She had no frame of reference. Her family never watched the news or read a newspaper. Although Afro- American, she didn't have a clue what the Emancipation Proclamation was. Her reading was on a fifth grade level and as we worked together it improved to a sixth grade. But the test was the challenge. We worked hard and she showed improvement when retaking it, but more work was needed. The next test was scheduled in June. Sadly for me, I never heard from her how she did.

By Christmas of my second year the Session decided to begin the search to find an associate pastor. My presence on staff had clearly served to demonstrate the need. I had mentioned that I would consider staying a third year, but that would need to be in addition not to fill the associate role.

When the new year came and weeks ensued, I began to hear you can't leave, we need you. Here I go again facing the unknown. Okay, Lord what's next? I began making overtures and connecting with the new Presbytery executive. Nothing was happening. A dear couple in the church who had a second home in Boone, in the mountains, approached that pastor asking if he would consider my coming. He expressed a keen interest, but explained to them his church was in the process of filling a desperate need for a youth pastor. Hopefully my joining that staff would be possible in the future.

Thoughts of Sequim, Washington always seemed to emerge. They were never far away from my heart. But now I had been so thoroughly blessed with five years of wonderful times with visits with the family and especially with the grandkids. Oh boy... heavy times again... the not knowing... another leaving.

Small groups now moved front and center on my agenda. I tried a six week series involving all the Sunday adult classes, meeting in the Fellowship Hall. I used one of Serendipity's introductory series, one that had specifically been developed as a starter for small groups. Previously I had met with the adult teachers and shared with them my goals. They willingly cooperated and were involved in leading the groups scattered about the room. We had a joint opening and closing and didn't hear many complaints. Out of that experience I then was able to launch some home groups. This study was focused on the Sermon on the Mount. Huw willingly used the same text for his sermons providing a sense of unity. With many folks involved, conversations about the lesson material occurred.

One of my groups was a real treasure. It was held out at Plantation Village, a retirement community where a member lived. That enthusiastic group became a highlight of my week as I looked forward with great anticipation to my times with them. There is something so gratifying when aging folks get turned on to the scriptures.

My son, Dan came to see me. It was delightful, having my own place providing a home for him to visit. He was in a time of his life where he was sending out resumes to various places and the answers seemed to be similar. "You are near the top of our list but we've chosen some one else." Ouch, that's tough.

Holy Week and Easter both years were highlights for me. Huw poured lots of thought, planning and prayer that resulted in making all the services deeply meaningful. Little Chapel had services for Maundy Thursday, Good Friday and of course Easter. My second year Huw was willing to have some drama in the Maundy Thursday service. I enlisted individuals to give five minute portrayals of specific people who had been touched by Jesus for the Maundy Thursday Service.

A community Easter sunrise service was held on the beach. Crowds poured down the streets heading to the spot on the beach where a flat bed truck was transformed into a pulpit area equipped with a sound system for music and speakers. While the sun rose over the ocean hundreds of people were singing Christ the Lord is risen today, hal-le-lu-jah. Powerful way to begin an Easter Sunday..... Keeping with a tradition, many before returning to their cars stopped at Little Chapel to enjoy the coffee and doughnuts. The regular services of the morning were full, rich in music and message.

sweet visits...

Bernice returned agan in April. This time we traveled east to the Outer Banks. Both of us found our stops at historic sights in Manteo and the great Wright Brothers' Museum at Kitty Hawk worthwhile. Of course we took in the well known Cape Hatteras lighthouse. We delighted in some tasty seafood meals and as always were so happy in each other's company. I had learned, while in Sequim, that as long as Bernice had something to read she was more than content for me to leave her and take the brisk walks I reveled in.

BJ had difficulty on the previous visit in making plane connections. I promised to eliminate that transfer, I would take her to Atlanta to board her plane for a direct flight to Seattle. Relatives she hadn't seen in years, lived in one of the suburbs. Her family was welcoming to me and of course thrilled to see her. I had never been to that area and was eager to do some sight seeing.

Lisa, my daughter-in-law's sister, invited us to stay with her. She lived just outside of Atlanta, off the freeway and gave us helpful driving tips to aid our explorations the next morning.

We toured the CNN building seeing the newsrooms and found them impressive. The Coke headquarters is based in Atlanta and both of us got a kick out of their displays showing the progression of their advertising through several decades. We found our way to the Civil War Cyclorama that comes alive while you watch the battle of Atlanta.

But for me the highlight was our visit to the home and neighborhood of one of my heroes, Martin Luther King. Our excellent guide told us many tidbits about Martin's growing up. The house is down the street a little ways from the Ebneezer Baptist Church and we were told that Martin and siblings would go upstairs on a balcony so they could their preacher dad coming up the block. When they spotted him walking home after Sunday worship, they would holler, "Mom he's coming." That meant they could all sit down at last to Sunday dinner. As Martin got up in his teens of course the balcony became a great escape place. We took our time at the church and the memorial. I wished they would have had some videos of his speeches.

After dropping Bernice at airport, I stopped at the Carter Center. There was a school group there and I tagged along with one of them, listening in on the guide's talk. It was obvious their teacher had done a good job in preparing her students. They were knowledgeable and asked excellent questions. The Center with its focus on peace had a serene quality about it.

Little Jessi came to visit Grandma two different times. She was almost three the first time and after the long drive, a little light supper and settling in, it was bedtime. When she was about to climb into bed she said, with some tears, "I want to go home. I miss my mommy and my blankets and my sheets". Oh boy, I thought, home is three hours away. Great wisdom emerged from somewhere and after some hugging and attempts at consoling her, I told her, " Honey it's too far and it's too late, but I promise we will go home first thing in the morning. We won't even go to the beach. I'll take you home." She was quiet for a few moments and then said, "but Grandma that would be dumb." Without another word or sob she snuggled under the covers and slept like a log. We had a great time at the beach the next day.

Later in the day I took her into the chapel. While entering the sanctuary she became quiet and reverent. We talked in whispers and then I took her up on the chancel area and showed her where I read scripture. When I lifted her up, behind the pulpit, she could look out over the pews. Precious memories. Our next stop was the preschool area and what fun she had checking out the toys.

In the spring a marvelous preacher came for a weekend at another church and I attended the Friday night service. He was a short, homely man, but when he began to speak his face became radiant as he spoke about his Lord. He was beautiful. His message was from Ezekiel and wasn't addressing anything about healing, but while he was speaking, I felt the Holy Spirit was touching me in a unique way. On my way home, I was still in awe and realized that something profound had happened, a healing had taken place. No longer was it painful at family gatherings. The sting had been removed from old memories.

Another spring event was a Franklin Graham Crusade and I volunteered as an usher, an inspiring event. An added bonus, one of the nights was the appearance of Franklin's dad and mom, Billy and Ruth. She quietly entered the arena before the program had begun. Some people spotted her and surprised her with a standing ovation. I was thrilled that she was honored this way because she was a spiritual giant to me. When Billy came out on the platform with the team, the roar of the crowd drowned out the preliminary music. Once again everyone was on their feet applauding. Billy spoke briefly as his son had asked him to, another special treasure.

my next church...

It was now May and I still didn't know what or where I was going when my two years were ended in June. Thoughts of two years ago returned. Hm. When I heard my phone ring and I was surprised to hear a cheerful voice on the other end. He was the pastor in Aberdeen and had been visiting his mother in Wilmington. Harriet, a friend from church was also visiting her. His father had pastored Little Chapel and they had both known each other from high school days. In conversation she mentioned me and my dilemma and he jumped at the possibility. Immediately, he invited me to come and meet with him and others, spending the night. He was certainly upbeat and sounded full of fun.

In our meeting the most urgent need described was in the Christian Ed area, including the Sunday School as well as an after-school program. Mike called the next day telling me that the vote was affirmative. Their plan to provide my room and board was once again, living in homes. There were advantages to this offer as it would place me geographically midway between the beach and my family in Concord. That sounded like a winner to me.

I soon learned at the interview, that the church had a strong connection with the Church of Scotland and over the last few years they had been blessed with a seminary graduate coming and serving at the church a year. This new intern was married and the two of them would arrive in September. The church provided them, an apartment and a car.

In June, the new associate was officially called thus closing the door to my staying on at Little Chapel. I knew my next step would take me to Aberdeen and Bethesda Presbyterian Church. My goodbyes were in earnest now. Little Chapel treated me to a lovely farewell my last Sunday, as well as a generous gift of money. Even more were the affirmations that included, "You know you really should me a minister". I had heard that before and knew that wasn't my calling. When I reflected on it, once again I realized that as a volunteer I could accomplish many unique things due in part to the freedom I enjoyed. That was not part of my Lord's plan for me. He had put me there at a crucial time in Little Chapel's history and that made me both grateful and humbled.

My last Sundays were after Huw and his wife had gone on vacation. I found myself in the pulpit, two consecutive Sundays loving and appreciating the challenge. Having my own place had been a treat. I had been richly blessed with a wide variety of family and friend visits.

Before leaving the beach a big dream of mine was fulfilled. Both of my oldest sons with their families spent a few days filling my house and heart to overflowing as we shared our love for the beach. I had always dreamed that someday I would be able to watch my grandkids romp on the beach and in the ocean. Kristen was eleven and Lindsay, nine. Jessi, almost five, thought it was cool to hang out with her older cousins. The boys were totally happy and busy either digging a giant hole of running into the surf.What a great time we all had.

summer interlude...

It was now time to head north and feast on sweet times with family and friends. I did my usual circuit in Connecticut and then onto the Baileys and the Grahams before coming back to John's.

Next, I boarded the plane to Washington and a visit to Sequim. There was obvious tension and turmoil in the church. One of my friends commented it was time to come back. I was needed. That always created a tugging at my heart but never dreamed it would happen. After all I was on board to go to Aberdeen.

I found myself dragging my feet in going to visit the Barnes and realized a total weariness of body, soul and spirit. These visits created an excitement in being with dear folks, but were two edged. I thrived on the deep sharing that took place while having to acknowledge that was coupled with the pain of having to walk away, having to relinquish them again. Letting go never gets easier. Once again I was thankful for the Lord's comfort.

A new pastor had been called and was eagerly awaited. Gerry, the associate pastor was in pain as he had hoped to step into that position. Yes, a strong mixture of hopefulness and disappointment hung over the church.

Before I had left Wrightsville Beach, Harriet and I talked about her coming out to Washington so I could show her around. And that we did. She was a most enthusiastic tourist and we enjoyed a memorable time together.

My friends, Dwight and Agnes were struggling with his condition. Significant changes were obvious. It was tough to see Dwight struggle to get out of his chair and then shuffle slowly across the room. Agnes, as always maintained her smile and acceptance of the decline. But I couldn't help but wonder what this was doing to her.

Once again, I found myself flying east ready to visits with my family and friends in Connecticut. And then it was time to head south as summer was winding down. More transitions again... another beginning... a new place. Will this be a "minding the store" year or will it have substance. I found myself ruminating about my future. Might there be an open door in a year or two taking me back to Sequim? Maybe the mountains of North Carolina would happen after this commitment? Hm, all these questions. Some meaningful words copied in the back of my journal jumped out at me and helped to quiet my soul.

Cultivate a willingness to wait and not wail. There is a need to balance the sacred skill of watchful waiting with holy risking. Jean Blomquist

Holy risking, hm, I respond to that, guess in many ways I'm living that and liking it most of the time, even with its highs and lows.

Bethesda Presbyterian '95...

After a super summer I was ready. Mike, the pastor at Bethesda, greeted me warmly and shared he wanted me to be comfortable and happy so don't fail to ask him if I needed something. The library became my office. It was a lovely room and I was able to position my desk in front of a big window. As I settled into my new nest and arranged my things it felt good and comfortable. I had splurged while in Sequim, treating myself to a painting of a ferry crossing the water with the mountains forming a backdrop. The art store in nearby Poulsbo shipped it to me and upon its arrival I found a perfect spot to hang it. Many times I would gaze at the picture and be filled with a longing for Washington State.

My first home was with a widow who I quickly discovered was not home much. She was very involved with her family and grandkids. Her stories fascinated me when she shared her experiences of hiking on the Appalachian Trail. Boy, that stirred up my spirit of adventure, wondering whether I would like an overnight or two on the trail and whether I could stand up to the challenge. Never got to find out, unfortunately.

Three small cities make up the area. Pinehurst, the most affluent, Southern Pines, a mixture and Aberdeen is more of a blue collar city. Naturally I was eager to explore. Easily I made my way around Southern Pines, stopping to treat myself to lunch. This part of the state is called the sand hills, generally flat but has a few gentle hills and an abundance of pines. I discovered a park with trails around the reservoir that quickly became my favorite walking place.

In the days to come I drove into Pinehurst and strolled around the town with its charming and expensive little shops. I checked out the famous golf course. The public is allowed only in the lodge. The hallways are lined with great pictures of famous golfers.

Bethesda is a lovely church endowed with a steeple. It setting is picturesque as it sits on a knoll overlooking a small pond. The property has lots of trees and combined with the landscaping makes an impressive presence. The building was well taken cared of and had many inviting classrooms for adults and children.

Folks were welcoming and encouraged fresh input. When I started to poke around below the surface I was not surprised to find the typical accumulation of stuff, old unused lesson materials etc. It was nice to have helpful hands ready and eager to help sort and discard.

The charming intern was just finishing up his year and about to return to Scotland. He had been a big hit with the youth, The church was now anticipating the arrival of the new intern and his wife. Their arrival would coincide with the church's traditional Homecoming at the Old Bethesda Church. The structure had been built in the 1860's and shared its spot with an equally aged cemetery. Ian and Kim were introduced at the worship service complete with bagpipes. Ian had been given kilts to wear and carried in the scriptures in a very traditional manner. Quite impressive. A special duet was so tender it brought tears to my ears as the voices resonated in the old building. Afterward we all feasted at long picnic table under the lovely trees. Good ole southern cooking was delicious and quickly disappeared off the tables.

The Watsons were warmly received. Kim was an immediate hit with everyone. Ian, more of an introvert was warm and gracious. Both I would soon discover had a good sense of humor. Kim's accent was more difficult to understand and when they were speaking together it was practically impossible to decipher their conversation. Our relationship took off immediately. We quickly became each other's support system.

At our first staff meeting Mike laid out some dates and direction. Ian and I would share the children's spot in the worship. The kids had been very responsive the few Sundays I had under my belt and I was eager to continue. That would be my only exposure in Worship as Ian, being the minister needed those experiences. He would be preaching monthly. Ian wasn't given much direction, but told to find his own niche and go with it. He was committed to work with the Youth and not tied down to anything else.

busy, busy...

My schedule didn't lack as I spoke or taught at Circle meetings and Sunday School classes. Of course I was very involved with the Christian Education committee. Mike received a call about a program called Divorce Care. He talked to me about taking on that responsibility. After previewing the program I was impressed and told him, yes. I liked the fact that it would be publicized and offered to the community. We launched the program in January and both Kim and Ian joined the team. Divorce Care is a taped series of well known teachers that presented the subject matter each session. The coordinator added some thoughts to the lecture that led to a small group discussion time. Although our numbers remained small the three of us felt the program was worthwhile.

Also, I was eager to offer the Caring Evangelism Program I had taken at Little Chapel. How precious that group became. It actually had a life changing effect on a few of the participants.

The need to establish rapport, the need to listen and not preach were eye openers. Again the Watsons were eager participants.

Kim joined with me to help in the after school program. That stretched her. She was naturally adept with teens but younger kids were a new adventure. Plus, we had some "high maintenance" kids in our group. Erma had been leading it and her style was to give long preachy lessons that essentially the kids tuned out. After a long school day there wasn't much hope one could expect them to sit still that long. Behavior and morale was a big problem.

Kim, Ian and I attended a lively and informative Youth Workshop in Raleigh. That was a brand new experience for them. The Youth Group was definitely giving them a hard time. There were a few middle school girls that were acting up and putting their feet to the fire. The three of us did plenty of talking, crying and praying together. Slowly things improved.

While at Little Chapel a couple when they found out I loved to play tennis made a weekly date to get together. I was now excited to find a new tennis pal as Kim was eager to play. On the weekends we were joined by a few others who enjoyed the sport.

Being in Aberdeen afforded me the opportunity to visit Wrightsville Beach. What a blessing to be able to get away and walk the beach. It definitely helps, when in ministry, to sort out and process all that is happening.

The other blessing was being able to continue to make frequent visits to Jim's. Just a few hours away kept me very connected. It was fascinating being there to experience these early years. Big sister's world was now expanding and she was such a delight as she faced her first dance recital. Little did we realize the number of recitals we would be attending together. It was fascinating observing the boys. I had never been around twins during their preschool years and marveled at the special bond they shared. They both watched out for each other and "usually" savored each other's company.

In November I splurged, treating myself to a few days at the Cove, a Billy Graham Training Center near Asheville. The attractive facility is placed on the mountain side. There was still some autumn color in the trees adding to the natural beauty. The chapel sits down the hill closer to the entrance and was lovely in its simplicity and elegance. What an awesome, sacred place to pray. There was such a sense of the Lord's presence making it possible to absorb the holiness and majesty of our mighty God.

The conference was about preaching and geared to pastors. What My attracted me the most was that the speaker, Rev Stephen Olford. During the pregnancy of my third son I was required to have bed rest. After the delivery my baby, Dan had serious bouts of pneumonia so we kept him away as much as possible from exposure to germs. My Sunday routine was sending my husband and other sons off to Sunday School and church. I would then do the necessary chores and care for the baby so that at eleven o'clock I was free to sit down and listen to Calvary Baptist Church's radio broadcast, coming from New York City. Rev. Olford was the minister there for many years and he became my pastor during that stretch of close to three years. I was richly taught and blessed and was given the gift enabling me to focus and worship at home, alone. At the Cove he was always surrounded with pastors wanting to talk to him. I noticed his wife standing by quietly and went over to her to tell her my story. She graciously assured me she would tell her husband and express my thanks and appreciation for his unknown ministry to me.

November, I moved into a new home. The family included two daughters who shared a room freeing up a place for me. What a contrast after a most of the time empty house to a very lively paced home.

a roadblock....

When December came, I moved onto Erma's in a most spacious and lovely home in Pinehurst. We got to know each other, working together with the after school group. She had her house on the market wanting to downsize and settle closer to her family. I had the lower floor which was more than roomy. I enjoyed a little frig, sink and stove as well as my own TV.

That sounds perfect, but I soon hit the wall as my hostess was a very difficult person for me. Her dinner routine included watching the evening news while we ate together. My dilema was that she was ultra conservative in her politics and I am really an independent and if I dared to differ with her viewpoint, even my Christianity became suspect. If I didn't offer any opinion I was wrong for my lack of interest. It was a certainly a no win situation. It was not the best way to enjoy and digest a meal.

There were other challenges. Whenever she would show the house all my personal items were removed and put in my dresser. One night, bless her heart, she accidentally locked me out. I enjoyed the privilege of a garage opener but being alone, she had installed locks that were anchored in the floors and when the bolt is pulled up it prevents anyone from getting in the house. After a long meeting one night, I pulled into the garage and tried to enter the door to the house only to find I was blocked with the special locks she used at night. Being hard of hearing she had her television turned up and she wasn't responding to the knock on the front door or the doorbell. Finally in desperation I squeezed behind the bushes and knocked on her window. Success at last. When I look back at all of this I suspect she was in the early stages of Alhzmeir's.

The Lord had a greater purpose in all this. Actually, in each of my homes I had experienced stress. Sensing I was over reacting, that made me wonder what was all this about. I gradually realized God wanted my attention. When I shared all these frustrations with Kim and Ian, I found comfort in being able to talk freely as I expressed my internal turmoil. That helped me to sort it out.

My next step was to sit down prayerfully and access what options did I have. Staying a second year was one, was Sequim a possibility? Bernice had told me their new pastor, Scott was doing great things and the church was growing. I was sensing the "gift" of being able to live with families and to make all the adjustments that are necessary had been used up. The apostle Paul gives us a list of gifts, but I always believed there were many more than he had identified. I knew that my ability to make the multiple adjustments in moving all the time as well as being without a home was due to my Lord. He had given me a special gift enabling me. With a smile on my face I concluded that my gift had been exhausted and I needed to make some adjustments. God definitely had my attention, a change was in order.

The next step would be to test out the possibilities of going to Sequim. I was in somewhat of a dilemma. I did not know how to spell the new pastor Scott's last name (Koenigsaecker) but did not want to ask Bernice how to spell it and raise her hopes of my coming to Sequim until the waters had been tested. I sent off a letter to him, introducing myself and asking if he would be interested in my coming as a volunteer. I had previously sent a letter to the Barnes asking if it would be possible to use one of the guest cottages as my home, but with the understanding that I would move out whenever the space was needed. Ruth had been quick to answer telling me they would love to have me come and stay in the cottage. I felt the need to clarify with them that I was needing to be independent, cooking for myself. Ruth responded with, "you sound like a teenager in desperate need of their independence. COME!"

One unique challenge came out of a staff meeting involving Ian, Mike and myself. Christmas is a difficult and painful time for those in grief over a wide variety of losses. Appreciating Mike's sensitivity to the need we felt led and decided to have a service for the hurting. It was held it on a Sunday evening prior to Christmas. We drew a few from outside the church family as well as some from within. Each of us had a part. The service was one of those sacred times. The three of us were blessed with the appreciative reactions we received.

After the Christmas Eve service, I jumped in my car and took off for the family. What fun the morning was with the kids as they squealed with delight while they opened their presents. What a treat to be part of the celebration.

a new year...

The new year started and with it came a call from Sequim. It was the pastor and we chatted about the possibilities of my joining the staff. Scott had already sounded out some of the folks that knew me from my earlier years and they were most enthusiastic. I joked with him afterwards that he had talked to all my supporters. By the end of the month it was a go and I could share with Bernice I was coming back. Needless to say she was thrilled.

Mike was very sad about my leaving, but understanding. My homes, now that my future was settled, were very special. In January, I house -sat and took care of a sweet kitten. It was fun roughhousing with her. I enjoyed having Kim and Ian over to dinner one night and we all had fun playing with the kitty. After the lady came home I asked her how the cat was doing. Ian happened to be standing behind her, facing me as she told me she didn't quite know what to think of the cat, it had gotten so frisky. He was cracking up and I had to struggle to maintain a straight face.

February, I moved into a lovely home complete with my room and bath off on the other side of the garage. The folks were leaders in the church and very warm and hospitable. We were all enthusiastic of our support for the UNC Tarheels basketball team. While in their home I was treated to a concert featuring the North Carolina Symphony and multiple lavish Sunday bruches.

March, I had an unique experience of living with a family with three teenagers, a mom who was a nurse and a dad who taught elementary school. Marty taught Spanish and the kids loved him. He was legally blind and had a seeing- eye dog which of course went to school with him. He had great stories to tell about the dog. Pedro would always sit by him when he was teaching and if any of the kids got up out of their seat the dog would stand up too, tipping his master off. One of the boys said to his buddies, "I told you the teacher can see".

Another story went back to when Marty went to Pougkeepsie New York to spend a week of training before he was allowed to bring the dog home. Marty quickly learned to be guided down the uneven sidewalks and to cross busy streets. All that was comfortable, until he had to take the dog into a large department store, he was surprised to find how capable the dog was in maneuvering through the crowded aisles. But even more surprised to find the dog take him up and down the escalator. Actually the dog was fascinated with it and Marty found himself being led many times to the escalator.

After only being in their home a few days, I received the shocking news that my brother, Rodger had died. Immediately the family engulfed with their love and sensitivity. I made the sad journey over the mountains to Tennessee. It was good to spend a some time with nieces and nephews I didn't really know.

family retreat...

Family Retreat was one of my highlights for the year. Intergenerational experiences always offer opportunities of bonding and creating great memories. Overnights I have found, accomplish something more long lasting between people and also deepens our walk with God. Years before when teaching VBS and Backyard Bible clubs I had discovered a greater impact as the relationships deepened when these events went into a second week.

There were lots of good vibes as I brought together a committee. An enthusiasm and sense of expectancy abounded as we enjoyed the process and shared the responsibilities. Marty played a great harmonica and we spent lots of time working on music. Realized I could relax, the focus would all be on him and not on my simple guitar. There was a nearby camp the committee checked out and agreed it would be a great place for the retreat.

Marty and Deb had both gone to Wake Forest and were friends with Jim Morgan. Jim is a gifted musician and song writer. He is very creative and original with lots of humor sprinkled into his concerts. His "Zit Song "is a riot and always requested wherever he performs. Here's a few lines that will give you the picture.

> *If God had to give me zits why'd he put them on my face?*
> *He could put them on my legs or on top of my head or any*
> *other place. You can talk about his love and goodness, you*
> *can talk about his grace. But if God had to give me zits,*
> *why'd he put them on my face?*

He graciously agreed to be our program for Friday night and was well received by the audience of all ages. We had crafts, games, skits all lined up for Saturday. A great time was enjoyed by all.

On the grounds, there was a small worship area with a rough large cross and log benches to sit on. We all lined up carrying our group banners that had been made and proceeded down the path in the woods to the opening. We had a short devotional, song and communion. A beautiful conclusion to a blessed retreat.

My year was winding down and while I reflected on it there had been frustration as I was limited in many ways in ministry, but thankfully the Lord opened up other avenues where I expressed and used my need to teach and share my heart. Both the Divorce Care and even more, The Caring Evangelism Course fed those needs. Once again I had experienced first hand how in both tender and awesome ways my Lord keeps his promise to supply my every need. I'm thankful as an old childhood chorus goes, he just keeps getter sweeter as the days go by.

April and May I wound up my time living with a family of three. Their home was situated on the edge of the old family farm. Next to their ample lot a large portion had been sold and turned into a lovely golf course. What an early morning treat, as I was allowed to roam around the cart trails before most golfers teed off.

I enjoyed lots of privacy in the finished basement as well as plenty of opportunity to interact with the young couple. We shared a common interest in clowning and the four of us did a clown routine on one of my last Sundays in the opening of Sunday School.

Now, it was time to pack up my things and this time not only would I be saying goodbye to a church, but family and friends on the east coast. Once again I had been blessed with meeting and sharing with many special people.

Okay, sweet lady cardinal..time to pack..we're heading west again...

Heading West '96

Ever charming ever new. When will the landscape
tire the view ... a Welsh saying..

The goodbyes were happening again.... farewell to Bethesda, my year there had been fulfilling.... On to the beach, spending sweet time with folks from Little Chapel that included being treated to many delicious dinners.... Kim and Ian had joined me for a few days and were surprised and delighted with the warm water, so different from their Scottish sea.... another goodbye...we had shared and cared for each other and this parting was painful......we talked about meeting again someday... Onto Jim and his family in Concord.... leaving the grandkids was the toughest of all.... It had been so great to be so close during those baby years. Before leaving, Jim told me he was proud of me and asked if I would please call him collect every night as I made my way cross country trip. His tenderness blessed me and was a balm to my soul.

Now it was time to turn north and make the long drive to my sister in the Pocanos. Lil was concerned about my going cross country and had even considered traveling with me, not wanting me to be alone. She had tears in her eyes when I drove away. My visit with Doug and family in New Jersey was a good one, as usual.

Next stop was Connecticut. I had planned to spend some time there and was staying with Dolores while indulging in quality visits with longtime friends along with dear folks from the church.

While in New Fairfield, I took the opportunity to take Kristen and Lindsay to Plymouth Massachusetts. First we toured the Mayflower then went through the Ocean Spray Cranberry facility. The next morning we stopped en route to Plimoth Plantation at a small amusement complex complete with some water bumper boats. We all got soaking wet as we laughed ourselves silly.

I had coached the girls before we arrived at the plantation that all of the people in costume could be approached and would engage in conversation if you asked them questions. Each person had studied the people they were posing as and would respond to their names. They were immersed in their characters and would not know anything that post dated their life time. We sat down on the bench with a woman, in costume, and chatted. Lindsay asked her what her favorite fruit was. She replied she liked apples. Then she asked "Lins" and her reply was bananas. The woman looked puzzled and asked what did they look like. She had never heard or seen one. We were both amused and taken back realizing her frame of reference differed totally from ours.

Kristen then thought to ask her if she could read. She answered emphatically that she didn't have to, after all the Reverend read and shared all the important information. That surprised us. We asked if her children could read and if not, would she want them to learn. She responded softly and thoughtfully with a quiet yes. Hm, that was intriguing. All three of us found the experience fascinating, appreciating the authenticity of the place.

After my Connecticut goodbyes, once again I was on the road headed for a few precious days with the Baileys in Maine. I found myself soaking up the beauty and charm of New England while savoring the sharing of hearts with dear people as they entered into my excitement about my adventure.

My last stop before heading west was with Geoff and Susan in their Vermont house on a hill. Now, after a few days... after all the visits and goodbyes ...it was time to leave. I rose early in the quiet house and sipped my coffee out on the porch. At long last the big day had arrived, one I had contemplated many times when flying cross country telling myself that some day I must drive. Those "old Daddy tapes" when he shared his desire to see more of his country, had planted seeds of pride in my country and a longing to experience more of it. I didn't necessarily imagine I would be doing this alone, but that's how God had it laid out for me.

The little Tercel was all packed and waiting. Geoff and Susan prayed launching me into my big adventure. Taking a deep breathe and heaving a sigh, I waved good bye and drove down the hill. With a prayer and a song in my heart, I headed west. Much thought had been used in making my plans and making several contacts. While I drove through tiny little Vermont villages I was tingling with anticipation as my adventure began to unfold. Headed northwest entering New York State above Lake Champlain I soon approached the border crossing in Cornwall. I was surprised and pleased, driving through this well- kept Mohawk Reservation.

My passage through Customs was smooth, with out any difficulty and now I proceeded in Canada. I had selected this route to avoid the congestion in the States, but was finding it somewhat disappointed as the drive seemed rather bland. First night was spent alone in a comfortable motel. The next morning the scenery became more satisfying when I started to pass some lakes and then began to see Lake Michigan and soon Lake Huron. Dropping south now, I crossed the border and reentered the U.S.

at Salt ST. Marie. The highway took me for a while through Michigan and then into Wisconsin. My destination was Green Bay. The plan was to stay three nights with the former youth pastor from Connecticut who I had worked with. Scott was now in a new position in a lovely church. A fun guy and good cook, it was a perfect place to stretch and relax. The next day we joined his middle school outing on a Lake Michigan beach.

The day after, he took me around Green Bay and of course we stopped at Lambeau Field to watch the Packers practicing on a fenced- in- field across from the stadium. Green Bay is famous for its rabid fans and the field was lined with folks of all ages. Several day camp groups were taking in the activity. When the team broke to have lunch, several boys waited for the team and offered the players the use of their bike to cross the road to the stadium where they would eat and relax. What a riot seeing those huge guys joyfully riding the undersized bike. How proud the kids were having their heroes choose theirs. Like them, I was thrilled to get a close look at Brett Farve and Rosy Grier.

Typically, I made an early start, having said my goodbyes to Scott and Sue's mom the night before. The drive was relaxing and pleasant as my route essentially took me through well-cared for farm lands. Both Wisconsin and Minnesota were neat and tidy. When crossing the state line into South Dakota, there was a marked difference in the scene, a definite change to "cowboy country". Seeing the cattle grazing on the wide open spaces reminded me of my two years in Central Washington. I spent the night in Chamberland on the muddy Missouri. It was apparent I must be near some reservations since when I walked a short way to get something to eat there were many native faces. The restaurant was dark and smoky, but the food was tasty.

The next morning, I soon left I- 90 to visit a tiny sod house. I didn't want to miss experiencing a small taste of "Little House on the Prairie." The front yard was packed with evidence of prairie dogs, unfortunately they kept their heads down in their burrows. Next stop was the Badlands that seemed to just appear out of nowhere. They are massive and incredible with multiple fascinating rock formations. There were well used tourists trails to wander about. It never ceases to amaze me at how much more you are rewarded when you get out of the car and walk the paths.

At Rapid City, I picked up route 16 to Mount Rushmore. The Black Hills were lovely, full of lush green trees providing a contrast to the wide open brownish prairie. Viewing the "presidents", I was struck with how huge and challenging that venture must have been. Next stop in Custer I found the Wood Carving Museum, a delight.

That night was spent in New Castle. The motel was tucked discreetly away on a quiet side street, full of lovely colorful flowers inviting me to stay. My timing was perfect. The Sagebrush Festival Parade was the big attraction the next morning. What fun! The main street was lined with flags and tables full of local wares and goodies to eat. The parade proceeded down the small hill giving everyone a great view of the action. The locals were decked out in western garb adding to the atmosphere. First came the kids showing off their pets. They were followed with the Shriners in their little cars revving up their engines and driving around in circle maneuvers while tossing candy to the crowd. A horse and wagon followed with folks tossing more goodies. A youth boot-camp group were impressive, marching in a disciplined tight formation. Their chanting gave me goose bumps. It was great to sense their pride in what they were accomplishing.

At the conclusion to the parade, five cowboys came striding into town preparing to rob the local bank. From the other direction came the local heroes and of course with guns blazing captured the bad guys. What a fun morning. I loved picking up the local flavor.

After leaving South Dakota, I made a stop in Buffalo at a museum depicting history based on the Native American viewpoint. When I left town, the Big Horn Mountains began to appear. Hunger and road weary I stopped in Sheridan. Just down the road was little Dayton, a community of less than six hundred. I was ready for a couple of nights to relax and visit with Denise's family. Her grandmother, Grace was most gracious and saw to my comfort and fed me as well. Denise's folks were in Russia so I had their house to myself.

The small town was in a festive mode also and in the midst of what they call Dayton Days. They had a parade that morning and other events that continued into Sunday. First I went to the small church and was blessed with the warmth of the people and good teaching. Grace met me in the afternoon prepared to watch the annual fire hose barrel competition. Rope was strung between two poles. A barrel hung from it. Two teams were competing, aiming their powerful hoses at the barrel trying to move it to the opposite pole. Grandma had experienced this competition many years and had strategically placed our chairs. As the struggle ensued lots of folks got drenched in the process. The competition was fierce and the audience supported their favorite team with whoops and hollers. Small town America at its best!

Early morning, before sunrise I said good bye to Dayton and started up the mountain. It was an unforgettable experience with the early morning light adding to the grandeur of the mountains. I was treated to lots of elk, moose, deer and of course some cattle. Climbed to 9,000 feet before a very long descent on the other side. I stopped to take in and savor an awesome waterfall.

Next stop was Cody, the home of the fabulous Buffalo Bill Museum. This stop would be a quickie I thought, but I was so impressed with the displays and presentations I spent several hours. In my Triple A book I had read that the approach to

Yellowstone from the east was gorgeous so I decided to take that route. It did not disappoint me and was thankful I had taken the time to go that way. I enjoyed being off the interstate those few days. My route took me through the park and when the traffic stopped that signals there's something to see. This time it was a black bear strolling down the side of the road. What a surprise and treat. I love seeing bears from my car.

A sudden wind and heavy rain made driving tough as I got back on I-90. My overnight was in Butte and then at last on the next day, I was pleased to finally be on familiar roads. Never having stopped in Couer de Alene I decided to spend a few hours there. I even took a boat ride out on that lovely lake. Finally, when crossing the state line into Washington, I let loose with a whoop and a holler, along with a sense of relief and accomplishment. Lots of miles, ahead but now on familiar turf, I was certainly getting close to home.

There is a great barbecue place east of Spokane that I couldn't resist. After indulging in a "yummy" meal I drove on through the rolling wheat country, passing through tiny towns, the stark area around the Grand Coulee Dam, followed by the ride over Disatel and the Indian Reservation before at last coming down the hill to Omak and finally Okanogan. Tollie and Woody were working in the yard when I pulled in and needless to say there were lots of hugs and excitement with a measure of relief on their part. Their wandering "child" had made it safely home. How precious they are to me.

My plans were to take a few days and visit lots of dear folks. People were happy to have me back in Washington. The pastor had contacted me before I left on my trip to ask if I would give the sermon on that Sunday. That was a privilege, another one of so many blessings the Lord poured out on me. Being with these warm and loving folks was a treat. Barbara and Colleen sang one of my favorites, "I Can Never Out love the Lord." The ladies also had a coffee time in my honor. This was a nourishing send off to my last leg of my cross country adventure.

Over the hill and through Winthrop and once again, the spectacular North Cascade Highway. The majestic splendor produced some tears as I anticipated what awaited me. This twelfth verse in Isaiah 55 resounded in my mind...

> *You will go out in joy and be led in peace*
> *the mountains and the hills will burst into song before you ,*
> *and all the trees of the field will clap their hands.*

Yea, I'm practically there.....thankful we made this trip together, Lord.

My route took me across Widby Island to the ferry, both of which I always enjoyed. Driving off the ferry, my excitement built. I was almost home, my destination was ever so close. I headed straight to Bernice's and was greeted with hugs and kisses. What an evening of sharing we enjoyed.

"home" again '96....

Okay, here I am in Sequim and it feels so natural. Running around with Bernice made both of us glad that she was perking again. It was delightful to see the old crowd, to walk the beaches and go out to lunch. Jean's Deli had moved into town and taken over the old Episcopal Church. Very nice, but I missed the old place, somewhat reminiscent of New England.

There were surprises in spite of the fact, that this transition was a returning to an area where I had roots. It was a place I was not only welcomed but loved. Many precious haunts to rediscover and enjoy but sandwiched in I was discovering an unexpected grieving that would require me some work to get through.

The church had been able to sell the building on Washington

Street. They spent a few years meeting at the Seventh Day Adventist Church and now at last had settled into their new location and new building. Innumerable hours had been given to help with the building resulting in a lovely structure. However, this was a difficult time. The associate pastor had been asked to leave, stirring up all kinds of both negative and positive vibes.

Personally, I found myself having to deal with "letting go" of the two pastors I had worked with my first time. Pastor Bill had taken early retirement due to health issues and was now found himself mired in the midst of a personal mess. Gerry had anticipated that he would become the senior pastor and when he found himself bypassed he struggled with a deep disappointment. Quite a predicament for a new pastor to handle all of that along with a multitude of things demanding his immediate attention.

Scott had now been the senior pastor for about a year. He was full of energy, vision and enthusiasm. He knew what he wanted and had a good idea how to get there. But his plate was overflowing.

Our relationship took a little time to jell. I had arrived early August and both of us still had a few weeks of vacation. It seemed that there had been little preparation for my arrival. When Ellie, the church secretary showed me my office in the library we discovered nothing had been set up. It took initiative on my part and some help from a friend to get a desk in there and to clear out stuff in order to get unpacked. Also, my cottage at the Barnes was still occupied, leaving me unsettled. Of course being with Bernice was comfortable, but essentially I was living out of my suitcase.

Experience had taught me that when faced with frustration I should   determine what other possibilities existed. Bernice and I decided to take a few days to do some sightseeing. First stop was Mount Saint Helen's. It was fascinating and encouraging to see how the foliage was restoring itself after the devastating eruption in 1980. Our next destination was the Columbia Gorge. The mighty river is so broad and expansive in this area as it approaches the Pacific Ocean. Along the Washington side are train tracks that create a picturesque scene especially when a train came through. Mount Hood dominates the Oregon side where there are multiple waterfalls, inviting you to explore. The "Gorge" is a favorite place for wind surfers and the two of us spent one evening watching their entertaining maneuvers.

When returning from our trip I was able to move in at the Barnes. I sensed Bernice was troubled and I suspected somewhat fearful that perhaps she wouldn't see much of me, once I settled into my new home. After a few days I surprised her by popping in late one afternoon and invited myself for supper. She loved it and began to realize I would not desert her or just be there to meet her physical needs... I would be there for her, emotionally, too.

My first official Sunday in August, Bob Goffrier, subbing for Scott, was in the pulpit. He was a retired chaplain from the US Navy and he and his wife had been in the church now for several years. We had connected on some of my visits. Marilyn was the church organist, making beautiful music. He was an excellent Bible teacher enjoying a fruitful ministry teaching the adult class. They both were an asset to the church. I was the scripture reader that morning and when I came up to read he introduced me and started singing, "Hello Dolly, we're so glad you're back where you belong." and everyone cheered. What an intro that was.

the new challenge...

Scott was back to work and when we sat down to talk he shared his serious concerns with the children's ministry. That definitely was the area that need attention and that became my first challenge. I visited folks who had been teaching and had struggled to keep things going. They were burned out and unwilling to be involved. There was only a handful of kids, but they needed teachers. After making many contacts I succeeded in finding some new faces, volunteers to step up to the challenge and staff the children's program. The last few years the church had conducted a Logos Club. I knew only too well from Sitka that demands involvement of many people to make a go of that. I felt the timing was not right.

In my initial talks with Scott I quickly learned that as we talked and made decisions, they might not be final. What appeared to me to be settled wasn't always a "done deal". The next morning I might find him in an entirely different place. His style of decision making was different from mine. While he's talking he's still processing. I could see adjustments on my part were necessary.

The Mothers Morning Out Program had been such a success at Wrightsville Beach bringing in some younger families into the congregation. I was optimistic that it would work here, too. One of my first moves was to start a "Time for Tots" modeled after that program. Young moms and families were the target group the church needed most to cultivate. After Scott's okay, I scoured around wanting to find a team of women who would help in this ministry. Thankfully I was led to the right ones and was able to get things going. It was rewarding to me to see in the coming years, that most of the initial group of parents joined the church and became involved.

Junior church was to be another responsibility and that took me out of the Worship service. I was unhappy. There was a quiet desire bubbling around, that involved adults. Was that a call, the Holy Spirit beckoning me to a new phase in my ministry... another Hm!

My next brainstorm was launched, a monthly big event night I named Supersational Saturday. At our first event we had thirty kids. The Barnes family from Okanogan had relocated to Sequim a few years before. They felt they should be near Bill's folks to support them with their hospitality ministry. They were dependable helpers for these monthly ventures. The oldest daughter, Carrie was already a teacher in the Sunday School. Each month the attendance at these events increased, making all the effort worthwhile.

One of my goals when coming to Sequim was to cut back on my hours to less than thirty per week freeing me to write. The thought of writing was scary to me. I was intimidated not knowing how or where to begin.

facing a new reality...

The mess with Gerry continued and we all felt the pain. Within weeks of my arrival he was asked by the personnel committee to take a four month leave and then move on. He had previously been asked to lead the Junior church, but had balked so that fell back in my lap.

My return was full of stress and turmoil. There was a deep pain that I kept experiencing that seem to linger in those vulnerable places in my heart. I was feeling lost emotionally, missing family and friends. The ever repeating question... where is my home...... is this really where you want me... how do I fit in? My elementary teaching days working with kids had been great but now having the experience of working with adults I had found a new niche that was both challenging and satisfying. I felt stuck in the quagmire like taffy, the more I tried to get free the more entangled I became. I was receiving positive strokes in my children's ministry projects, but it came at a personal cost to me. Bill and Gerry's pain also had an impact on me.

Upon my return I realized my dear friends the Masons had entered a new phase in their lives. Dwight's condition had worsened and the family intervened finally convincing Agnes that he needed to be in a nursing facility. Memories are such a powerful faculty a two-edged sword. It transports us back to precious times and places where we can be enriched and learn from them all over and over again. How excruciating to observe a loved one whose memory is slowly but surely slipping away. There is a prevailing blank look and a "knowing" that dear person is lost to himself and to you. Also, it provokes a quiet fear in all of us. Will this happen to me?

My first visit to the nursing home to visit Dwight was painful. He was alone in his room seated in a chair with wheels that he could propel with much effort. He made no eye contact, staying engrossed in looking at pictures in an album of his grandkids. I wondered what does he see, does he recognize them, does he know them at some level. I hadn't expected him to know who I was, after all I hadn't seen him for more than a year. But it was still heart wrenching when I confronted this new reality.

On another visit to see Dwight, I brought some Sunday School kids with me to sing. He always had a big heart for kids as well as music. Each new grandchild was a grand occasion. He always kept a supply of candy for them in the top drawer of his dresser. When we walked in he was slumped in his chair in the dining room while Agnes struggled to get some oatmeal in him. He looked so dejected and absent. When she saw us come in she said to him, "Dwight look the children". What a transformation. He sat up, flashed his beautiful smile and the twinkle was back in his eyes. While they sang "Jesus Loves Me" he sang right along with them. Fascinating. So much is unknown about how this memory thing operates. I've noticed with many, that the words of the old songs never get lost.

A favorite haunt was shopping at Sunny Farms, a local market that continues to grow. Fruit and veggies from the Sequim area as well as produce trucked over the Cascades from sunny and warm central Washington was always in abundance and sold at reasonable prices.

The store has a meat counter where you can buy a piece of salmon, just the right size for one or a third of a pound of freshly ground hamburger and much more. The place evoked memories of my childhood when I would walk down the street, less than two blocks to the corner, to the butcher, grocery and ice cream stores. It was the grocery store I enjoyed the most. Eddie, the proprietor, would engage me in talking about my beloved baseball team the Brooklyn Dodgers. I was eight years old and always short for my age so he would set me on the edge of the counter and have me go through their lineup telling their positions and batting averages. Pee Wee Reese shortstop, Billy Herman second base, Pete Reiser center field, Dolph Camilli at first, Dixie Walker right field, Ducky Medwick left field. Cookie Lavagetto third base, Mickey Owens catcher and Witlow Wyatt pitcher. Still can rattle them off. Memory is an incredible gift. I would listen intensely to Red Barber and Connie Desmond describe the game on the radio and then when Dad got home be able to tell him all about what had transpired.

Eddie's affirmation was significant to me. The store fascinated me especially when he used his "grabbers" to get an item down from a high shelf. They don't make stores like they used to.

Dan came to visit in mid-October. We both enjoyed the Spit and the ocean beaches along with meeting my friends both in Sequim and then in Mount Lake Terrace. He realized he had goofed by making his trip too short... I was also enjoying monthly rides to Kingston, hopping the ferry to Edmonds and sharing a dinner together with the group from Terrace View.

To inject some enthusiasm in Sunday School I initiated a drawing. Each child upon their arrival would write their name on a slip of paper, drop it in a hat and then later we would draw one out. That entitled the winner to a treat at Dairy Queen. I picked them up at school and off we went, know the one on one time created good connections. It was a big hit! One of the boys, Gabe loved the fact that we beat his school bus home, arriving ahead of his sisters. To celebrate Halloween I decided to split the group and have the younger kids have their party at the church while taking the fourth- sixth grade kids on a treasure hunt on the grounds at the Dome. Again the Barnes family was a big help. Each of the kids, all teenagers, led a small group around the grounds searching in the dark with only a flashlight for the clues. Both Bob and Bill were stationed at certain points and did a little "spooking".

I began to settle in and find a good groove and it seemed like it was Christmas before I knew it. Another wonderful trip home to spend the holidays, first stop was with Jim and Denise and the grandkids. When I exited the plane, there they were. Cole was the first to spot me and we quickly were hugging each other. How special Christmas is with little ones.

While home, I rented a car and headed for Wrightsville Beach. Folks there had experienced two major storms since my leaving and there were lots of stories to be heard. Little Chapel was spared any significant damage for which everyone was thankful. Then I headed drove north, stopping at Doug and Judi's and then onto Connecticut. Such a blessing to be with family.

January '97

Back "home", the new year began with new challenges. With Carrie's assistance, I held slumber parties in my cottage in January. Boys' night first followed by the girls a week or two later. There was lots of laughter and a good time was had by all, including a big pancake breakfast at the Dome.

Still bearing the responsibility of the children's ministry I found a healthy balance in conducting two women's retreats. First one was with my Terrace View friends. A couple opened up their home for us to enjoy even though they now were attending another church. Their house was situated on a bluff overlooking Lake Washington. I found myself waking up several times during the night to watch the twinkling lights on the lake from my bed. My second retreat was in Sequim. Fourteen women crowded into my little sitting room on Friday night. Some of the women could not come on Saturday so our numbers were down to nine. That really was a better fit in our meeting room.

A church committee was engaged in searching for the right person to fill the key position of Minister of Music, Arts and Drama. Steve Potter was called to the challenge. Our team was complete. The critical missing piece was now present and what music would ensue. It didn't take long for him to begin planning the addition of a contemporary service attempting to attract younger families.

Scott reassured me that by January '98, Session expected to add a half time person in children's ministry free me to go full speed ahead in the adult arena. That boosted my morale as I was ready for a change and a new challenge. Spring and summer my schedule looked full, leading me to decide to go back East in April.

It was spring break in Connecticut providing the opportunity to take a trip with the girls. Kristen, Lindsay and I drove to Philadelphia for an overnight. Unfortunately Independence Hall was closed needing repairs but we saw the Liberty Bell and explored the Ben Franklin Institute. That was a big hit. My girls were now teens so we hit the mall in the evening.

a great adventure....

While I traveled cross country in my own car I had drawn up a list of places I wanted to see and experience. Denver, the Rockies and the Grand Canyon were a high priority. Mickey, a close friend of Bernice's had moved to the Denver area shortly after I had arrived in Sequim. She was located north of the city and was pleased to host us. We spent some time with her as well as venturing out on our own to explore some of Denver, Boulder, and Estes Park. I was thrilled with the mountains. The next day I connected with my niece, Peggy who lived up near Nederland. She met me in Boulder and we drove around enjoying the scenery. At one spot, I asked her to stop so I could get out and observe the rushing stream. What a delight watching the crystal clear water tumbling over the rocks. The whole scene was breathtaking.

Peggy, when in her teens had gotten "into" horses. That interest had only intensified and now she was immersed in the raising, training and breeding of horses. She proudly, after first showing me her lovely home, led me out to the stable. What an ideal place for them.

The next phase on our itinerary was to travel south on I-25 to route 160, then west to Cortez where Gerry, our friend from Sequim was now settling into pastoring the local Presbyterian Church. We spent a few nights there enjoying his company. Gerry's family was finishing up the school year and he was lonely and very pleased to see us. We all went together to explore Mesa Verde to view the cliff dweller homes and the impressive canyons. Bernice was unable to do some of the walking due to the extremely steep paths. I was glad to have Gerry to share the experience. There was a mysterious aura to the place, a sense of walking on sacred ground.

Before leaving the area BJ and I drove to Durango to check out the various shops full of western and Indian regalia. We would have loved to have taken the steam train ride, but learned that had to be booked a long time ahead.

Indeed, it was a treat and joy to see Gerry in his new church and to sit under his teaching. We had a sense that our visit had not only been special for us but meant a lot to him.

Now, we were heading west and south, stopping at Four Corners where Colorado, Utah, New Mexico and Arizona all touch. We were in serious Navajo country and certainly high dessert. What a vast land it is, full of tumbleweed and sagebrush and most of the time, little else.

We arrived at the Grand Canyon early afternoon eager to explore, but first were challenged to find a parking place. Finally we located one. The entire area was congested and when we hurried over to catch our first glimpse of the canyon we felt hemmed in and somewhat deflated. We soon learned there was a bus that would take us along the canyon's edge to multiple viewing areas. Cars were prohibited from that stretch. While the tour bus made its way, there were frequent stops where folks could get on and off, at will. I stayed with Bernice for the ride.

After our full day, en route to the motel we stopped at an Imax theater and were thrilled with a viewing of gliding over the canyon, folks riding the donkeys down the narrow steep trail and people riding rafts down the river. The whole adventure was breathtaking. The next morning we went back to the park. Bernice, sensitive to my needs, offered to stay at the Visitors Center while I hopped the bus and spent a few hours viewing the canyon. She had reading material with her and urged me to go. It was perfect... getting on and off the bus at different stops to walk along the edge in uncrowded areas. I loved the solitude while drinking in the beauty, having a time of praise and thanksgiving. I returned in time to share our lunch and then pull off at a less crowded viewing spot to enjoy a special time together before bidding the canyon farewell and heading north into Utah.

When we arrived in Moab it was raining so hard you could scarcely see. That night, we settled into our motel near I-70. In the morning we proceeded east over the mountains back to Denver. We lunched in Vail and even though we still had some rain, we enjoyed poking around the shops. It was in between seasons there and everyone seemed laid back while they replenished their shelves and tidied up their shops. At the end of a street when I looked up I was startled to see a ski slope right before was eyes. Standing at the bottom of the hill I couldn't imagine someone skiing down it. There still was some snow, but it was mushy and rather dirty in spots, at that stage. Back on the highway we then proceeded climbing higher before starting our descent on the other side.

Now back at her friend's, the next morning Bernice chose to stay with Mickey while I took off for Colorado Springs. First stop was the Air Force Academy. I had seen West Point on many occasions and Annapolis, now it was the Air Force's turn. What a perfect setting the Academy has sitting on level land in the shadow of the mountains.

From there I located the Olympic Training Center. Unfortunately it was Memorial Day weekend so many of the athletes were away. There were a few of the men's gymnastic team working out however and I enjoyed watching them practice.

My last stop that day was at James Dobson's impressive complex. I found it interesting wandering around looking at their displays that tell of their extensive ministry, Focus on the Family. Returning to Mickey's, Bernice and I took our hostess out to a German Restaurant where we indulged in a delicious dinner while we were entertained with an accordion player. Our trip to Denver had certainly been most fulfilling, packed with awesome variety.

back to work...

Steve, our new minister of music had joined the staff in April. The family came in June after the kids completed their school year. The planning for a contemporary service was underway. Steve already had a worship team that would be leading the singing of contemporary songs, setting a new tone. Scott had streamlined the traditional service eliminating a few features earlier, but in the new anticipated contemporary service there would be more radical changes ... no hymns, no reciting the Lord's Prayer or singing the doxology etc.

My busy summer had arrived and I was blessed while preparing for Vacation Bible School. There were people eager to help, many who communicate well and love the kids. In participating and observing numerous programs I had noted that it seemed the preschoolers, due to space problems, were usually jammed into small quarters and didn't receive much attention. The focus was understandably on the elementary children. After the success of Time for Tots, I decided to schedule a separate three day VBS that would precede the older kids' program.

The down side of that was it made more work and required more staff. Plus parents would have to bring their younger children at a different time than their older siblings. I felt the advantages were worth testing out. We took over the whole facility. The Calvin Room was unique as it was primarily designed to be a choir rehearsal/ warm-up space. It had long rows of rising steps. I had the chairs removed having the kids sit on the lower steps. The sanctuary had always been used before at large group time, in the smaller room the voices weren't lost and the kids in both sessions responded. With the pre kids I had each age group come in at their own scheduled time and geared the story to them. There's a big difference between three and four year olds.

We used the spacious narthex as our recreation place. One of the favorite times was when they enjoyed the colorful parachute. Each teacher had their own room for their group where they had their craft time and refreshments. The following Sunday morning in the first service only, the kids sang, succeeding in bringing out lots of parents to our newly initiated contemporary service. Everyone involved as well as the moms felt it was great.

The next week the kids entering first through sixth grade came. Adventures of Paul was our theme. Each day I chose a different teacher to present the story of the day. They were given the scripture text and ran with it. We had a jail made out of a huge cardboard container and enlisted Scott and Steve to play the part of Paul and Silas on one of the days. The pastors made great 'jailbirds' and the kids ate it up. I enjoyed a great staff and was able to delegate many of the major responsibilities. Becky, the youth summer intern came up with exciting crafts.

Small groups met outside in tents with their leaders and that was a big hit. On Thursday we took the kids to the Spit making a great setting for telling the story of Paul's shipwreck. Each group had a great time creating their own dwelling out of the available logs that were on the beach. I was pretty exhausted at the end of my two weeks, weary, but well rewarded.

On the last day everyone had fun with water balloon fights capped off with snow cones. Sunday morning the group sang in both services while many parents came to hear them. The presence of Worship team and band leading the music was appreciated.

Supersational events had been enthusiastically enjoyed. They included a gymnastic night, a movie night and a bike rodeo where I had a policeman come and talk about bike safety as well as lay out a course for the kids to maneuver. During the summer I planned two events. One was to Fort Worden where the younger group had fun on the beach while two of us had the older ones climb up to the bluff and let them play in the old World War II bunkers.

Fall '97...

My son, Dan came for a second visit the end of August into

early September. When I picked him up at the airport we were experiencing a few rainy days on the peninsula so we headed over the Cascades to sunny Okanogan. Of course, we stopped in Leavenworth to enjoy some great sausage etc. After two nights with Tollie and Woody, we returned by way of the spectacular North Cascade Highway, after a stop in Winthrop.

This visit I was house-sitting in a lovely home on the ridge that had a great kitchen and deck with long views of the Strait. Dan stayed longer than his prior visit enabling us to visit all the "biggies", the Spit, ocean, Hurricane Ridge, Seattle, Victoria, and last but not least Mount Rainier. Dan told me we could skip that having already seen so much, but when we started up the Mount his reaction was like mine, every time I go. One of awe, amazement and wonder remind me my God is soo BIG and yet he knows and cares about each detail in each of our lives.

Steve started Sound Express. This program was for elementary kids who would like to sing. His program included a devotional that became my responsibility. That was a joy as well as observing Steve's gentle and effective way of working with the kids.

I heard from Jim and Denise telling me that Jessi would need to have heart surgery again. I quickly booked a flight for November around Thanksgiving Holiday, wanting to have some time with them.

adult ministry...

The Session had voted, as promised, to add a children's position. Mid- September, Scott told me a very capable and talented mom had applied for the position. After he interviewed other applicants he felt Erin was the "right fit". Choosing staff is another area of Scott's giftedness. Erin was hired and assumed her duties in October, freeing me to make the shift into Adult Ministries.

Reflecting on my time with the children it was plain to me that I had been right where God wanted to me. Yes, there were frustrations, but the joys were by far greater. Now was time to experience new challenges.

Almost immediately, Scott asked me to fill in for him and take the Tuesday morning group next week. Now... that was intimidating. This was a mixed group, largely retirees who showed up for breakfast at seven, followed by an hour Bible study led by Scott. He was definitely the major draw. He totally enjoyed this venue where he could share his stories and open up his heart in this relaxed atmosphere. Everyone loves his sense of humor as well as the depth of his faith and knowledge of the scriptures. Sundays the sermons were crafted with the visitors in mind. Tuesdays mornings he was free to go deeper. I was both pleased that he felt I would be able to do this, but very uptight. How could I possibly be accepted by this group and live up to their expectations. The Lord in his grace, softly assured me to accept this challenge, relax and don't attempt to be another Scott. I was to use the gifts God had blessed me with allowing him to shine and speak through me. One of my subbing Tuesdays, I shared with the group that there was no way I could be a second Scott, besides the world couldn't handle two. There was a roar of laughter.

Next, I was asked me to give the sermon on December 28th. This was a most wonderful birthday treat. It's great when you can dream and plan ahead for a sermon still a few weeks away. I've always been impressed and curious about Joseph, Jesus' step dad He must have been an incredible man, one of strong faith and character. While considering and praying about my message, I found myself thinking that the Sunday between the two holidays is really unique. Christmas is over and yet still present. As my thoughts developed, I became willing to risk doing something a little different. I would present a monologue, portraying Joseph's mother, Jesus' grandmother. This way she could lay out the qualities she saw in her son and share the anticipation for the newborn babe. I received many positive comments from folks... and loved doing it.

My granddaughter, Jessi was operated on Christmas week. This was a tough on all of us. Denise's dad and step mom were there to support them and care for the boys. Jessi came through in flying colors and hardly missed any school.

1998....

A new year was beginning and new opportunities opened before me. Erin asked if I was willing to offer a young moms Bible Study during the Time for Tots program. That ministry turned out to be a cherished one for me. A few in the group were well-grounded, but most were very much on the edge of their faith. A special chemistry evolved as we opened up to each other. God richly blessed us. Next, I offered the Caring Evangelism Course. There existed enough interest to warrant both a morning and evening session. Once again, enthusiasm ran high in both groups.

I was thoroughly enjoying "my nest" at the Barnes. At Christmas I had put up a little tree and entertained local friends as well as the group from 'the other side'... Terrace View.

In February, Bernice fell and broke her hip. She was taken to the hospital and when the news reached me I hurried to Port Angeles finding her in the ER. Her son and wife came the morning of the surgery. Since it was Sunday and I had responsibilities, I didn't get to the hospital until afternoon. She did well but the strong pain medicine gave her weird dreams and caused her to be incoherent. The next day when I visited, the nurses were discussing her condition and concluded her behavior was typical. My timing was perfect as I informed them her behavior was not typical at all. She was usually very sharp and very much "with it". I sensed the staff assumed her erratic behavior was normal for her but when they heard my input, they cut back on the pain meds and shortly after she was her old self again.

Terrace View had invited me to once again lead their women's retreat. This time we had it at the Gibsons. The fellowship was rewarding full of a healthy blend of the serious and laughter. Another treat was a Singles conference held at the Doubletree near Sea Tac Airport. The workshops were outstanding and although I probably was the oldest one there I picked up much stimulating information. The topics applied to ministry in general, not just singles.

In April I was more than eager to get home and see Jessi and everyone. Spring is the most beautiful time in North Carolina and it gave me an excellent break. Once again I was able to include the beach in my visit.

Scott and I had been engaged in an ongoing conversation during the prior months about my staying a third year. He was hoping for an associate pastor but was also wanting me to stay. The church was growing and his plan was to build a separate facility that would be a combination worship place for the contemporary service and a gym that youth and kids to use. A top notch sound system was a must, as well. These ambitious plans required growth and money. The Lord responded to my prayers in letting me know that I was right where he wanted me to be. My work was not done. There was much for me to add to the mix while experiencing rich personal blessings and significant and growth.

on the road again..

Another giant adventure on my list of 'must things to do' had included driving the coast of California. That was a biggie, a dream long anticipated. Bernice was not able to make this trip, but I decided not to let that stop me. I would do it alone. Of course, I never really felt alone for the Lord was always there with me enjoying my pleasure and wonder. While I was in the planning stages, offers of homes to stay in opened up, promising to enrich the whole experience. Armed with my Triple A maps and guide book, I plotted my strategy.

With great anticipation, I left the Peninsula and traveled south to Vancouver Washington spending my first night with cousins of the Barnes. It was fun meeting them and sharing stories. The next day I had an early start and made it down I -5 into California to Placerville where Jan's folks were waiting. That's south and west a little from Sacramento. I had a most delightful time with them . They drove me around the area as well as fed me. Childhood pictures were brought out and "mom" shared stories of Jan growing up. I felt so at home with them.

Also, I picked up some guidance as to the best way to Yosemite, my next destination. The scenic way was worthwhile. Upon my arrival. I checked into the motel for two nights, unloaded my gear and eagerly headed for the park. After passing through the entrance heading toward the Visitors Center, I remembered my first impressions of my Grand Canyon and much earlier Niagara Falls trips, when reaching a most extraordinary scenic site I was engulfed in a mass of people and vehicles. The congestion robbed me of the solitary experience I had anticipated and longed for. After I parked my car, I fought off the crowds and took in the sights. The next morning I went into the park early and was rewarded, sharing the area with only a few 'early birds'. This provided the opportunity to take in the roar of the waterfall , absorb some of its spray on my face while letting my appreciation and thoughts head heavenward.

Yosemite is huge and I discovered it's a long drive through the park before arriving in Fresno. After spending an overnight, I then cut across the state heading towards the coast. The early morning drive winding through miles of farmland and tiny towns was interesting, but I was getting itchy to reach the ocean. At last I pulled into Morro Beach and easily found my motel before exploring the area. Then I leisurely walked the beautiful sandy beach, devoured a sumptuous seafood dinner while sitting out on a deck overlooking the water and roamed around the town enjoying the pleasant little shops.

In the morning, I enjoyed more beach time before heading up along the coast to Carmel and Monterey. That stretch of highway probably is one of the most spectacular. I wanted to make that roundtrip and it paid off for me as I savored the ride with its hairpin turns and breathtaking vistas. Carmel was charming with blocks of little gifts shops and places to eat. The seventeen mile drive at Pebble Beach satisfied my desire to see the site of the many golf matches I had watched on television. The streets were lined with spectacular houses all positioned so they faced the ocean, picture perfect. Later in Monterey I found the location of the Cannery, Steinbeck had described in his famous book.

After an overnight in Salinas, my next destination would be San Francisco. Since it was a Sunday morning I decided to drive into the city, hoping the traffic would not be overbearing. I had been in the city on two different occasions, but had never driven there. It was rewarding especially when leaving when my route took me across the Golden Gate Bridge. There was a viewing area where I pulled off and parked that provided me time to drink in the scene. What a magnificent spot and view of the harbor and city. It certainly lived up to its reputation as a one of a kind place.

Now I was ready to experience the northern California coast. The road was varied with very steep, curvy descents. Most spectacular. I had to stay totally focused on the drive, but I was living my dream and loving it. I was disappointed when I stopped at Muir Woods only to find no parking was available. The day was long and demanding partly because I had no sense of how far it would be to find a motel. The rugged cliffs and sandy beaches, however made it all worthwhile. I pulled off the road at a little rustic place high on a cliff looking down at the water. I still can taste the clam chowder and picture the great salad loaded with a variety of goodies.

After a long day I finally found an overnight place when the road turned inland. Food and sleep were much appreciated. There had been some off and on light rain the previous day. This new morning, however was blessed with warm sunshine. I kept finding unexpected coves that beckoned me to stop and check them out. They never disappointed me. An added feature in these coves were the abundant wildflowers giving a splash of color enhancing the scene.

The road continued to be challenging with its twists and turns, causing some distress with my inner ear. If I ever get to do this again perhaps a day off from driving, just vegging out on the beach would have eased some of the dizziness I experienced. The next stretch of road didn't hug the coast providing a nice break en route to Eureka. Fortunately, I had planned to stay there for a couple of nights. It's quite a bustling industrial city, but I quickly found a barrier island where I could enjoy the beach. Looking east my view was full of billowing smokestacks and factories, but westward the clean fresh salt air and the ocean filled my eyes, my heart and my soul.

From Eureka I traveled through Redwood country, making a stop. While I walked a short trail, I paused, quieted as I felt I had entered into a cathedral created by those magnificent giants that towered above me. I bowed my head and heart and prayed....

Oh God, I don't know how but in the midst of this vast land and awesome beauty, I know your eye is still on me. You

*are filling me up to overflowing and I am thankful for
your presence so real, so dear.*

My thoughts turned toward my dad, remembering him
talking about seeing and enjoying this great beautiful USA. "Yes
Dad, I'm doing it and loving it. Thanks for planting those seeds
in my heart".

Leaving California I couldn't help being deeply appreciative
of all the wonder and beauty I had observed. The experience left
me more than thrilled with the adventure God had blessed me
with. I had touched base with my hostess in Bandon Oregon.
She sounded warm and gracious on the phone and I was ready
to be in a home again and have some company.

When I passed into Oregon I was now retracing my glorious
trip Georgie had treated me to, back in '84. I arrived in Bandon
earlier than I expected so after a bite to eat, I headed for the
beach. A heavy shower popped up causing me to flee and head
to some shops I had noticed. While browsing my eyes feasted on
some lovely art paintings, jewelry, pottery, wood carving . Great
place.

My hostess was waiting for me when I arrived at her lovely
home situated on a high bluff overlooking the ocean. Rosemary
was warm and vivacious. Her stories of her husband and family
were a delight. Her husband had pastored a church for twenty-
five years in Sacramento. They had done lots of backpacking
as a family. She drove me around in the evening and showed
me her church hinting that perhaps I could come here as a
volunteer. Have to admit I did play with the thought when I
headed north.

While driving north along the famous Oregon coast I
remembered a special gift shop that sets out on the bluff
overlooking the beach. Georgie and I had stopped there and I
was eager to see it again. Next I explored for the first time the

Three Cape area and loved it. Then onto Canon Beach that was so jammed I quickly hopped back in my car and continued north to Sequim.

Now home again my first stop was checking in with Bernice and catching up with her news. When we went out I was pleased to note there was much improvement in her walking. I returned to my house-sitting and fulfilled my duties watering plants both in and out. It felt good to be home again and relax in my lounge chair while viewing the man-made waterfall and garden. That area served as a buffer between the house and the golf course. Occasionally I would find a stray ball that had been mis-hit. My time in their lovely home was a treat. Every time Bob and Marilyn called to see how I was doing, they would remind me to please use the food.

Another piece of news was that one of the moms in my Momentum group, had been hospitalized in Seattle. This sent me on a mission to go see her. Without difficulty, I located the hospital in the University District. She was overwhelmed by my visit. She had been experiencing hallucinations and was typically having other medicine problems prescribed for her ongoing struggle to manage her bipolar illness. Fortunately she was able to get a pass allowing us to leave the hospital for a few hours. Our first stop was at a nearby Starbucks. Our conversation deepened as she opened up her heart sharing concerns about her boys. Soon, this led her to share even more, expressing thoughts and questions she was struggling with about God. Our conversation was intense and it seemed I was able to bring about some peace, reassurance of God's faithfulness to her. We were then able to relax and share a lovely meal together before she had to return to her room. My heart was both heavy and full when we said our good-byes. I was thankful I had responded to the Holy Spirit's nudges by taking the time to make this visit.

My inner ear distress continued after my trip to California

caused me to lay low and get extra rest. Thankfully it gradually subsided and didn't prevent me from working.

A few days later the Momentum group was treated to a lovely lunch. A member of the group, who at that time lived with her parents, had a most beautiful home up on the hillside. They laid out a lovely buffet for the young moms. Even baby sitting was provide down in the "rec" room. We also were all treated to a twenty minute massage. Talk about being indulged.

9

Sequim '98

If only I may be firmer, simpler, quieter, warmer...

Summer had arrived and with it came new challenges. Scott asked me to develop a six week Bible Study for small groups. He was realizing that he needed to relinquish some of his responsibilities freeing him to put more energy in other pressing areas. The care and oversight of the Small Group ministry was my responsibility. This favorite of mine was now on my plate. Another joy, I was asked to take the pulpit one Sunday in July.

Bernice was slowing down in her thinking as well as her movements. The changes were subtle, but real, confronting me with the aging process in a person I loved dearly.

Again the pre school vacation Bible school was rewarding. Enrollment the second year increased to nineteen. I was blessed with a wonderful staff and everyone had a great time. This age group was such a delight to work with. They are not only adorable but so responsive. Everything you do with them is an adventure.

Pastor Scott was on vacation during July. I was busy setting things up for the Fall as well as spending significant time with a wide variety of people.

There was a missionary couple who was in need of housing that summer and I willingly moved out, able to house-sit for a stretch. While away, I needed to get into my cottage at the Barnes to find some papers. When Ruth took me it my reaction was intense. Emotionally I felt blown away. The furniture was all changed around and everything seemed cluttered. I experienced a sense of being violated, my place had been invaded. In reflecting on this I recognized once again there was that deep longing for my own home. Every transition I made, evoked some pain and feelings of being lost.

Fortunately my next move was to Elmer and Cry's. At least this was to a home I had spent significant time in and loved dearly. Also, the timing was great as I was anticipating a visit. Susan was coming with her daughter and granddaughter. How special that we could be in this lovely and spacious home. I was surprised with some emotions that surfaced in the visit. This was a new dynamic, having to share her. She, too was struggling with stuff that seemed to emerge with the setting and group dynamics. We did have a great time as I showed them the sights. Susan wanted to do the Loop which takes you over the North Cascade Highway to Winthrop then south to Leavenworth and before returning west over Steven's Pass. It's an awesome, but exhausting full day of driving. I had prearranged to spend the night with Lynn, a friend from Mount Lake Terrace, that put us in a good position to visit Mount Rainier the next morning.

When we all were getting up I was thrilled and grateful as I saw the bright sunshine and clear blue skies that promised that the Mount would be not be shrouded in clouds. What a spectacular day the Lord had provided. I had prayed earnestly for this kind of a day. When Susan and her granddaughter Elizabeth came up from downstairs, Susan approached me. Her daughter, Jenny was positioned behind the two of them as they proceeded to tell me that they had been talking and were so weary they wanted to skip Rainier and get back to Sequim and "crash". Jenny was mouthing, "oh no I want to go". I dug my heels in and said I knew they were weary, but I had prayed for this perfect day and I didn't know about them, but my car was heading south to the Mount. Susan was somewhat taken back with my proclamation. We all backed off and gave each other some space while loading the car and taking off for Rainier. Jen told me in private, how much she wanted to go and was pleased with my decision. She had spent a summer working at Denali in Alaska and was eager to experience Mount Rainier.

When we arrived at the park, we made a pit stop. From that place there is a view where you begin to sense how huge the mountain is. Elizabeth's mouth opened and her eyes wide with wonder excitely told me she so glad I had made them come. Susan was equally enthusiastic. When we reached Paradise at the five thousand foot level we decided to split up and go off on our own. Jenny and her daughter went in one direction. I went on another path and Susan did her own thing. Once again the experience was awesome. Every visit I find a "humbling." I'm overwhelmed as I contemplate how huge my God is and small and insignificant I am and yet I know.. his eye is on the sparrow and I know he watches me.... What a weary bunch we were when we finally arrived home that night. No one wanted to budge the next day, content to back off and lay low for a while.

Before their visit was complete I needed to move again. This time it would take me back to my cottage. I was more than ready for that. This would be a first however... moving with company would be a new challenge. Saying good bye to a home always provoked a mixture of feelings and demanded an emotional adjustment on my part.

On our trip to the airport they were eager to do a little shopping so we stopped at a mall in Silverdale. I was pleased as I found some things for my cottage. I was beginning to sense that when I left Sequim, I'd be heading east to settle at last, would have my own place and would welcome some homey items.

a seed is planted...

The summer was just about over and I was anticipating a visit from Kim and Ian. Their plans were to fly from Scotland and spend two weeks with me before going east to Aberdeen NC and visiting there. I had fun fixing up my place, making it more me before bringing my next guests home. They were weary after their long flight, but oh my... how great to see them.

Again I was going places and showing off my great Northwest. Previously I had arranged to go to Okanogan and take in the County Fair complete with a rodeo. Kim and Ian had seen some of the East their year in Carolina, but to see central Washington would be a most unique event. While driving over the Cascade Highway we were talking and Ian was telling me, "you know we are hoping you will visit us. You could come as a tourist or ..." I picked up on that 'or' and said that would be interesting, I would welcome the challenge of working with him if we could arrange that out at both ends. I thought Scott would be open to that, but first Ian had to run it by his church he was now pastoring.

After the Watsons left I felt the need to make a quick trip to Connecticut. It was good to go home and drive around Bethel where I had raised my family and taught school for seventeen years. I enjoyed visits with long standing friends as well as the family. All were replenishing. I certainly had a full summer, especially blessed with my company, but the respite was good.

Now it was practically October and as Scott and I touched base I told him about the possibility of my going to Scotland. He was supportive and hoped I would wait until 2000 when he expected an associate pastor would be on board. He also was encouraging me to start up an adult class during the second hour on Sundays. Singles' ministry was another challenge. Both of those were not totally comfortable or satisfying to me, even though I agreed they were important. I was continuing to thrive on the times of " stepping in for Scott", taking the Tuesday morning class for him . In addition were the Momentum moms and more preaching opportunities. Busy, busy. As Scott noted "they wound my clock". Yes, they energized me.

Serious problems were becoming visible among the younger group at church. Depression touched several, as well as martial problems of varied sorts. I was finding my "one on one "ministry expanding.

My times with Bernice were frustrating at times. I took her weekly to the Safeway, to shop and came to realize that she required lots of time to make decisions. The socializing was also important. It would have been so much easier if she gave me a list and I shopped for her, but she needed the mental stimulation. We all have an inherent need to have some control and sense of independence. I realized a good solution was simply to drop her off and then take off for SARC, the recreation center, to workout on the machines and return just about when she would be ready to be picked up. Thank you Lord... this was injection of wisdom.

I continued to enjoy meeting the Terrace View gals monthly in Edmonds for dinner. Okanogan gave me an invite to come over and lead a women's retreat. So October took me "over the hill" and treated me to some autumn color. The house we had the retreat in was great. The hostess was open and welcoming except that she didn't think of offering morning coffee etc. so when Tollie came she picked up on the fact I was operating on empty and she quickly remedied that.

It was satisfying to see the positive things occurring in that small church under the leadership of their new pastor. He was a hunting and fishing type a great fit for the men in the congregation.

The Fall months were full and fruitful in Sequim. I was blessed as I spent some time with a sweet couple, Howard and Irma. She was an encourager par excellence. The music ministry was evolving and it was always a huge blessing to me. The worship in the contemporary service was opening up. There were noticeable changes in the singing as folks became familiar with the new songs. What a joy to be part of it all. The Christmas Program was marvelous. I was given the privilege along with Bob Goffrier to be a narrator for the Nativity part. Another blessing.

Christmas saw me headed to Concord NC. The kids were growing up too fast and I wasn't about to miss out on Christmas morning. I took Jessi, now eight, to our "Shoney" breakfast. Shane chose to go to the church with the graveyard and playground equipment. He and Cole had attended pre school there. He was fascinated with walking around the tombstones and reading the dates on them.

Cole chose to go to the park to shoot baskets and ride his new bike. The boys were now five and when they all came to meet me at the airport on the way home they were telling me their poppa was going to set a trap to catch Rudolph. Shane begged me , "Grandma, he's your son tell him not to do that." I then proceeded to tell Jim he better not do that or I would have to really spank him. He responded "okay mom I'll be good". That scenario was repeated for several more years. Actually it was elevated and became a tradition.

I made time to drive down to Titusville to spend a few days with Dan. We took in the beach and Vero Beach where I was thrilled to walk around on Dodger hallowed ground. Don't follow baseball much anymore, but my old Brooklyn Dodgers still excite me.

My flight back to Sequim turned into one with lots of long delays due to weather. When the plane finally arrived in Seattle it was too late to pick up my connecting flight to Port Angeles. An even smaller plane was covering for Horizon Airlines and was entered from the rear of the plane. Passengers and luggage were all weighed before anyone could board. When everyone was strapped in the pilot announced this is a nonstop flight to Gig Harbor and we all cracked up and had lots of fun on the short flight to P. A. The stretch between Sea Tac and Gig Harbor was the Puget Sound.

a new year '99

It didn't take long to get back into the swing of things. My Sunday class, "Boundaries" continued to be positive. Attendance was consistent. Folks were sharing more of themselves. Bill continued to be a help with his input and comments. The attendance at the Singles events was erratic and I was discouraged.

Filling in for Scott on Tuesdays continued to be a blast. It seemed whenever I was the one teaching the scripture for that week was dealing with some heavy duty sexual stuff. It got to be a source of humor when I would walk into the room the "guys" that sat up in front to my left would say, "here she comes, oh boy what's the class about this week". They also took great delight in bugging Scott about the content I had to wrestle with. Lots of laughs.

I experienced a painful scenario when I started to attend a Wednesday women's class. That group was made up of moms with school age kids. Most of them were already well established in the church. The teacher was excellent and I appreciated the way she handled the lessons. She went to Scott upset with comments made to her from one of the woman in the class. The woman complained that I was dominating and turning off discussion. He told her he would share this with me. When the two of us met I sensed he was troubled. He had a tough time relaying this info. As he told me I kept my composure while feeling hurt. In that class as well as generally in other settings, I never sought the limelight, preferring to focus on other participants' struggles and insights. What feelings of failure those comments created in me. Scott later shared that he had dreaded telling me that. I withdrew from the group, but as Scott, the teacher and I looked back we came to realize my accuser was one to be leery of. She was adept at playing the passive/ aggressive game. She was always sweet to me and actually had baited me in the class to speak up . Needless to say after apologizing, I avoided possible contacts with her. I suppose we all experience toxic people in our lives.

One day Bernice and I had enjoyed a pleasant lunch in P.A. and then drove out to Lake Crescent. It was a sunny day and there hadn't been snow anywhere, but when we approached the lake we began to notice some along the edges of the road. What a surprise awaited us as we approached the lake. The tall cedars and pines were encased in ice, creating a winter wonderland. While we drove along the windy road that hugs the lake we were enthralled with the scene. Surprisingly the road was clear. What a feast and magical ride, one we commented on for years to come.

Bernice was feeling very weary and experiencing troubling bladder infections. Her doctor ordered some tests and then called her in to talk about what he was finding. She wanted me to go into the examining room with her so I would hear what he told her and ask questions if I wanted to. He had determined her spleen was enlarged and her blood count was low and ordered medicine to correct that as well as an antibiotic to stem the bladder infections. There was some improvement.

In January, I had asked her if she could go anywhere where would she like to go. It didn't take her very long to say I would want to go see my grandson Doug. He lived near San Diego. Enough said we made our reservations and in May we went. I had told her that I would really like to visit that area so it was a great combination of touring the city and having some very sweet family time. Doug and his wife invited us over to their house and treated us to dinner. A few days later they came to our motel. Doug and his daughter, Taylor enjoyed the swimming pool as did great grandma enjoying their squeals of delight and rambunctious antics.

Bernice then took us all to dinner. When Doug asked her what had brought us down to San Diego she had answered that I had wanted to come. I took him aside later and told him how much she wanted to see him and how much she yearned for him and his dad to be reconciled.

Each morning I walked the beach at Carlsbad while BJ was getting up and ready for the day. One morning, after breakfast we rode the train into the city and took a trolley tour. We then had a long walk back to the train station. This was difficult for Bernice, but she pushed herself hard to see some things. I would love to go back some time and revisit the city, feeling like there was more I would have liked to see. The beaches were lovely as were the houses and yards. We both enjoyed a harbor cruise, amused with the large lazy seals languishing in the warm sun.

On Sunday we went to the Presbyterian Church in Solana Beach and were able to hear Roberta Hestness, a well-known Presbyterian minister. She had just been a featured speaker at a Baptist Seminary near Littleton Colorado where the tragic shooting took place at Columbine. She shared how her secretary always puts some sermons in her brief case on a certain subject and had mistakenly placed one that didn't fit the topic of the conference. Being in the midst of the tragedy she was surprised when pulling that one out finding it was most appropriate for that day. The whole service was very moving and we were pleased we had gone.

In April, I was invited to housesit in a most lovely home located out on the bluff overlooking the Strait. The view was so expansive and incredible. In the evening watching the shades and hues of color that were splashed across the western sky left me speechless and made me think how wonderful it must be to be able to paint that view. I took advantage of my home entertaining some friends, wanting to share "my" humble abode. Another fascinating sight was due to the setting, high on the bluff. I could look out the front windows and observe eagles floating on the wind currents at my eye level. God is good, what treasures he's provided for me.

While housesitting I always like to browse the book shelves and also enjoy the cook books my hostess has. On one of the shelves I came across a quote that jumped out at me

"On our own we can't do much more than 'Michael, Row the Boat Ashore', but with you, Lord, suddenly we're more capable of much more than we ever dreamed."

This was a continuing experience of mine especially when I step into the pulpit. I was again savoring in the prep time leading up to a upcoming sermon. It was always awesome how a message would unfold while I walked the beach or while I submersed myself in the scriptures.

Mary Beth, the youth director, initiated a program that connected older folks in the church with teenagers in her group. I volunteered and was paired with a junior in high school. I opened my heart to Mandy and enjoyed our relationship. She loved the beach so we went many times out to the ocean. We also enjoyed going out to eat together. She was somewhat reticent and I wondered if she might open up more if I invited another girl to go with us to Victoria British Columbia. The other teen was very outgoing and a fun day ensued. Their agenda was to do some shopping and what a kick we had as they tried on expensive dresses and then paraded them in front of me. Mandy, on the way home, did open up. My hopes and prayers were answered. The girls had many things in common. Their parents had been divorced and remarried and both of them were living with one parent and a step parent.

In May, I was given the responsibility to plan and organize a Prayer Vigil. The expectation and hope of the staff was that people would commit for a specific time block starting at five a.m. and ending at nine p.m. The roster wasn't filled, but the day was full of surprises as unexpected people showed up to fill in empty spots.

short vacation...

The end of the month saw me heading for the East coast. My time at Wrightsville Beach was always a great way to get relaxed and rested while tapping into friends and church folk. Little Chapel was now under construction and it looked huge to me. Once again I savored great walks by the ocean. Many leisurely conversations and indulging in east coast seafood were enjoyed. Going to church on Sunday and being welcomed warmly fed me in my deep places.

Driving back to Concord I was more than ready for my grand kids. Now all three were into baseball. Jessi was the catcher for her team. Cole was totally into his game while Shane wandered around the outfield oblivious to what was happening.

Mom and Poppa escaped to spend a few days at the Myrtle Beach campgrounds. We meanwhile enjoyed swimming in a friend's pool, splashing around in their own wading pool in the backyard and playing lot of cards. "Go Fish" was the big attraction and I kept losing. I feinted some tears and they all enjoyed my drama. I declared, "you know not only am I losing but Cole you are creaming me." Well that caught on and became our mantra. When Dad came home and asked whether the kids had been good I told him yes, except for Cole. Panic swept across his face until I quickly explained he not only beat me but he creamed me. We all burst out laughing and Cole knew everything was all right.

While there, I went to watch their swimming lessons. The instructions were to swim from a designated spot to the side of the pool. Jessi and Cole complied but en route Shane did a back somersault in the water. His instructor asked "what was that all about" and his answer was "that was my grand finale". Oh boy, I don't think she liked it, but it tickled me.

Next leg was heading north for Connecticut making stops to see both my sister and my brother. My sister-in-law was considering flying to Seattle to attend a conference and started plotting a visit to me, prior to her scheduled meeting.

Finally arrived in Connecticut, anxious to see my "growing up" granddaughters and of course their parents. Kristen was now working at the Bagel Shop and she lit up when I came in to satisfy my bagel hunger. Lindsay was very much into her soccer. The timing was right for me to get to watch her in action. That was a double treat because the proud dad was always with me.

My longtime friends, Gary and Gale, who had been in New Hampshire for several years had moved to Maine and failed to send me an address. I had wondered how I could track them down. Even though Gary had stepped out of the pastorate I was hoping by calling the denomination office someone there would know how to locate him. When I called, I was surprised to hear their friend on the other end of the line. Frannie immediately gave me their phone number and we both had to smile. She had just returned that very day from an extended vacation. Another of those coincidences that God has a way of arranging. Gary, Gale and I enjoyed a reunion together in Maine.

I returned to New Fairfield before leaving the East. In visits there I was saddened to hear of some problems in the church. On my last Sunday, the service I attended, in came someone I had been anxious to see. We had worked together when I was in the church and he was going through a very painful time in his personal life. We were able to spend a few hours talking and praying together. It never ceases to amaze me how the Lord orchestrates where I am and who needs a little TLC.

The end of June, I flew back to Sequim. It had been beneficial for to have a break from being saturated in Bernice's needs. Refreshed, I was more than eager to have our time together. I was coming back to face a very busy and productive time, especially with BJ. My first order of business was to tackle the job of putting her garage and patio in good shape. After much urging, Bernice was now wearing a Lifeline. Sometimes she would inadvertently set it off and I would go flying over there not knowing what I might find. In spite of that the Lifeline was a comfort to me.

Scott and I had a chance to get caught up with each other before he left for his much needed vacation. Even though it was summer my schedule was full... small group responsibilities... working on a sermon... teaching some breakfast Bible studies... and involved in a wide array of "people time". I was thriving with my full plate of challenges.

Sadly, my beloved Dwight died. His dear family had surrounded him on his death bed, lifting up their voices singing his favorite hymns. I was thankful to be able to spend a day with Agnes shortly after. Seeing loved ones die while knowing they are with the Lord eases the adjustment.

reflections..questions..

Blessings... the flow of affirmation for my ministry came in a multitude of ways... Linda's visit from Terrace View... so gratifying to observe her opening herself to the Lord in deeper ways... knowing I had a part in that process... back at the Barnes indulging on the yummy raspberries... people telling me they missed me and were glad I was back... walks on the Spit... the ocean beaches... numerous times of healthy exercise ...precious times of reflection ... and most of all...the keen awareness of the Holy Spirit's presence....

Scotland... if I go... how long should I stay? ... what about Bernice's needs? Seemed like with a support system she would be able to stay in her home and not be faced with relocating until I returned... what about the church?

Revelation 3:8 jumped out at me, "See I have placed an open door that no one can shut."

Gradually my prayers were answered and my thoughts crystallized. When I filled Scott in on what I was thinking he was comfortable. I suggested I would be gone from July to January. Included in this time frame I would visit my family on the East coast before leaving and after returning from Scotland.

In the meantime the search committee was earnestly looking for an associate pastor and it made me wonder if they chose a woman to fill that position would I become excess baggage. My role on staff was unique because I was the only one on staff that had a history with the church. It was evident that many of the older folks who had played such dynamic roles in the church were either dying or at least incapacitated. Often in staff meetings I would share some stories of this older group filling in some blanks.

Terrace View celebrated Pastor Dick's thirtieth anniversary in ministry in August and it was fun for me to participate. Of course there was an abundance of good natured kidding and laughter as well as other surprises.

Dan came in September and I planned a special trip . We headed south on I-5 seeing Mount Saint Helen's from a distance and down into Vancouver where I had arranged an overnight.

He loved the Gorge and we treated ourselves to the steep climb up Multnoma Falls and were awed when we viewed the cascading water from that vantage point as it bounced from rock to rock. The next day we went to Yachata and stayed in a motel on the Oregon Coast. Our few days were great while we enjoyed vigorous walks together both in the woods as well as on the beach. Returning to Sequim we indulged in a few "laid back" days. Per usual it was difficult when the time for leaving came but when he left I felt "filled up" for awhile with the sweet time we shared.

Another extended request to house sit while the folks were traveling came from Vic and Muriel. This provided a positive change of routine and I enjoyed having a kitchen and cable TV. Later when I returned to my little nest I went on a "weeding out" tear, getting rid of some accumulation. Incredible how easily that happens.

The church was growing and several mature Christians were adding stability to the congregation. It was an answer to pray and a delight to be a part of what God was doing in our midst. The music ministry continued to develop. Steve's energy, vision and know how made for a winning combination.

Small groups were expanding also. The monthly leaders' meeting was a outright joy for me and in many ways filled a personal void. In essence they became my support group. I had made a goal to visit each of the groups as part of my duties knowing that connected me with both the leaders and the people. Again, the dynamic of visiting in homes provides more understanding and insights.

A couple in the church was willing to host a group, but felt inadequate to lead it. I was happy to step up and fill that role. They were most gracious hosts and we all looked forward to our weekly meetings. As the weeks progressed the couple was eager to talk after the meetings seeking my input into how to develop more open discussion. I explained how vital listening, allowing questions and concerns to be expressed was. How jumping in with pat answers cut off the discussion and inhibit growth. After a few months of meetings our group dynamics changed when a new couple joined who were quite dogmatic in their statements and I had to work on keeping the dialogue open. We all bonded and was saddened at year's end to hear our hosts would move to be closer to family.

Bernice's health continued to falter. She took a couple of falls that caused no injury, but definitely undermined her confidence. Her hearing aids were also a source of frustration. She still was teaching her Monday afternoon class, but so many of the older ladies spoke in such soft voices it became more difficult to hear them.

The Momentum group continued to be a blessing. Our sharing was deepening and I could see helpful. A special relationship with one of the moms developed and we would meet for breakfast occasionally. She needed a mom for a while and that was precious. So now I had an adopted mom and an adopted daughter. I have learned to say if you are missing something in your life, reach out.

Thanksgiving arrived and I was invited to join the family at the Barnes. There were nineteen of us around the table and it was fun to be a part of the celebration. The next few days found me busy decorating and putting up my little tree early as I was heading home for Christmas. Also, I helped Bernice with her decorations.

Scott enlisted a few younger couples to share in the morning services, how they came to join the church. I was surprised and pleased when one young couple mentioned me and the 'Time for Tots' as a main reason for their decision.

Christmas again and it was great to be home. Family visits are always a top priority. I was able to squeeze in a visit with

Charlie, a college friend. It was fun to see her and her husband and share our stories. Once again my old buddy, John, from New Fairfield and I were able to get together. Things were still difficult and he was facing tough family times. I was glad to lend a sympathetic ear.

2000...

Back in Sequim and a new year and a new century had begun. I had heard from Ian that all systems were go in Scotland, coming in July would work for them. Scott told me the Session would give me two hundred dollars a month to help with my expenses. The church wanted to have a part in my mission. The search for an associate pastor intensified. The committee charged with this responsibility expressed concern that person might prefer not to have an assistant. That we thought might be my role. Scott assured me if that was the case he would plug me into being his personal assistant. High praise and affirmation. It was obvious he wanted me to return.

Another challenge on my plate was with getting the "Keenagers" organized and going. This was a senior group who wanted monthly potlucks with a variety of program. Their committee was full of plans and happy to have my involvement.

I had a blast going to Jan's (Barnes) class and leading a few workshops on clown ministry. She was teaching third and fourth graders in a nearby Christian school. We prepared a skit for the clowns to perform in their weekly assembly. Once again I stressed the significance of the white face and the concept of giving oneself away to serve others. Her class that year was a most delightful one and it caused me to remember that I used to say in my school teaching years that some years I felt I should be paying for the privilege of working with my students, they were such a delight. Of course there were a few times through my teaching years that were just plain tough, requiring many really deep breaths before entering the classroom.

The end of January the group from Terrace View came for an overnight, a real all girl slumber party. Lots of laughter and significant sharing.

In February I attended my second Single Adult Ministry event. It was in Orlando this time and Dan picked me up at the airport. We went out to dinner and he stayed overnight providing us a nice visit with each other. Once again the conference was loaded with stimulating sessions and inspiring messages. An illustration was given by one of the speakers when describing mission trips. He said it's like tooth paste. When the tube is squeezed of its comfort zone it can't ever revert back to what it was. It will never be the same. Great illustration. My favorite workshop provided some instruction and tips on storytelling. That's always stimulating stirring up some creativity genes.

After being saturated with dynamic messages I thought it wouldn't be possible to get too excited about any thing more on the agenda. It felt like the whole crowd was rather spent. Wrong ! Tony Evans, a well known pastor, speaker and writer was the last on the program. I thought what a tough spot that would be. However, it didn't take him long before we all were rising to our feet as he laid out for us that we should and could be supermen for God. Amazing! Thrilling!

The next day Lil and Dave came and picked me up taking me to their Florida home. It was a treat to see their winter place while soaking up some sun and spending time on the wide sandy beach while observing the lovely aqua color of the Gulf.

a great home.. a great dog...

"Home" again... one Tuesday when I was filling in for Scott I mentioned that I enjoyed house sitting. At the end of the class a couple approached me and asked if I would be willing to sit for them. They told me they had a German Shepherd and would put her in the kennel so I wouldn't have to worry about that. They had no way of knowing that I had been wishing I could have a dog, even though that wouldn't have worked with my lifestyle. I quickly exclaimed, " oh I love dogs and would enjoy taking care of her." I was invited over and shown their fascinating log house that was beautifully decorated and met a very special dog.

The entire back of the house was windows that faced the mountains. I soon learned they had been in the Army. Andy had been a doctor and Judy a nurse. They spent significant time in Germany and was able to do lots of sightseeing. Their photos of the Alps were breathtaking. On many occasions they had purchased some lovely pieces of furniture. Some handmade wooden beauties.

I fell in love with Fendie the dog. Every day I would take her to a huge empty field and throw sticks for her to retrieve. What fun to watch her run and romp. Upon their return they insisted on paying me for the care of the dog. Too much!

When the news got out about my going to Scotland, King one of the new men in the church came up to me and said. "Ruth, that's fine, but only if as you promise to return".

Ralph, the associate pastor candidate and his wife came for interviews in April. Scott wanted to make sure the staff would have some quality time to interact with him. We all went to lunch and after we ate, he removed himself so we could have some alone time with Ralph. He had been told that Scott was difficult person to work with and if you weren't a yes man you would be unhappy. I spoke up and shared that Scott was full of ideas and directions, but sought and wanted your assessment. He also is one who keeps on processing so when the conversation ended and you were at one place when you saw him again he often would be in another. If you didn't continue the discussion the next time you might misunderstand where he was coming from.

Scott respected and wanted your input and would support your decision. Later Ralph shared that my response had been a factor in his decision to come.

Every time I would slip away and head for the Spit there were always special delights. At times the tide might be coming in and the waves would be large and impressive. At other times there might be no waves at all. At low tide I usually was treated to seeing Smitty Jr. and that was a delight to watch him swimming around and splashing. One early morning while walking along the beach out around the four mile spot there was an eagle perched on a log. Usually when these birds spotted a person they would fly away. This fellow didn't budge. We both eyed each other while I quietly walked past him. He sat not more than four or five feet from me. I was thrilled that he allowed me to come that close and surprised me again when on my return he was still there. Spotting eagles was always a huge pleasure even in Alaska, where every time you were outside you see several, the thrill never ceased.

There were other surprises, special serendipities the Lord blessed me with. One morning I was sitting by a log looking out at the horizon and saw something in the water heading on the diagonal towards me. As it came closer the light dawned I was seeing a whale. Fortunately he decided at the last minute to turn or he would have been beached.

My full schedule continued. I asked two of the young moms if they would co-teach while I was in Scotland. Reluctantly, they agreed to the challenge. I hoped the group would continue while I was gone.

It was tulip time in Washington and Bernice and I drove to La Connor to enjoy the spectacular sight. We stayed overnight in Bellingham after enjoying a lovely dinner in a restaurant high on the edge of a bluff looking over the harbor. BJ at eighty-eight was still eager to go and do.

Mary Beth, the youth director, generously gave me access to her computer and showed me how to send and receive e-mail. This served me well as Ian and I could readily communicate with each other.

My friends, Bob and Ruth in Connecticut told me that their daughter Jessie, now twenty-one, was en route via Am Trax to Seattle. We had discussed this possibility and I was eager and excited to be part of her grand adventure. I met her at the ferry in Seattle and brought her out to Sequim I was staying at the log house when she came and she chose to sleep in the loft on the floor. Her parents had given her a great camera and she was thrilled with snapping some eagle pictures at one of their favorite spots along Marine Drive. It was comical as it seemed like the eagle was posing especially for her.

I took her around taking in some of the sights and then drove her over to the ferry where she planned to take a bus to Portland. It made me nervous to see her go off on her own, but I told her to call me if she ever needed a helping hand and wherever she was I would come and pick her up. When she returned to Seattle, a few weeks later, once again I met her at the ferry and brought her home. This visit we went to Victoria and she enjoyed it. While on her own she hadn't done any sight seeing. It sounded like she did lots of hanging out with street people. I was glad to put her on the return train and know she was safe.

plans develop...

Ian e-mailed and asked me if I would lead the Caring Evangelism course as well as do some teacher training. I shared that was great but I had assumed, he would only want me working with woman and kids. His reply was he was open to more than that.

The weeks were flying by. Easter we had three services with a large attendance. The music, the drama and the preaching were inspiring.

Led another retreat with ten gals from Terrace View at my cottage. The topic of ordaining homosexuals was a burning issue in the church at that time and there was much discussion.

A big celebration pot luck was a success for all the small group participants. We had lots of fun and everyone was enthusiastic about the whole year. The Lord's timing for the arrival of the associate pastor was ideal. Ralph and Cindy arrived the same Sunday I was leaving to go East. That was ideal because I was removed from the scene as he would now assume many of my duties. People needed to look to him.

The staff gave me a sweet send off with gifts. As always there were conflicting emotions when I made my goodbyes. Excited, thrilled to go, sad at leaving. Of course this time I would be coming back.

Time at home passed quickly while I made the rounds of family and friends. Goodbyes were said and the excitement was building on every one's part. When my son, John was hugging me he shared how proud of me he was. It was time to board the bus to JFK. This time I needed my passport. My flight was a red eye to London.

Hey, there she goes that cardinal again, going to unexpected places.

10

Scotland 2000

We have to be braver than we think we can be, because God is constantly calling to be more than we are....... to break down our defenses of self-protection in order to be free to receive and give love.
Madeline L'Engle

Here I was about to board a plane at JFK. Memories of that first flight west to Seattle, way back in '83 came to mind. This leaving would be another first for me as I was saying goodbye to the USA. I would be flying across the Atlantic Ocean. Except for Canada I had never been out of the States. Never in my wildest dreams could I have imagined this scenario and was more than a little excited when the plane began to proceed down the runway and began to lift off. With some tears in my eyes and a heart that was pounding I took a few deep breaths settling back in my seat. The first leg the jet traveled north and I soon spotted Cape Cod. Then when the sky was darkening the plane headed east over the "pond". The night was a long one. I didn't sleep much only dozing off a few times. Before dawn the flight attendants came down the aisles passing out warm washcloths that felt so good when washing my face and neck. How refreshing. This was followed with a light breakfast and some much welcomed fresh coffee. As the plane approached England, right on schedule, the sky showed some early traces of morning light.

Upon leaving the plane I was in a pack of passengers that moved aggressively to a steep flight of stairs, then hurried out the doors and onto shuttle buses. I didn't have a clue where I was going, but made sure I stayed with the crowd. The bus transported the group to another terminal and then everyone was herded up more stairs and down a long corridor to wait in line to go through Customs. I had my passport ready and the officer asked the purpose of my visit. When I told him I would be serving in a church he asked me if I had any "details" with me. I was puzzled and he explained that meant papers, teaching materials. I was allowed to pass through and then found my way to my connecting flight that would bring me to Scotland. This section of Heathrow Airport was smaller and much less intimidating.

This flight from London to Glasgow was short and I kept my eyes peeled out the window, catching my the first glimpses of Scotland. Bursting with excitement, I spotted Kim and Ian waiting for me as I came down the steps. How good to see them, to know I was safe, but much more than that. We all shared a genuine love for each other. After much hugging and chattering Ian led us out to where the car was parked. They wanted me to sit up front so I could see better. Oops, I realized the passenger side is on left. Of course I was eager to see where I would be living and learning all about Scotland.

The ride to Caldercruix went quickly and my first language lesson was beginning. My luggage had been put in the "boot"... Ian checked the "petrol"... and under the "bonnet"... and we took the "dual carriage way".... out to the "motor way". Driving on the 'wrong' side of the road, maneuvering the "roundabout", all presented me with a new vocabulary. I would need to learn quickly.

Home was a small village about half way between Glasgow

and Edinburgh. My eye spotted a steeple down the road and Ian informed me that was the church. When we approached the village I could see that the steeple towered over all the other small buildings. The manse was set back from the road making for privacy. It looked quite contemporary. The church was foreboding. It couldn't have been more opposite from my small and simple church of my childhood. Ian took me inside and it felt cold and very formal. He was so enamored with the pulpit and climbed the steps up to it to impress me. I dubbed it his throne.

After bringing my gear in and seeing the house we all went out to lunch at a "nursery". These were common and I found them charming and pleasant to browse around after eating, enjoying the flowers and gift section. We then proceeded to drive in the country to Linlithgow to see the ruins of the ancient palace that dated back to the 1400's. This well visited spot sat next to an old church that was a popular wedding place. Just as we started up the hill a wedding party arrived, complete with a bag piper properly attired in kilts. Now I really knew I was in Scotland. I teased Kim and Ian saying I was impressed they had this all orchestrated to impress me. The site was set up on a hill with multiple paths leading down to the "loch". The three if us enjoyed walking around the lake observing the ducks and geese. I was to return on my own on several occasions, enjoying a vigorous walk, browsing through some shops and treating myself to a pleasant lunch.

This had been an ideal way to adjust to the five hour time difference and the overnight flight. I took a quickie nap and then settled into my new surroundings. A few days later I was introduced to the church and at a potluck presented with a lovely cake decorated in red, white and blue. Everyone was very warm and gracious, but oh, I was having great difficulty deciphering their brogues.

A committee had been organized to see that I was well taken care of. The three of us were invited to one of their homes to enjoy an elaborate dinner. Our meal began with starters, a choice of soup or sliced melon served with a sweet sauce. The main course offered choice ofd beef, chicken, lamb as well as a variety of potatoes that include french fries, boiled and mashed. Most of the diners took some of each. Veggies and rolls also were served. Next course was a salad and then dessert or "pudding" as it is called. This was followed by a choice of tea or coffee. Later, with a flourish a brand new box of chocolates was opened up and passed around. This I learned was the standard company meal.

Quite elegant..

Kim took me out in the car as I was anxious to learn how to shift with my left hand and drive on the left side of the road. It was after dinner so the roads were pretty empty. She was surprised how quickly I caught on. How good it was I had always driven a "stick". Getting used to shifting with my opposite hand seemed quite natural, but driving on the left hand side of the road took some time. The next day we went into Airdie, the "big" closest town, to do some shopping and to get more oriented. I managed the two roundabouts. They were challenging. Ian took me to the bank and helped me open up my own account. Now I had some money.

While in North Carolina both Ian and Kim's family had visited them so when Ian's folks came it was fun to see each other again. Ian and Kim had timed their "holiday" (vacation) and made plans for the three of us to do some traveling around their country. We packed the car and all climbed in with their little dog and began our trip, driving north. The terrain reminded me somewhat of New England with its rolling hillsides except here in Scotland, their hills were usually dotted with sheep. Ian told me there probably were more sheep than people in Scotland. He informed me that wherever there's a village you will most certainly see the church steeple. If you're looking for castles, in or out of towns, they will be always be located on high points. Of course this made it easier to defend. First stop we visited some family members in Aberdeen (quite industrial) and then proceeded on to Peterhead, a charming small city both located on the coast. There we stayed with friends, a clergy couple. I enjoyed getting to know them and seeing that area. Unfortunately I was stressed with a painful foot problem that limited some of the walking I would have enjoyed.

We all went out for a lovely dinner. The potatoes and vegetables were served family style. Dessert was an 'icky sticky' pudding with both ice cream and whipped cream on top. This was typical and it didn't take a rocket scientist to see why I was noticing lots of plump people. On the drive back to their house Pauline had us drive past her more contemporary church that was located in an upscale area.

Leaving the next day we drove along the coast and made a stop at Penne, a tiny village tucked into a cove. I was told a movie had been filmed in this picturesque spot. It also had quite a history as a favorite hide out of smugglers. While traveling, I became aware of the lack of variety in the structures. It seemed that all the villages had long rows of stone "attached" houses.

We arrived at the home of more "clergy" friends. While we were conversing the husband mentioned that there was a nearby minister from the U.S., that was filling in that year at a nearby church. When they told me where he was from and his name, I burst out, "I know him." After a quick phone call to them and an invitation they joined us as we all sat around talking and eating dessert. I had spoken about my VIM experience at his church on Widby Island in Washington at a mission potluck. He remembered me when I mentioned being a baseball fan, especially the Dodgers. It had been World Series time and both of us were checking the scores during the evening. Later the conversation led to a discussion of the health of the Church of Scotland. The three men shared a strong sense that it was dying. A sorrow and sense of helplessness was expressed.

We returned to Aberdeen where Ian's sister and husband took us out for a drive in the country. We all were hungry and when they spotted a pub we all decided to stop to eat. When we entered and stepped into the dark dining area, we all noted the pleasant aromas. I loved the cozy atmosphere and enjoyed a most savory "boozy", (beef pie). We all took a walk along the River Dee and once again my foot became swollen and painful. Next day with foot elevated and iced I laid low and read a book about a most unhappy married woman whose husband saw nothing immoral about sleeping with other women. Her way of dealing with this was alcohol. She also detached herself from her kids. A tragic story for sure. Later when talking with Kim about it she shared that the story unfortunately, was quite typical.

The next day we traveled across Scotland, touching the southern portion of the Highlands, en route to Oban located on the west coast of Scotland. I began to notice some houses (detached) were standing tall and alone. We drove through some charming villages with small shops that beckoned to us and I enjoyed the many "lochs" (lakes), we passed . We had to hurry along as we needed to reach Oban to catch the ferry to the Isle of Mull. After parking the car we almost ran to get on board just in time. The boat was about the same size as the Coho, the Victoria ferry. Karen, our hostess was on board with us. She and Kim shared a longtime friendship and they had much to talk about. Karen was a comfortable person to be around and made me feel most welcome. The next day she drove us to the only village on the island, Tobermory. It's a charming little spot right on the water snuggled into a cove that is a natural harbor. We enjoyed our scones and coffee and had a good time checking out the shops. The store fronts were painted a variety of attractive colors instead of the traditional gray.

Sunday we attended her small church that was full of tourists. Karen and a friend led the soft and mellow music. In the afternoon we drove to a beach with a very wide stretch of sand. There were sheep grazing on the hillsides at both sides of the beach. On Mull I was introduced to country roads. Karen would pull way over to allow an approaching car to squeeze by. I was soon to find roads like that on my trip to Wales. Our return trip, after the ferry ride we were back in the car. On our way home we passed Loch Lomond.

Sonny, the dog was extremely placid and didn't express much emotion. Couldn't help to wonder about him. Kim doted on him. Ian displayed some extreme sternness and I observed rigidity in him that made me wonder how he would be with his own kids.

The Watson "holiday" was over so now it was time to talk about my role and glean information about the church and how Ian saw me fitting in. "Holiday Club", VBS to us was held the first week of school. They had discovered that time worked for them, the vacation time didn't.

I was eager to get to spend some time with Julie, a young woman who loved to work with the kids. The feeling was mutual because she was eager to learn all she could from me. The three of us went to visit another church who was in the midst of their VBS and was using "The Go For Gold" material This was an Olympic year and it made for a great theme.

Ian wanted me to be visible and so it was decided that Julie, Ian and I would take turns doing the Children's Message. I also had the joy of reading the scripture and giving one of the morning prayers. The congregation responded to the variety. I heard positive comments as the time went by from the women who particularly responded to having a woman up front.

When I settled into my room, which doubled as my office, I became more acclimated. I was becoming accustomed to Ian and Kim's routines and as so many homes in my past, finding my space. Kim went off to work early every day traveling to Edinburgh. With Ian's directions I was already enjoying a walk from the house that led me out of the village and to a reservoir or as the locals called it the "reser". I took that walk often, as usual, loving being around water. The abundance of heather and thistles added to my delight.

Ian's office was in his home. After his instructions on sending e-mails I learned to get in there when he was out to meetings or visits. That worked well. Got a kick out of the mailman delivering mail through a slot in the front door. There were many things that brought me back to my childhood. People tended to be short and stocky and in their midst I wasn't short anymore. Kim is tall, but she came from the Highlands where there is lots of Scandinavian blood.

The houses were small and modest. The manse stood alone while most of the houses in the village were "attached". There were a few stores in the village and a community center that was encased in barbed wire. Much graffiti in the public places gave off negative vibes. Ian took me to the community center and introduced me around. Their office was a place I could make use of their copier, and became well acquainted, needing class materials on several occasions.

A group from the church had "hired" a small bus to take folks into Glasgow to a concert called "Prom Praise". It was a fund raiser for the National Bible Society of Scotland. The lovely new concert hall was endowed with superb acoustics. The All Souls Orchestra performed, led by their most enthusiastic conductor. Audience participation in the singing of praise songs was accompanied with a great piano and sax. I thoroughly enjoyed the evening as we sang a wide variety of songs, many contemporary and familiar ones as well as many traditional selections.

Kim took me to the Leisure Center in Airdie and after some negotiation I was allowed to come and use the exercise equipment. Outside there was a quarter mile track so I usually would work out on machines and then use the track for my walking. I now had been promoted to using their old car, solo providing me with a welcome freedom.

Both Ian and Kim began to share their concerns about some problems in the church. I sympathized with their struggle and wondered whether the people and they would be open to change. I expected it would be frustrating, since I knew from experience that was all part of the process.

On Sunday, I was settling in, adjusting to new routines. It was comfortable giving the children's message and pleasant to begin to recognize more people. The church building was nicely kept, but the adjacent fellowship hall where we would be having the Holiday Club, always made me wish for some cleaning up and paint as well as posters etc.

Edinburg...

A big day arrived, today I was going to explore Edinburgh. I had many thoughts of my beloved family doctor, back in Connecticut who was from that city. Kim dropped me off near the Royal Mile showing me where we would meet for dinner. I was on my own and psyched. Eagerly I walked up the steep climb to the Esplanade, eager to visit the castle first. The parade ground was packed with tourists, buses and people. I got in a queue (line), purchased my ticket and joined a tour. The guard garbed in kilts, of course, paraded out to the entrance as I approached. The castle was impressive with thick walls dating back to the 12th century. It had been a favorite residence until 1603, after Elizabeth's death, when James VI succeeded to the throne becoming James 1 king of both Scotland and England and to the chagrin of the Scots resided in England.

After my tour I left the castle and began my exploration of the many little shops along the Royal Mile. I found a "wee" place to have a lunch of a salmon, cream cheese and cucumber sandwich. Next I got a kick when I took a city tour on a double decker bus. So British!

The palace is located on the opposite end of the Royal Mile and that was my next stop. There were lovely impressive throne rooms, magnificent art work and handsome pieces of furniture. The Palace is used by the Royal Family so much of it is off limits. When one of them comes to town there is a royal flag flown and visitors are not permitted at all. Prince Andrew is a favorite and often visits. I enjoyed strolling through the well tended gardens.

Ready for more, I started back up the Royal Mile. A few blocks were closed to traffic as a celebration called the "Fringe" was occurring. A wide variety of entertainment was taking place and I delighted having a great time watching the various acts and antics. There was a group of about twenty adults, kids and mentally challenged folks working together in harmony presenting their show. I found that very inspiring, their look of pride and delight was apparent while they all functioned as one unit. No one missed a word or a step.

Later I came upon a bronze statue of a man that was drawing a crowd around it. I laughed at some kids when they approached him, for they jumped back startled when he suddenly winked. His routine continued as he revealed he was real. He was brilliant !! The Children's Museum was another enjoyable treat. The displays showed samples of toys dating back through the century with everything imaginable. My fascination of old toys was well satisfied.

After a long day alone I now met the Watsons at an Italian restaurant. It felt good to sit down and enjoy both the delicious food as well as their delightful company. Then we got in line, queuing up for about an hour before the gates to the parade grounds were open. We were all anticipating seeing the "Military Tattoo". The Commonwealth was to be the theme, but we didn't quite know what to expect. The program began appropriately with bagpipers. They paraded out of the castle immersed in a swirl of fog. Then the various nations from the Mounties from Canada, the Zulus group, the Maori from New Zealand, a string band from the Caribbean and an Aussie band all took their turn. All the performers were precise in their movements and the wide variety and richness of the music was extraordinary. The timing was perfect as one group would leave another was making its entrance. Ian had never gone and was as thrilled as I was. He kept saying I'm so glad you wanted to go, this was phenomenal. For the grand finale all the performers came out one after another filling the parade grounds. This was followed by fireworks... and then the lights were dimmed. A hush ensued... a spotlight focused on a lone piper. He played Auld Lang Syne. Tears, goose bumps and a huge lump in your throat was a common experience. Unforgettable, unbelievable !!

I spent a pleasant day with Christine, a school teacher who had been to the States a few times. She had volunteered at the church to take me sightseeing. Fortunately, she was pleasant to be with and easier than most to understand. Her car was comfortable and it was obvious she liked to drive. We drove up to Crief, north of Stirling. I enjoyed the rolling hills and lovely vistas. We ate lunch with a friend of hers that worked in a retreat center. I enjoyed poking around the shops and taking a good walk along a river.

On their visit with me In Sequim, Kim and Ian had shared how anxious they were now that they were back home, to have a family. They had begun the long process. She shared how difficult the uncertainty and the endless waiting was for both of them.

a really big adventure...

Before going to Scotland I had shared with Ian and Kim that before starting at the church I wanted to take a trip to Wales. My plans were now taking shape. Ian helped me make some Bed & Breakfast reservations. There were a few nights he wasn't able to book. The car rental would be expensive, but there was no other way of doing this excursion. Before starting on my journey Ian had told me, it was fine to tell people at the church I was traveling to Wales, that would be well accepted just don't mention it included a few days in England. Hm!

Early on August 17th, Ian drove me to another town where I would "hire" a car. Then I followed him to a gas station and he helped me to fill up with "petrol". I messed up on the round-about finding myself heading north and quickly turned around and now was on my way... and ... on my own. Scary, excited, with a touch of feeling this whole experience was a "wee" unreal. I was thankful for the comfort and reassurance that my Lord was with me.

My destination was Wales the birthplace of my paternal grandmother. I had reservations in a B&B in a village named Ruthin. That was a coincidence and made me curious what I would find there. Surprised to see a Burger King along the motorway, I decided a Whopper would hit the spot. While picking up my order In my excitement without realizing it, I dropped my credit card. Fortunately a kind man picked it up and turned it in at the counter. Whew, I realized I better settle down and get hold of myself. The next stop was Chester where I turned off the motorway to enjoy some quiet lovely country roads.

Now I was in Wales, and fortunately my destination, Ruthin

was easy to find. Upon my arrival, I filled up with expensive "petrol" then parked the car and walked a short distance where I was able to ask for directions to my B&B. It was part of a long "attached" row of houses. When I walked up the few steps to the massive wooden door with a brass knocker I was pleased and relieved when my hostess greeted me warmly. The hallway was rather dark and spacious and she led me into a warm and inviting sitting room, offering me a spot of teaand"biscuits" (cookies) before showing me to my upstairs room. The beautiful staircase was wide and curved before you reached the top. When my hostess opened the door I entered a large and inviting room. The bathroom was down the hall and shared with other guests which I quickly found was typical in the U.K., (United Kingdom).

After settling in and relaxing from my long day of driving I began to explore Ruthin. It was a charming place with a village square and lovely looking Georgian houses and gardens everywhere. My hostess gave me tips on where to eat and the one I settled on was excellent. The restaurant was located upstairs and had two large old stone fireplaces, dark wood beams and candelabras. After my satisfying meal I did some more strolling around town noting the"Dispensing Chemist", (the pharmacy), the English Presbyterian Church and another Presbyterian church.

The next morning going down to breakfast I was treated to wonderful aromas. It was interesting to meet the other guests and to hear their stories of what brought them to this place. One couple from LA were tourists. Two retirees from the States were volunteering in Holland helping on the Community Bible Study staff. They were taking a brief"holiday". I would have loved to talk but I was anticipating a full day, a once in a lifetime day.

My drive took me west where I was treated to being in the rugged green hills and lovely valleys. Caernarfon Castle, a 13th century fortress, looms over the busy town. Its famous polygonal towers makes a most impressive sight. I found a parking spot and made my way to the entrance. The walls of the castle are extremely thick and seemed impenetrable. There were a myriad of windy staircases that fascinated me. These led to a variety of lookout spots that I expect had been well used in times of danger. There were also some grand rooms where gatherings were enjoyed. The guide proudly told us that Prince Charles had visited the castle. When I proceeded back to my parked car I was treated to great views of the sea on one side and mountains on the other.

I had seen a flyer describing a slate museum. Curious, I made that my next stop. After climbing into a cage that descended down into the mine, I found various interesting displays. Small groups formed and then followed a well mapped out course stopping at ten sites to listen to a cassette tape explain what you were looking at. It was close to being as good as having a guide. After that we got back into the lift and was taken up to ground level. I can't imagine how difficult it would have been to spend all those hours underground. Up top there were a few shops that were replicas of previous times where you could buy some items. On my return to Ruthin I passed through many villages and was struck by their sameness and dreariness.

Next morning, Swansea, the actual birthplace of my grandmother, was my destination. It's located on the southern shore of Wales. situated on the water. I found the city and the harbor extremely busy and congested. I roamed around a bit, but was anxious to locate a place to stay that night. After a few brief hours, I headed west out of the city, hoping and praying to find a room. After a scary roundabout where I inadvertently cut someone off, I pulled over and just sat still. After scolding myself, I decided next time when circling and not sure where to exit I would simply keep going round and round until I figured it out.

My plan was to find a way that would take me to the Gower Peninsula. I left the motor way and headed into a town. Kept driving and lo and behold I spotted a place I hoped had a room waiting. Yeah, there was one room available that night. Whew, I was relieved. Thank you, Lord. After moving in, I decided to take a walk and quickly realized this was a rough part of town. It made sense now that when I parked my car it was in a fenced and locked in area. After dinner I did get my car and took off in one direction having no sense of where I was. Surprise, surprise I found a beach. I also spotted signs leading to the peninsula and realized I was in a perfect spot for my departure the next morning.

The new day dawned and I was eager to go, curious what the beach and the sea would be like. I always had such a profound love for the beach, certainly tracing it back to my Uncle John and Aunt Daisey, but also wondered had that been passed down from my paternal grandma. I had heard many stories about her character and love of God and that she had taught Bible studies. Dad, often mentioned she never spoke a bad word about anyone, always looking to find the good in every person. Quite a legacy I was given.

The road was easy to find and when I reached the Gower Peninsula I wished I knew whether grandma had ever been there. What a most comfortable morning, I was blessed with bright blue skies as I continued my journey passing through small villages and farmland. Of course there were the ever present sheep. I was surprised to find the road changed to a narrow one way lane. Reminded me of the "one way" experience on the isle of Mull. Within minutes I was shocked to spot an approaching tour bus. The lane had no room as it was lined with hedges that weren't about to go anywhere. I pulled over as far as possible and when the bus squeezed by it caused some damage that I had to pay for when I returned the "hired" car. The experience left me shaken, but I certainly had to keep on going and hope I would soon be on a two way road. What in the world the bus was doing there I'll never know!?!

Soon I stopped shaking and calmed down. I was happy when shortly the beach appeared on the horizon. Always have said whatever car I'm driving knows how to find the water. The location was rather isolated with no signs of any facilities. The beach was flat, wide and long. Of course my shoes came off and I enjoyed a great walk along the water's edge. An added delight was there were some novice surfers being taught by an instructor. It was fascinating and occasionally amusing watching the class.

Perhaps this area was more like it might have been in grandma's day. It intrigued me and wish I could have spent a night there. I had read in my tour guide book that on the other side of the peninsula there was a beach with boardwalk and amusements. That would have been interesting to check out, but I didn't have time.

Needing to get going again I the drove off the peninsula and picked up the motor way to Cardiff. Signs to Welsh Folk Museum had caught my eye and I'm glad I followed them. What a treat. On the grounds there were on display a series of small houses from the different periods of time. My favorite was a small cottage complete with a thatched roof that beckoned to me. When I poked my head in I spotted a guide seated on a low stool. He was grandfatherly person and facing him was a darling little four year old girl seated on another stool. They were telling each other the story of Goldilocks. How captivating that scene was.

In the gift shop I was delighted to find a "Little Book of Welsh Sayings" that give me a chuckle when I read it. The introduction relates, *there are no listeners in Wales only tired talkers waiting to get their breath back.* My visit to Wales was much too short there were many more places I would love to see.

England...

Back on the road again, I drove over the bridge to Bristol England where was paternal grandfather had lived. Somehow once again there was another "round about". This one sent me off towards Bath. I hadn't really planned to go there, but figured... why not. Little did I realize the adventure that awaited me. It was a Sunday with no reservations, certainly was a major concern. Bath was getting closer and at every lodging place I stopped to inquire I was told they had no room. I kept looking, praying, but was not meeting with any success. When I entered the city, I drove down a main thoroughfare and caught a glimpse of a sign reading "Rooms". Now the challenge was to get turned around and find a parking place so I could pursue my lead. Thankfully, I found a rare spot and walked back to the large house. After climbing up a steep hill I spotted a sign directing me to go to back door. There another note instructed me to knock and come in. I made my way down a long dark hall and found a couple sitting in comfortable chairs rather disheveled looking from an afternoon of working in their garden. They smiled and invited me to sit down and relax. When I inquired about a room they told me they were full, but a friend of theirs would be coming around six. She would have a room, after she checked me out first. Whew, what a relief. The gentleman, after giving me something to drink, walked back with me to get my car and led me through a maze of alleys to the rear of their house. Now I was parked in their driveway and would be ready to go with the lady. I never could have found it on my own and again was so thankful for their kindness.

An eating place was just a few blocks from their house. Now fed, safe and relaxed I returned to the house to wait. The couple were delightful and in the course of our conversation I found they were both college professors with PHDs. It reminded me to never jump to conclusions about anyone or anything.

The English lady arrived prim and most proper. We talked a little and she quickly decided I was safe and was willing to have me follow her out of town and spend the night. She had come to meet an Australian couple who would be going with us. When they arrived we left to go to her place. I followed her while the Aussies followed me. Her car was a little Rover. When she turned onto the main rode she floored her gas pedal forcing me to keep up while still needing to be concerned about the folks behind me. Fortunately there was a roundabout plus some traffic lights that aided me. I still have to smile as this was another unexpected experience. I was weary from a long day, but found her a delight to talk to. She had been widowed a few years now and had lived with her husband on a large estate further out in the country. She wanted to be closer to town. Her friends questioned and cautioned her about having strangers come in for the night. That wasn't safe. I encouraged her by pointing out that she had a perfect setup working through her friends who certainly functioned as a safety screen for her. People didn't knock on her door.

After a tasty breakfast armed with good directions, I easily slipped into Bath locating a place to park. It was early still and tourists were slow in arriving. Knowing there wasn't much time to spend I took a bus tour. York would be my next stop and at least there reservations had been made. I had no idea how long a drive it would be. The first part of the tour went up a steep hill overlooking the white Roman buildings. There were numerous beautiful Italian homes with lovely gardens everywhere that were a feast to the eyes. The guide on the bus pointed out Edwardian windows. They were very large and passerbys were afforded clear views of the inside of the house. Bay windows were then created to keep people 'at bay' and not allow them when passing to see inside. I then strolled around Bath a little, but was anxious to leave.

Back on the road on my way to York, I somehow missed a turn and wound up heading for Shakespeare's Stratford. That was a disappointment because it was impossibly congested. I was able to get some clear directions, the English accent was understandable and reached York in the late afternoon. My hosts, the Bradleys had told me to call them if I had difficulty finding them for the area around the city is most confusing. After a few attempts on my own, I called and they came to where I was and led me back to their home. Their place was only a short walk to the walled city and after parking I didn't need to move the car again until leaving. Exhausted I skipped an evening meal and fell into bed. I stayed two nights there which gave me a break and also helped me to really appreciate York.

The morning brought a heavy thunder and lighting down-pour. While enjoying breakfast and observing my hosts I couldn't help, but note the Bradleys were the quintessential British couple. Both were handsome, proper, refined, and gracious. The rain let up and garbed in my raincoat I walked down through the city gates and began to explore. England had survived many invasions in their history. Bath was Roman, York showed remnants of the Viking era. There was a 'Disney' type ride in a boat to view the displays. When I joined the queue to do this there were two men garbed in Viking regalia going up and down the line spooking people, generally adding to the festivities. For a quick change of pace I took in the Castle Museum. It was an excellent display tracing British history, dress and customs that was on the level of the Smithsonian in D.C.

I typically find myself drawn to transportation and found the Railroad Museum that housed a terrific huge steam engine that must have been quite a sight when huffing and puffing it pulled into the station. Also, I was fascinated with the Royal plush railroad cars that were specially shaped to handle the many canals the tracks ran by. There were many activities geared for kids. I indulged in a charcoal grilled hamburger, making me think of back home, along with an ice cream cone. Later in the afternoon, a scone and some tea were satisfying.

The York Minster dominates the scene in the walled city, dating back to the 1200's. It took two and a half centuries to build. It is the largest medieval building in the UK with the finest example of Gothic architecture and treasured stained glass windows It's been described as 'poetry in stone' and 'chiseled lace'. I was definitely awed by its magnificence. I returned a second time to be blessed with a choir rehearsal. The unforgettable sound resonated through out the structure. The tourists were restricted to a certain area and left me feeling shut out and thinking I was glad the Lord doesn't prevent us from approaching His Holy places. I walked away thinking how lovely...how very formal... how devoid of emotion...how very controlled.

The next morning in my devotions I read in Zephaniah 3:14b *"Be glad and rejoice with all your heart.....The Lord your God is with you. He will take great delight in you and quiet you with his love. He will rejoice over you with singing...at that time he will bring you home."* What a comfort.

My last leg of my journey I stumbled onto Seaham, a small village complete with a charming tea shoppe. Yes, the scone was good. It was situated on the coast and I spent some relaxing time on its lovely beach.

In Newcastle, a large and congested city, I got lost, but luckily was given some excellent directions from a man in an auto store. At last I was back in Scotland driving up hilly and winding roads en route to Edinburgh. There were numerous open fields dotted with many sheep. It was easy now, passing Edinburgh and onto home.

How great to see Ian and Kim, share my adventures and settle into my home. While I was gone there had been more meetings related to the upcoming adoption of the children. There were some family problems surfacing with Ian's mom especially having difficulty accepting the concept. "If they just trusted God, he would give them children". Ian and Kim spent some time with his parents and openly talking about it and this helped to ease some of the pressure that had been building.

"home" in Caldercruix...

Ian had told me while they were visiting me in Washington, that the clergy had the privilege of going to the public school and provide religious instruction. Ian did this regularly speaking to all the children in an assembly. While discussing the possibilities of my coming he explained that he could see me stepping into that role thus freeing him from that weekly commitment. School now had started and we went to visit. First stop was the Catholic school where he enjoyed an open invitation. We were guests at their assembly and Ian told the kids about the upcoming "Holiday" Club (Vacation Bible School) inviting them to join us. While he was speaking a few of the kids were inattentive and antsy. The staff was distressed and vowed the children would be disciplined for their rudeness.

Next we visited the public school. The old building had a mellow well cared for feel to it. The walls in the gym were a pleasant blue and the buffed floors shone. Everything was neat and tidy. Ian's a natural with kids and he was warmly received. An invitation was given to come to the "Go For Gold" Holiday Club. He also introduced me to the children explaining that I would be coming to see them.

We then sat down with the "head teacher" (principal) and talked about my involvement. I offered to come two mornings a week, if this was okay and visit individual classrooms. She was pleased and surprised that I would commit to that much time. I asked her whether there was any curriculum. Her reply was no, but perhaps I might tell the stories of David and Goliath and Daniel in the lions' den. I listened and then offered that I thought it was most important that the children hear about Jesus. That would be exposed them to what Christianity was all about. She quickly agreed. My plan was to sing a few songs with the kids followed with a gospel story. I would visit the three classes of younger kids one day taking about twenty minutes in each room and then the second day do the older two, taking about thirty minutes.

After our meeting Ian expressed he was finding he had some "letting go" problems. He was faced with mixed feelings, wanting to be relieved of the weekly responsibility while knowing he would miss this visits. We both agreed that he shouldn't step back entirely, he needed to remain visible, after all my time would only be a few months. Both Ian and Kim were finding it challenging to release some things even though they had expressed frustrations. Change is painful.

a magical cottage...

I had identified places I wanted to see while in Scotland. My plans were in the works to go with Kim to Inverness, fly to London, and drive to St. Andrews. Ian had a friend, another Christine, located near there that he knew would love to have me come and stay a few days making the drive to St. Andrew only about an hour from her home. It was Labor Day weekend when I started out to visit this place I had heard much about. Once again my directions were easy to follow and as I pulled off the narrow road, parked my car and walked around to the front door I knew this was going to be special. The cottage looked like something out of a fairy tale and was surrounded with flowers of all sizes and color. The shutters and the window boxes as well as some ivy on the house all added to the charm. It brought me back to Aunt Belle's summer home on the Susquehanna River in Pennsylvania. Christine responded to my knock on the door and welcomed me like I was a long lost friend. She had enjoyed Kim and Ian when they had served in her church. The inside was even more delicious that the outside. There were multiple corners that invited you to snuggle up with an afghan and devour a good book.

Christine was a few years older than me, a big sister and had been widowed several years ago. She taught school for several years and had enjoyed extensive travel in the U.S. Her sense of adventure was apparent as we talked. She was impressed and enthusiastic about the States.

I rose early, eager to explore St. Andrews. Ian had told me that the renown golf course is a public one and open to everyone to stroll on and/or play. Tiger Woods had just won the British Open in the summer. I'm not much of a golf fan, but do watch some of the big tournaments.

The drive was lovely and well marked, finding my way was no problem. When I drove into the small city I did have difficulty finding a parking space, but got lucky and found one without a meter. What a picturesque place. I found myself on the water's edge and followed a path that took me through the remains of an ancient castle that led to the main part of town. When I arrived I found it full of inviting shops begging to be explored. I broke down and purchased a woolen jumper,(sweater).

The buildings of the university were interspersed through out the main part of town adding to the charming atmosphere. In my wandering around I found a coffee shop brimming with students, that also served tea and scones. I walked out of that area and strolled along the bluff spotting the golf course and the "Chariots of Fire" beach off in the distance. The opening scene of the racers training for the Olympics had been filmed there, a scene which continues to inspire me. I have quoted that line that Eric Liddel said to his sister " When I run I know it gives God pleasure." I think of that in so many situations in my own life, when teaching or in the pulpit as well as when I've discovered an awesome place I never expected to find myself. I know my pleasure pleases him.

Now, I headed back to the car and drove over to the beach. There was parking all along the bluff overlooking the water. Leaving the car I eagerly hurried down the path and went to the water's edge overwhelmed with thankfulness to my Lord who pours out on me an abundance of blessings. After pinching myself, I began to realize that I was strolling along that beach, that I was in Scotland the whole thing was incredible. Of course when no one was looking I ran down that beach hearing the famous music in my ears. Later I walked over to the golf course and strolled around thinking of the greats; Jack Nicholas, Arnie Palmer, Tiger Woods and many others.

There was multiple charming places to eat and shops to explore. The next day I decided it would be good to drive south along the coast and check out some of the villages the tour book had named. It was a warm sunny day and I discovered some of the villages were touristy and some were commerical fishing spots along my route. The seafood was especially delicious.

Sunday morning while strolling around I was kicking myself that I hadn't checked with Ian as to where I might attend church. There were two Churches of Scotland near each other, but I found myself still in a quandary, unsure of where to go. As church time was getting near I began to notice several students garbed in red capes that they wore over their jeans, running helter skelter in my direction. Ah... I began to follow and came to a building that didn't look like a church from the outside, but noticed the students were entering in. There was a short line of tourists types queued up. I got in line and within moments the doors opened up and we were ushered in. Saint Salvador Chapel was long and narrow and I found myself a seat on one of the long pews that lined both walls. The organ and choir were not visible as they were situated in a loft. When the music began flooding the sanctuary with beautiful sounds, chills ran up and down my spine and tears filled my eyes. *Awesome*, is the only word that fits.

It was the first Sunday before classes would begin and some of the faculty paraded in dressed in their academic robes. The chaplain and another person in a robe carrying the Bible followed. I appreciated the formality, it certainly fit the setting. The chaplain gave the message, challenging the students as they were to begin their new year. He used passages from Genesis 12 and Hebrews 11:8 that describe how Abraham obeyed, left his home and went, even though he did not know where he was going. I could relate to that. Neither Abraham or myself had a clue where or what God was calling us to. I've reflected many times wondering what if I hadn't listened and obeyed. Wow, what I would have missed in my life. I believe God has multiple blessings we miss out on because we are so preoccupied with ourselves, setting our own agendas.

Back at the cottage my hostess and I enjoyed good conversation. Her story read somewhat like a fairy tale. When she was in her late teens she had attended a Christian camp or conference and met a young man whom she was very attracted to. They both shyly noticed each other and engaged in some conversation. When she returned home she then entered into her schooling in preparation for teaching. He went back to helping his dad run the large and demanding family farm. They didn't keep track of each other, but she learned he was married and had a family. She enjoyed her teaching never meeting anyone and remained single. Imagine her surprise when in her mid 30's received a call from him. His wife had died and he had never forgotten her and wanted to see her. It didn't take long before they were married, neither one of them wanted to risk losing the other again. She had a huge adjustment to make leaving her career, moving to the farm and living near his family while raising his children. Her stepchildren love her dearly and keep close touch with her.

In some of my reading and in conversations I was picking up an animosity between the Scots and the English. I asked her how she would describe the differences between the two. Her reply was many of the English in the southern part of the country had some German/Prussian blood. The relationship was strained enough due to the defeats they had inflicted on Scots but their arrogance and elite attitudes continue to be offensive.

Scots, Irish, and Welsh sprung from the Celtic/ Gaelic. Christine went on to share that her people, the Scots, typically tend to have a kinship with the underdog. Usually they are excellent workers, but never produce strong leaders because they are too busy disagreeing among themselves. They are always quick to say to anyone who might exert themselves, "who do you think you are?" The "outsider" (any non Scot) was appreciated, everyone always feeling they knew more. How fascinating that was to me as I listened intently I caught glimpses and insights of my parents. My mother was of German and English descent. Old tapes from childhood play in my mind of her telling us kids that we were better than others and hence we shouldn't do such and such.

One author stated their character was confusing for these elements coexisted: dourness-- humor, meaness-- generosity, arrogance-- tolerance, sentimentality-- hardheaded, humor both subtle--sarcastic. Of course I feel we all have a unique mix.

Their democratic tradition didn't prevent maintaining their taste for arguing. I could smile with these descriptions. They fit, but the measure of their quiet humor, their deep love and appreciation coming and being a part of them was demonstrated to me in abundant ways.

When it was time to leave I realized how much I had loved this entire time and I sensed that St. Andrew would be the favorite spot and my time at the cottage, most special.

En route home I knew Kim and Ian were away on holiday and I was looking forward to having the house to myself. Shouldn't have been surprised when I returned home that they were still packing the car. I had previously observed they took forever when leaving on a trip. Once they were gone, the two cats soon found their way to my room, even more frequently... giving me company.

I spent some fascinating time watching the Olympics. It was interesting, hearing and seeing the events from their viewpoint. The presidential election was also approaching and I certainly got teased about that especially when all the tallying of the votes turned into such a mess. Global warming was a hot tissue and although I found nothing but affirmation as an American, they were troubled with the USA's stance on that topic. With the time difference I was missing out on football and baseball playoffs and the World Series. I started setting my alarm and watching in the middle of the night. In dire need of a sports' fix I began to watch their football,(soccer) and rugby. What a rough sport that is. British humor on TV gave me some good chuckles.

"Go for Gold", the VBS, was a great success with eighty kids involved. Even more significant was a number of boys in the older group. Julie was a natural teacher and it was a joy to see her in action and give her the feedback she was seeking. She was eager to enhance her teaching. I urged Ian to have the parents come the last night when awards were given out and have the kids sing. Light refreshments would also be appealing. He kind of dragged his feet on that, anticipating a poor response. He had no problem if I wanted to handle the preparations. I enlisted a few women to handle refreshments. The open house was a huge success and Ian was thrilled. I kept stressing the need to get the parents and their children in the church and then you have the whole family. I'm glad they didn't pass up on a natural occasion to expose them to Ian and the church.

In later conversations Ian was recognizing that he was experiencing an erosion of hope, a settling down. He shared he hadn't realized a dulling of his spirit that was characteristic of the village, a resignation that change wasn't possible. Why bother to put all that energy into something that won't really be worth it. For me, I saw a familiar role of my coming in from the outside and lifting peoples' spirits and expectations, being a catalyst, an energizer. "Let's work together and then you'll be able to keep it going on your own" was my motto.

Krazy Kids, a weekly evening group, started up the following week. It had been an ongoing ministry the last two years and was well attended. Lots of energetic kids showed up and the evening was quite exhausting. The church really was reaching the kids, but there was a drop-off of the older boys. They needed more action, more program sensitive to their needs. Girls will hang in there longer while the boys just disappear if their needs aren't met from church activities. The age span from ages five to eleven was too wide. I convinced the team we needed to have some small group time dividing up the grades during part of the program. We met in the fellowship hall and the facility desperately needed some attention.

Next I launched "Caring Evangelism" and was pleased with nine members. Unfortunately four or five probable folks had made a previous commitment to another series of meetings. Once again I found a joy and rich blessing in leading this study. Just as in the States the Stephen's Ministry material was enthusiastically received. The delicate balance of practical truths and how to apply them is awesome. There is a part of each session that involves small group interaction. The group found this a challenge, a stretch. Even though they knew each other they were reticent, unaccustomed of sharing deeply. It was rewarding to witness much growth in this area.

One gentleman, after a few weeks, hung back after the session and told me with tears in his eyes he had to withdraw. He went on to explain that he felt he was dishonest with his small group because he was afraid to expose his past. He had been sexually molested as a boy and had never talked about it. Only his wife knew. While opening up to me, much anguish and pain spilled out that had been locked away all those years. My heart ached for him and I was profoundly touched by it all. I counseled that he needed to share this with Ian to alleviate the pain and burden he was bearing. It was good to see that happen. What a personal affirmation, that he felt he could trust me. Thank you Lord for that privilege.

Another person in the group came to me sharing, though mature in her faith and a person of prayer, she had always been afraid to pray out loud. After she shared her heartache and I prayed that there would be a breakthrough. Part of the following session one of the exercises was for partners to share a concern with each other and then pray together. There was another woman in the group that was both quiet and gentle so I teamed the two together. When everyone was returning to their places at the closing, up came the one with the problem with tears rolling down her cheeks followed with a big smile. "I prayed", what a huge victory she experienced. "Lord, thank you for blessing upon blessing". It's times like this that all the homelessness and homesickness are more than worth it.

challenges...

Early in September Ian wanted me to come to the meeting of leaders and elders and share my insights about the church. When I entered the room I noted that the woman all sat on one side while the men were on the other. Committee reports were given. The "fabric committee", which translated means the building committee gave a report also. Never could put those terms together. Then it was my turn to share my observations. It wasn't difficult to have many positive comments to share and that I was happy to be with them. I echoed their acknowledgment of the need to attract young families. I complimented them on their outreach to the children in their village, but recalled Jesus' question of the man that had sat next to the pool and claimed there was no one who helped me into the pool after an angel stirred the water. Jesus' question was ...

Do you (really) want to get well? John 5:6

Do you really want families? I suggest you walk through your church and out to the Fellowship Hall and try to see everything through the perspective of a young couple with small children and think... would I find this a safe place, a place where I would feel good about leaving my children? This led to some discussion and Ian shared when the women were dismissed, the elders continued to talk.

This led to an invitation to come to their next meeting. Oh boy, confess to some feelings of intimidation. I certainly had done this in most of my churches with the leaders, here however, the elders were all male and women just didn't carry much weight with them. From their point of view, that's how the Lord had ordained it to be. With some fear and trepidation and a huge amount of prayer seeking wisdom and calm, I went. We all sat in a large circle in a rather poorly lit room. Ian laid out to the group that he asked me to share my insights Unique to this church was that once an elder you always remained an active elder. This put on the board fathers and sons, men in their thirties to some in their seventies.

I had done my homework, visiting the schools as well as

talking with their Sunday School teachers. I found much frustration as the teachers informed me they had many times told the Elders improvements were needed, only to find that again and again no action ever ensued.

My opening were full of the positives and points of agreement. They had a viable ministry to the children of the village. We all agreed there was a critical need to reach young families. That was vital to the growth and future of the church. I began with praise for their ministry to the children in the village. I shared my observations of the well maintained schools and then I came with the big BUT… " But when I see the fellowship hall, the dark and dingy walls, unsafe tables piled precariously in a corner, no hot water, bathrooms with no way to wash your hands… it makes me wonder how serious you are about attracting young families.

As a grandparent and former teacher," I continued, " that if I visited with my children I don't think I would return because of unsafe conditions." When I finished there was a deafening silence. Then one of the senior member spoke and said he thought Jesus really wouldn't mind that the bathrooms weren't complete or the walls not clean. Another man thought we needed to be winning souls and not worrying about a building.

My knees were still shaking and I felt depleted and crushed. After a few more of these 'Jesus comments' one of the younger men spoke. He stated that he thought since they had invited me over from the States because of my experience that they should be open to what I was saying. He then proceeded to say he would be willing to head a committee that would get bids on painting the hall, he would get a dumpster and everything would be taken out of the room and evaluated before going back in. "A-N-D this needed to be done immediately." He would hire a painter to do the Hall. Many of the younger men spoke up, approving his direction and there was a huge mood swing from dreary to enthusiastic. Yes, we can do this. Someone stated the church had always stepped up to a challenge and contributed when members had been asked. Money would be available. There was an energy in the room and I felt it time to leave and let them work it out.

Kim was excited when I returned home and shared what had happened. Ian, about an hour later came bouncing down the hall to where we were chatting and said, "I MUST come to all their meetings. He had never seen so much get done so quickly before". Yes, I believe in miracles. When I was in the planning phrase of coming to Caldercruix I had wondered what would get accomplished in five months. I was beginning to see that God was using that as a plus because the mindset there was to be ever so cautious in making any changes.

Christine, my ever faithful church friend, took me on more sight seeing outings. I enjoyed her company as well as her thoughtfulness. While we spent time together she began to open up more and share her frustrations. She was discouraged with the many negative thoughts and comments in the church. We also indulged in some teacher talk as she was a first grade teacher. The schools didn't have the special ed, and speech therapy that we take for granted in the U.S.

Observing children at home or out shopping and other public places I was noticing that the little ones generally were very placid. They were kept in strollers and high chairs much longer than we do and seemed to always be sucking on a bottle of whole milk. The kids in school were typical,but more like our kids in the 1950's. Many homes had computers and of course TV, without the selection of channels we are accustomed to. Unfortunately as the children reached their teens the same problems as we have, drugs, drinking, unwed mothers occurred.

One Sunday morning, I knew we would be having a communion service. When entering the sanctuary early I was surprised to see white tablecloths draped over the front pews where the kids usually sat. They were expected to move to a different spot and it made me wonder what subtle message that gave the boys and girls. The communion table was decked out in white linen. Just before the service began the grim faced Elders, dressed in black suits, paraded in and were seated on the platform. The organ was the only instrument used and the music was somber. Ian's keyboard was given a rest. Tradition was this service was grave. Ian longed to inject some joy into the ceremony. Communion only happens four times a years. The Elders are mandated to visit everyone and determine their status in the faith. Both the Elders and Ian were extremely uncomfortable with this practice. To be barred from communion is unbearable, definitely a disgrace.

Soon I discovered how easy it was to go to both Glasgow and Edinburgh on the train. I would drive to Airdie, park the car on a side street and hop the train into Glasgow. The station is right in the middle of everything and I returned many times. I found a Borders and a Christian Book store. There were many nice places to eat. Later I located a Museum of Transportation that featured many models of a wide variety of ships and small boats. Glasgow has an impressive history of boat building, claiming the honor of constructing both the Queen Mary in '36 and Elizabeth in 1940. It was a daily bombing target for the Nazis in WW II so during the war many British ships were docked in NY Harbor. I remember, well, my dad taking us to see them and how much pride he took the "Queens". Edinburgh was in the opposite direction and equally accessible and I took full advantage, enjoying the "get-aways".

At long last Kim and Ian appeared before an adoption committee and were approved as foster parents. This whole process was slowly moving forward and certainly exciting. Kim was leaving her job, sensing that soon she would have children to take care of. She had been having difficulties at work but she knew she would miss many of her co- workers.

Ian's parents came for dinner and it happened that it was one of my nights to cook. I had made a stew we all loved and used some cooking wine in it. When we sat down and began to eat Ian's dad commented how tasty it was and what had I put in it. His parents are vehement in their anti- alcohol stand. Ian kicked me under the table to remind me not to mention the wine. He was having difficulty keeping from laughing. Of course all the alcohol evaporates in the cooking process.

Several invitations were extended from different folks to come for dinner. Ian and Kim were included, easing the language barrier. We all enjoyed a lovely meal at the Armstrongs. They had invited two other couples and it made for a lively evening. Salmon was served as starters followed by the main course that included both lamb and brussels sprouts, all favorites of mine. Their home was a single dwelling and more spacious than most. Jim was the Elder that was heading the committee working on the Fellowship Hall. After dinner he told me the painters were coming tomorrow. Wow, I was impressed and pleased.

busy busy...

This next stretch would be full. I had organize a committee to plan a Christmas celebration that they called a Christmas Cracker. Santa would come, there would be a variety of crafts, music, games and of course, refreshments. I would do a devotional. The Hall was now a soft yellow and looked warm and inviting. I had purchased and put up some posters on the walls and everything was clean, neat and tidy.

Also, I had scheduled some teacher training workshops that I conducted on a Friday night and Saturday morning. My efforts were well received and it seemed it had been a delight and rewarding time.

When the Watsons returned we had a spaghetti night for the Krazy Kids and their parents. We didn't get much of a turn out ,but again these were bold steps in reaching out to families. One of the older men, Tommy told Kim he wanted to pay all the expenses for the night.

My passion for 4th-6th graders led me to have what we called 'Torch Night'. I passed out flyers when visiting the classes at school and even one of the teachers urged the kids to show up for this. Ian willingly offered the use the sanctuary which was very dark and somewhat scarey at night for a spooky game of hide and seek. "Torches", flashlights, were the only lights allowed. A great exciting time was enjoyed by all and next week the kids were asking, what's next. Julie, Ian and a mom helped with this and were ecstatic at the outcome. The ladies continued with this age group after I left and caught the vision that they needed to plan more activities with the boys in mind.

I spent a great day with a mom and son going to Stirling. They kept a camper outside of town that they stayed in. We climbed up the steep hill to see the castle. As the day unfolded Margaret opened up sharing lots of painful hurts and "faith" wonderings.

Social Services contacted Kim and Ian in the middle of October. Kim and Ian were to consider three sets of children, choosing one. The first pair was a four year old boy and his two year old sister. They were malnourished and neglected. The second choice was two boys and the third was two girls. Kim, an only child, felt somewhat intimidated with boys. I had spent the day away when this meeting occurred and when arriving home the two of them, about to burst with excitement shared what had transpired. They asked which of the options did I think was right for them. I chose the brother and sister and they looked at each other grinning from ear to ear. That had been their choice. We all shared our joy, wondering how all this would transpire.

They had told the social workers they would be willing to take two or three kids and I spoke up and cautioned them that three would be too much. Their adjustment would be challenging enough. Glad the Lord handled that one.

Going to the schools continued to be a rich experience. The older kids loved their Gospel of Mark that the church gave to them. My first visits going into the classrooms the teachers generally would be at their desk engrossed in correcting papers. I began to observe though, as the weeks went by, that there occurred a subtle change, they began to listen to my teaching. That was rewarding bonus to me.

Early November, I led a women's retreat in a lovely facility in Crief. What a joyful time we had. The church had never done that before and there was great excitement and anticipation. Our study and sharing blessed us all. The meals were delicious and well appreciated by the women. Saturday afternoon after we checked out, some of us did a little shopping in the charming town. I was thrilled when I spotted a figurine of a young ballerina with dark hair pulled back in a pony tale that made me think of Jessi, my granddaughter. I quickly bought it and had them wrap it well for the long trip home in December.

Three ladies, Cecilia, Lizzie and Irene took me to New Lanark, situated on the River Clyde. The village was founded in 1785 and features displays of the life of people in the 19th century that worked in mills. There were tributes in the museum that recognized Robert Owens, a well known and respected gentleman who concerned himself with the welfare of his workers and was instrumental in implementing reforms. We had fun together exploring the various buildings and displays. Then they treated me to a lovely lunch followed with a serenade of a "piper" heralding a wedding party.

Another treat was a trip to Inverness up in the Highlands. Kim and I enjoyed the time together as well as the visit with her delightful Aunt Janet. What a gracious hostess she was, cooking the infamous haggis I had heard so much about. Actually I found it delicious. The city is lovely, blessed with a river running through the middle of the town. We enjoyed strolling around seeing the sights. The next day she took us out on an extensive ride through the Highlands including Loch Ness. Of course Nessie, the infamous dragon was not to be seen. Later we parked at the bridge that takes you to Skye and walked over it so we could say I had been to Skye. Wish I could have spent some time there but my days were rapidly evaporating.

The Guild is a women's group that like those in the states, has a history of supporting mission with their projects and with their money. I was asked to speak at my home church as well as at a few other places. I was privileged to meet many lovely women of faith, but like most in the U.S., stuck in a time warp. Those women's organizations were not attracting the younger ladies and they couldn't seem to make major adjustments in the way they conducted their programs.

Women in their fifties dressed very matronly. Pants were hardly seen. Folks were generally puzzled about my age. With my white hair and talk about my grandkids I just didn't fit into their age categories. When shopping in Airdrie for groceries I would find women dressed in stockings and "old" women shoes. The men would be in suits and ties even. In the larger cities of course there were more exceptions in the way people dressed looking much more "with it".

There was a strong current within the congregation that opposed change. It was held almost as strongly and passionately as one would defend a doctrine of the church. A simple logical matter of removing pews from the back of the church to open up an area where people could visit was shocking and earth shattering. I'm sure there were many, although appreciative of my ministry, breathed a sigh of relief when I left. One couple

291

in particular viewed change as an enemy of the church. Ian was acknowledging more and more how he was gradually giving in to the prevailing attitudes. They do erode one's vision and undermine enthusiasm.

trip to London...

November had arrived and another big adventure was about to unfold, my much anticipated trip to London. It began with a rather frantic ride to the airport, west of Glasgow. Ian had failed to fill up with petrol and we were late in leaving. He was anxious and unsure we would make it and not run out of fuel. Fortunately when we arrived at the airport the tank still had a few drops left. I had an inexpensive flight on Ryan Air and immediately joined the line. There had been lots of heavy rains and flooding in the greater London area. When landing, instead of getting on a "sky train" I had to catch a charter bus that would take me to Liverpool Station and there hop on the "underground". I found my connections and now walked around Highgate checking out the area before heading to my lodging. There were posted signs warning of pick pocketers that I found rather intimidating. Trash bags were all over the place perhaps due to the storm.

Using my directions I walked about a half mile to the Mission House. The neighborhood had changed into a well kept one. The houses and trees were pleasant, but I felt I wouldn't want to be taking this walk after dark. The lodging was a few stories high with big old rooms on the first floor where folks could sit, have a cup of tea and read magazines and newspapers. I also found it a great social spot where I could exchange information about places to see and directions etc.

My room was a single one on the second floor with the bath down the hall. I was told they were beginning to create some ensuite rooms (rooms with private bath). Friends of the Watsons had stayed at the Mission and told us there were special rates for people in ministry, retired missionaries and clergy. The next morning, breakfast was in the basement. People were assigned seats that were moved each day affording everyone an opportunity to interact with folks. The first morning I was seated with a young couple with small children and it was fun watching their eagerness.

I learned that if my arrival at the underground was too early I had to pay more and even a greater penalty, fight the crowds. The trains were jammed and you had to be determined you were going to make room for yourself. Directions are clearly posted and I had no difficulty making my transfer. Every stop the train made you heard 'Mind Your Step'. My destination was Victoria and when I climbed the stairs I found myself in a wealthy area. After checking out bus tours I decided to walk to my first destination, Buckingham Palace. Some gift shops attracted me along the way.

Upon my arrival at the palace I watched with fascination as elegant limos pulled up to the impressive and massive gates that opened before them. Watching the well coffered passengers dressed in furs exiting the vehicles I could only speculate that perhaps they were there to attend some function with the Queen. It was too early for the Changing of the Guard so I strode across an adjacent park, just enjoying the morning and appreciating where I was.

When I returned to the palace, I settled into a good viewing spot to watch the show. First came a military group garbed in gray, followed with a group on horseback. Their medieval headgear and red attire were impressive. The ceremony went on and on and I wandered away after an extended time. I came upon the Museum of the Royal Guards that happened to be free that day. After my visit I went into a gift shop that was full of figurines and toy soldiers. They still fascinate me bringing back memories of being allowed to play with my older cousin's castle complete with a draw bridge and his soldiers. I spotted some queens and purchased one for my grandson. He and I played chess together and I had found two knights in Inverness, but was tickled when finding a queen.

I continued walking and soon found Westminster Abbey. The architecture is breathtaking and I found myself walking reverently through the building appreciating the history as well as the structure. My first glimpse of Big Ben and Parliament pleased me. The lines were hours long so I got a quick look at the Thames and then hopped the underground to the Tower of London area. There I enjoyed strolling along the river and later taking a river cruise.

Next day needing my rain gear I went directly to the Tower and the place was just opening and there was a short line. I decided it would be foolish not to take the tour and definitely found it rewarding. As one enters through the gate, groups are counted off and assigned a guide. My "Beef Eater" was tops. He was garbed in medieval dress and immediately began to weave the story of the Tower, attempting to both frighten and intimidate the group with all the gory details. The complex had a grand history as a residence of the royalty, an armory, treasury and most famous as a prison for enemies of the crown. My guide with great gusto, told many tales of horror as to how prisoners were tortured and beheaded. When the group gathered around him he looked around at each of us and then picked out two because they had long necks and stated they would be prize candidates to be beheaded.

He was a gifted storyteller blessed with a great sense of humor that kept the group close hanging on to his every word. We paraded through the different buildings. When entering one, we stepped onto a moving belt to view the crown jewels that date back to 1661 era. It was a most effective way to move the people through the display. The most celebrated residents of the tower were eight black ravens that legend states the tower would fall if they are not present.

After the tour I delighted in an adjacent gift shop where I purchased some Christmas ornaments and gifts. My challenge was to keep items small and light in weight so it would fit in my gear when leaving Scotland. Later I took the interesting tour of the Tower Bridge. Where ever I went there seemed to be many lively school groups taking tours. I noted their behavior was a contrast to the more somber children I had observed in Scotland.

After a full morning I wandered around and decided to splurge on a special meal. A lovely Indian restaurant featuring a lunch buffet drew my attention. I savored the experience, appreciating the service, the linen tablecloth and napkin, the delicate water goblets as well as the delicious cuisine. In the same area was a marina with a variety of boats and little shops. There was a coffee shop with a second floor that had a delightful view. Later I discovered a Hagan Daz ice cream shop that I found myself drawn to on more than one occasion. It was extra bonus to have an ice cream cone. I've often said that in Heaven, Hagan Daz will have no calories.

The sun had come out, but it was windy, whipping up the river enough to cause the river cruises to be canceled. I loved strolling along the promenade and sitting on a bench looking at the water and the view pinching myself to make certain I wasn't dreaming. One of the mornings I wandered around Piccadilly Square the famous crossroads packed with garish advertisements and fast food places. After more walking I found myself in an area renown for their elegant shops and hotels. It was fun exploring. Later I was impressed with the British Museum of Natural History.

My last breakfast I was pleased to be eating with an American from Chicago. It was great to hear "American English" spoken and stirred up longings to go home to the States. On my agenda that morning was a boat ride to Greenwich. The Old Royal Observatory dates back to 1884 and sits importantly near the dock. It now houses a museum. The area is full of maritime and royal history and I got a kick out of being on the spot where the world's time is measured.

Now it was time to head for the airport and take the return trip to Scotland. The day was long and exhausting, but I had no difficulty in finding my way. Christine and a friend met me at the airport and it sure felt good to get home.

adoption...

Now that the selection phase was accomplished the next step was for Ian and Kim to meet the children. The hopeful parents-to- be were nervous, anxious, excited all rolled into one big knot in their stomachs. The darling wee two year old Amy responded immediately even climbing up on their laps but Jordan, the four year old held back, more cautious. Ian has a way with kids and gently enticed him near. By the end of the visit the lad warmed up.

A meeting, without the children, came next with the foster parents and that was full of good news. The children had come from a totally nonstructured home and required work on developing basic routines. Sleeping in a bed, eating family meals at the table and simple table manners were established. Their behavior was stable, much progress had been made quickly and easily. Next on the agenda was the big visit of bringing them home for the afternoon and evening meal. Again the kids seemed to immediately be comfortable and were already calling them mummy and daddy. They did not want to return to their foster home and cried some. The second visit the children stayed overnight. The whole process was happening at a greater speed than typical.

After years of wondering and praying, whether they would ever have the joy of parenting, it was happening. Both Ian and Kim admitted to feeling overwhelmed and a little scared. Adjustments in the process were made by Social Services. They were named foster parents and that allowed a transfer to be made. The KIDS came HOME. What a joyous day that was! However, a big hurdle faced them. The natural parents still had visitation rights while the adoption process began. Both of the children, when taken on supervised visits with a social worker came away deeply distressed. Jordan was totally wiped out. His behavior when he returned from a visit was full of anger and crying, totally distraught. Fortunately the case worker saw this and the judge stopped the visitation rights.

My role, while still living with them was a supportive one and I kept a low profile realizing they needed to bond with Kim and Ian. Also, I would be leaving shortly and that would mean they would suffer another loss. I offered to go stay with someone during those last weeks, but both Ian and Kim welcomed and appreciated my support. In the evening when the kids were in bed we would talk about the day and I would encourage the way they were interacting with the kids. After several days I felt I should remove myself from the scene and return to that special "Cottage" and revisit St. Andrews for a few days. I savored that little trip and it gave the new parents more confidence in their parenting skills.

Early November I began to notice more and more difficulty with an old nemesis, my inner ear. In the fellowship hall the sound really bounced around the room and I had difficulty even in an adult meeting understanding what people were saying. I could hear the sound, but couldn't decipher their words. Of course Krazy Kids, especially when playing the active games was straining and stressing my ear. I adapted by staying for part of the time and avoiding the noisiest portions.

The Christmas Cracker was a huge success with over a hundred folks in attendance. My committee was excellent. Unfortunately, because of my ear problem I had to miss most of the evening, choosing to just being there in the beginning and then coming toward the end to tell the story. The committee, Julie, as well as Ian and Kim were thrilled with the large turnout and everyone's delight with the whole event.

I received news that there were unhappy rumblings in the church in Sequim. Other happenings were that Bernice's son had come to see her and took her to visit assisted living facilities informing her they decided to move her out of her home as quickly as possible. An apartment unexpectantly opened up the end of December and they moved her the first days in January.

farewell time..

Ian surprised me when he asked me to give the sermon my next to the last Sunday. That was a huge stretch for him and the congregation to have a woman in the pulpit. He even offered me the use of his "throne", but I was much more comfortable speaking from the communion table.

The school kids and staff including the head teacher all marched over from school on a very cold and rainy morning to the church. That was a custom for them to come to the church both at Christmas and Easter. When they paraded in, I found it so moving and unbelievable to see school children coming into a church. The kids sang Christmas Carols and presented me with flowers, a gift and cards they had made and signed. The head teacher thanked me for my visits. I told them a special Christmas story. As they left the building I received many hugs and still get choked up as I picture and relive the scene. This was one of my most cherished parts of my ministry in Scotland.

My last Sunday was a brilliant day. I had the joy of giving the children's message and one of the prayers. Thankful the Lord blessed me with calm. I was called up to the platform and given a proclamation, a tribute for my ministry with them. It was a great honor. A luncheon followed and I sat with my back to the wall easing the stress to my ear. Presents, hugs, well wishes, and "will you ever come back" was ringing in my ears and warming my heart.

That evening, the service was a tribute to me. Ian started it off by saying that I had accomplished everything he had hoped for and had rekindled his vision and purpose. Others also spoke. John identified that my strong characteristics were love and humility. I found that very humbling and had to fight to restrain the tears. Jim wrapped up it all up and had me laughing by sharing that when he first saw me he wondered what in the world this little gray-haired lady would be able to accomplish. Ian, when telling the Elders about me, made him expect another Billy Graham. Then he looked at me and said, "well done".

Five months had been just the right time. More had been accomplished that I ever could have expected. It was time now for this young family to have its privacy. It was time for me to be home. Sequim was definitely calling.

One last time Christine had another big treat for me, a lovely meal complete with starters and choice of puddings. The Watson family came to the airport to see me off. Words are inadequate when trying to describe the feelings of my incredible sojourn.

East coast USA...

Once again I was in the air and flying across the Atlantic. This time returning to my country. After landing at JFK, I walked wearily to the baggage area more than ready to get to Danbury. My smaller bag had not come home with me and I would have to do without for a few days. Of course that was the one that held my winter things. I took the Connecticut Limo to Danbury and Dolores, picked me up taking me to her home in New Fairfield.

We both had lots of news to share. She was progressing nicely toward her goal of selling her home and returning to her roots in eastern Washington. How special now to see my family and spend time with them and dear friends. Kristen and Lindsay were such lovely girls and of course busy in their teenage world. What delights I had in sharing my experiences and how good God had continued to be.

I rented a car to get around in and delighted in my solo drive up to Kent and over to Litchfield and back. There was a light dusting of fresh snow that added to the scene. The charming surroundings I was observing stimulated a new appreciation of the variety of homes and the lovely hills and trees that make up the Connecticut landscape. In many ways this area would always be home but I was sensing an impatience to return to another significant home in Sequim and be settled in my nest and back into the ministry that awaited me there. Susan, my longtime friend from Vermont met me halfway near Boston for a brief visit. Our times together were always nourishing.

Of course I was also anticipating Christmas with my family in Concord. What fun to take my "Shoney girl" to breakfast and Cole to the park and hot chocolate sitting on the high stools in our special shop. Shane was eager to go to the playground and graveyard at his old preschool . Christmas was great with all the excitement.

New Year's eve I promised Jim and Denise that I would take care of the kids so they could go out. When I arrived in the afternoon I found the family had a brand new puppy. Zazbo, she was named, wasn't much trouble and to this day a delightful mellow dog just what the family needed.

11

Sequim, A New Year

Wonderful thing about grace is that once it comes into our lives we are set free from a preoccupation with ourselves... set free from worry of whether we are doing enough to please God. We are free to serve him in love.
C. Swindoll

When the plane landed at Sea Tac, I made my way to catch a connecting flight to Port Angles only to be told there were strong winds and the flight might have to be canceled. After a brief delay the announcement was made that the plane would attempt the flight and if unable to land would bring us back to Seattle. I had been away for six months on an adventure of a lifetime and was eager to get home. I spotted a woman from church who also was returning from an extended trip. We chatted while we boarded. My seat was on the opposite side a few seats ahead of hers. The planes used on this route were small jets. We took off and immediately were coping with a VERY bumpy ride. We hit one with quite a drop and she called out to me to ask if I was praying yet. A man in front of her answered saying he didn't know if Ruth was praying, but he sure was. Everyone got a good chuckle out of that and it helped relieve some of the tension. We landed successfully, it was definitely a flight to remember.

My first priority was Bernice and I found her, already moved at the Fifth Avenue, an assisted living complex, in her new apartment. All the furniture was in place, pictures hung on the wall, clothes in her closet, but her living room was piled high with boxes and she looked like a little lost lamb sitting in her chair as I approached her. We hung onto each other and shed a few tears sharing a most tender moment. I settled in on the couch as we chatted away peering around the stacked boxes. The next days were spent unpacking, discarding or finding a place for her things. My grief over losing her house surprised me. I had made it my own in many ways. We both had some adjusting to do.

She certainly was struggling to cope with some health issues involving both bladder and intestinal difficulties. She complained of being exhausted all the time and that sent Dr Crist , her long time primary physician, delving into possible causes. After some testing,he arranged for us to go see a specialist at Virginia Mason, a hospital in Seattle. The diagnosis was a nonaggressive lymphphoma that hopefully could be treated with a pill. Her hearing was becoming progressively worse. She was needing lots of help. I still marvel how God had brought me back to be her strong support.

It was good to be home and seeing dear ones who had both written and kept me in their prayers while I was gone. Ralph, the associate pastor had settled in and had assumed many of the responsibilities I had before. Scott and I had good talks about my new role and challenge as well as sharing the challenges he was confronting. My position now would be focused on the women.

A new worship schedule began the beginning of January. Three services, 8:30, 9:30 and 11:00. The early services were contemporary and 11:00 o'clock, a traditional one. The music was outstanding in all. Steve was developing the music program in an awesome way. He used three or four rotating teams in the contemporary services. One of the groups was made up of both high school and college girls and it was a wonder, observing their development. He was creating a beautiful sound from his mostly senior choir that sang in the traditional service.

I jumped right back into the young moms group much to the relief of my subs. It was sweet to be with those women again. Upon my return I had found myself questioning if I would be really needed and was there still a place for me. Once again I was reminded to open my eyes and see... all the new opportunities... new challenges. These questions didn't have much of a chance to survive. Quickly I was deeply engaged.

Two women approached me telling me they were so glad I was back as they were eager to have a women's retreat. The men already had two and Scott had promised that I would take on the challenge upon my return. There was no difficulty gathering a committee that turned out to be a huge source of joy. Each person was a willing helper and we became a small group in that we shared and prayed for each other each time we met. The room also filled with wonderful laughter. I found myself eagerly anticipating our meetings.

Ralph and I teamed up and led a Lenten series we named the "Journey to Easter". We shared the teaching and received a wonderful response. The classes were offered Sunday morning and repeated during the week on an early afternoon. I also was taken aside and asked to be part of a mission team going to Helene on an island off the coast of Honduras. That was not on my agenda at all, after being away those months but I soon came to realize it was in God's plans.

Keenagers, the senior group, wanted me to speak at the next potluck about my time in Scotland and what a joy, showing my slides and telling my stories.

Former pastor, Bill Klink had come to have a memorial service in Sequim for his wife Barb after her unexpected death.

We met at Pedals for lunch and we both enjoyed a special time together.

Quickly my plate was more than full. It was always special when my group from Terrace View came for a retreat. Good news was that Pat would be moving back with her new husband, Ray to Mount Lake Terrace. It blessed me so to see Pat, happily married. She had endured more than her share of heartbreak.

During one of our staff meetings, Scott had the team do some "bonding" exercises to enable us to become more cohesive. He valued having a staff that respected and cared about each other. Our activity was to write on slips of paper two words that described each person in the group. When these were read mine were compassionate and encourager, genuine and warm-relational, kind and wise, creative and spiritual guide. That's an awesome affirmation and I've treasured those comments. I appreciated that the staff after their weekly meeting, once a month, we all went out to eat together. On the other weeks Scott took one of us out to lunch providing us the time to engage in one on one conversation.

Early June, Scott and I during the traditional service surprised Bernice. That special lady had been teaching most of her 89 years. We presented her with flowers and a gift certificate to enjoy a meal at a lovely restaurant. The congregation gave her a standing ovation. She was surprised and deeply moved by the honors bestowed on her. Her health problems were troubling. It seemed there were endless doctor appointments and tests needing to be done. The diarrhea kept her fearful to go out, even to church. The plans for the Mission trip were progressing and I was concerned about leaving Bernice at such a critical time.

summer '01...

I was able to make a trip home and spent a few days at Wrightsville Beach. This time I stayed in my old house next to the church. The R&R was beneficial and seeing dear people nourished me. Next stop was with Jim and Denise. They went off spending two nights alone providing me with a great time with the kids. I enjoyed watching both Jessi and Cole who were now involved in gymnastics. Shane performed his magic tricks and had us all chuckling as he used Cole to be the one who disappeared in a large box scenario. Cole beat me in two straight chess games and was ecstatic telling his mom and dad he had beat me finally. We all had our rounds of "Spoons" and "Go Fish". It was as usual a special delightful time.

Heading north, I stopped off for visits with both my sister and then my brother. Arrived at John's to see Kristen graduate from high school. Her parents threw a lovely party out on the patio. Unfortunately it rained, but they were able to put up some canopies that saved the day.

I visited the New Fairfield Church and had a happy time chatting with several dear folks. Susan and I spent a night together in a motel in Brattleboro. We had much to share with each other, we hardly came up for air. My friend, Ruth and I took a train, to the "City" and enjoyed a visit to the Statue of Liberty and Ellis Island. We were impressed and touched with the history of those sites. We snapped pictures from the boat of the New York skyline showing the Twin Towers never thinking that in a matter of weeks they would be gone.

Upon my return, Scott was now on vacation and Ralph and I sat down together. He told me that Bible Study Fellowship had ended their women's ministry in Port Angeles leaving a huge vacuum, an opportunity to step up and fill... something more to pray and consider.

On the 4th of July, Bernice and I were going out for a drive. As we walked down the hall together and were near the front desk, she tripped and fell. I was right near her and felt so helpless that I hadn't been able to stop her fall. EMT's were called and they determined she was stable enough to ride with me to the ER for stitches. The receptionist shared with me that many at the residence had feared she would fall, it was obvious she was unsteady on her feet. After the accident I insisted she needed a walker. She knew I was serious so reluctantly agreed.

I took my turn in the pulpit in early July. I met the challenge of three services. What a surprise when the choir sang a song I had been blessed with in Scotland, "We Are Singing". Actually the song is from Africa, but I will always associate it with Scotland.

When Scott returned from vacation we had some long talks about the Women's Bible Study, shifts in my ministry and other problems on his mind. I formed a committee to prepare for the new venture. This provoked mixed feelings. I realized I would have to give up my occasional dearly loved, Tuesday morning Bible Study.

News reached Bernice that her doctor, wanting to do some mission work, decided to take early retirement. I set up an appointment in early August before he left, noticing she was becoming more frail and complained often of being very weary. Doctor Crist was well aware of her enlarged spleen and felt strongly she needed surgery. Bernice found it difficult to say good-bye to her beloved doctor after all those years she had enjoyed his tender care. The next doctor appointments were in Seattle, in a few weeks.

Bernice and I drove out to Lake Crescent to enjoy lunch at the lodge. When we returned she received a call from her son telling her that Jo would come to get her for her upcoming appointment in Seattle and then bring her home to Sequim the following day. She was most stressed by this for two reasons. She was going to have to drink the infamous cleaner outer and that would be embarrassing at Paul's house and she wanted and needed me to be there. She had told Paul this but he had said there was no room for me to stay at their home. After some hugging and crying together Bernice called her son and told him she wanted to stick to the original plan. We would meet him in the hospital. We had already decided to spend the night in a motel since she had an early appointment. All this emotional turmoil added to everyone's stress.

Paul and I had lots of time together to talk while we sat together in the hospital waiting room. I felt better after sharing with him about his mom's concerns and deepest wish to stay in Sequim. Bernice rallied and marched through a most strenuous day of appointments and tests like a trouper. The results and decisions was that surgery would not be helpful. The diarrhea was the cause of the fatigue and new meds were prescribed. I realized that all signs were green. God wanted me to be part of the mission trip to Helene.

Prayer kept me going. The Lord quieted my thoughts as I breathed deeply and focused on him. *"Dear Father in heaven, you are my rock and I know my storms are not greater than your comfort. Help me to be strong and comfort Bernice. Touch Paul and Jo . Keep me from judging, keep me loving and help me to let go of my bruised ego. Amen".*

mission trip...

Now at last all systems were GO, I was to be part of the mission team en route to Helene. Charlie and Liz had gone a few weeks ahead of us. They were committed to staying five months. Before they left the group had shared a meal and evening together. Vic and Muriel had a granddaughter who joined us in Houston along with Bud, a dentist from another local church. Carolyn had been his long time assistant and had told us he was eager to be part of the team. We gathered in the church parking lot, standing in a circle holding hands Vic, a retired minister who was part of the team, prayed. Then, after loading up our gear, we climbed into the van and headed for SeaTac.

Lois, Liz and I had met a few times planning the crafts we would do with the children. All of us traveled with two suitcases full of supplies for the mission as well as own gear. The trip went well. We "moteled" it in Houston and found out quickly our gear was formidable. The three men struggled with it all. The next day we had a short hop to Roatan, off the coast of Honduras. Landing over water evoked memories of landing in Sitka.

Big Dan, as he was called, led us out to an old rinky dinky bus and we all helped to squeeze in our stuff. We traveled several miles to where we would spend the night. I was intrigued with the homes and scene. Roatan is a large island and is well known as a great scuba diving destination. When we drove through the tourist area the scene changed to upscale houses, hotels and eating places. The single women stayed in private quarters up the hillside. It was more than warm, we were now near the equator. I was glad I had bug spray as the mosquito population was robust. The group was treated to a tasty seafood meal sitting out on a lovely dining deck, enjoying the warm gentle breezes off the water. Quickly I observed that the hours of daylight and night stay about even through out the year. It seemed strange being in "summer time" and darkness falling around six p.m. Up early, I showered and headed down the hill to find some coffee. There was a small eating place with tables and chairs placed outside under the trees. One of the staff filled my coffee mug and I enjoyed some alone time, sitting quietly listening to the sounds of a variety of birds while sipping the hot brew. I had a chance to take a walk along the water's edge while pondering and wondering what new experiences awaited me.

Breakfast was unappealing to me, yucky banana pancakes. Next was another long bumpy bus ride that made a stop at a grocery store with a very gross rest room. We were all desperate and told this was the only place until we reached the pier. Dan had arranged a diving boat that would transport us. Blessed with calm seas the trip was delightful. It took about ninety minutes before the boat turned into a dock along the shore when we spotted Liz and Charlie running down the hill waving furiously at us. What a great reunion.

Helene was a small island off the island of Roatan. The Mission was housed in a well-planned, well built facility and blessed with a great setting on a high spot overlooking the water and some of the village houses. One long dirt path that went about a mile in both directions was the only "road". We dubbed it Highway 101. There were no vehicles with the one exception, a bicycle. Of course there were many that owned small fishing boats. The people were beautiful, all black tracing their heritage to slaves that had served their masters many years ago. They were part of Honduras, but spoke some English and pig Latin, no Spanish. They felt neglected by the government.

The school was less than a quarter of a mile down the road and was in deplorable condition. The dirt floor had lots of deep ruts in it. You really had to be aware of the unevenness when you moved around the room. Supplies were extremely scarce. Teachers came over from the mainland and often you would see the kids in their uniforms walking down the road from their villages and then walking back, for no teacher had shown up that day.

We had arrived on a Sunday so we all attended the evening service at the small church located adjacent to the Compound. It was rough on all of us as the service went on and on lasting more than two hours. We had experienced a few long days and were weary. The singing was robust and seemed that the louder you sang the more you were valued. Being on key really didn't matter.

Most folks came to church with a wash cloth that they

would wave around to ward off the bugs. There was no glass in the windows giving the bugs free reign. The bugs loved church services. People were warm and pleased to have us.

We soon learned that there had been an almost constant parade of mission groups all summer and we found the staff worn out and unprepared for us. Many of the teams had been teens needing lots of supervision. It was necessary that the crew needed to make a shift in their thinking. I was very frustrated as we sat around for a few days before getting really started. My expectation and hope had been to conduct several Bible Clubs in the various locations, but Jen, a staff person, had not expected that. We had to depend on her to take us and to be a liaison in the villages. She definitely was a key person. She went with us as we walked the dirt paths that connected the tiny villages. Upon arrival she would gather up the kids that hadn't already spotted us coming up the trail. We found the kids were very responsive. The more energy and drama I invoked the more they listened intently. We all had fun playing games, singing doing the story, singing. My team was excited and involved.

Jen was from Mount Lake Terrace, and knew my friend, Lynn. She had been in Rainbow Girls with Lynn's daughter. Dan was from Shoreline, near Seattle. Our doctor and nurse team found plenty to do, but Bud was totally frustrated as the people had not been told a dentist would be available to them. Carolyn spent a bundle of energy cleaning up the dental equipment and area.

Similarities between Helene and Scotland were noticeable. The workers slip into the village mentality without realizing it and take on that nonchalance... no hurry, no urgency. Expectations are lowered.

Early the next morning after arriving, I took my first shower and it turned out to be quite an experience. Following the instructions we had been given I pulled the cord and got enough water in order to put shampoo in my hair and then when I pulled the cord to rinse off, there was none. To compound the problem the water was soft and the suds were abundant. I jumped into the other shower hoping to get enough water to rinse off with only minimal success. In desperation I was forced to use the water in the sink which was only to be used while brushing our teeth. What a laughable, inauspicious start. Charlie was quick to fix the problem. The absence of hot water wasn't a problem because it was warm out of the tap. Water was limited. Our instructions were when using the facilities to not flush if the water was yellow, that was mellow. Only brown should go down. Yes, we were definitely in third world.

We were blessed with a capable cook, but she needed to make changes in her meals to accommodate an older audience. Our team was a different breed than usual.

Unfortunately we had hardly done very much when I picked up a bug and was overcome with diarrhea. Anything I ate would trigger a reoccurrence. Great way to drop some pounds... not great for the situation. Unbelievably the Lord blessed me with energy to walk with the team to the villages, jump all around telling the story with the kids, come back to the mission and then collapse on my bed. This kept me isolated from meeting some of the people and was rough.

I loved to climb up the outside steps to the crows' nest on the third floor. It quickly became my early morning routine, sipping coffee from a fat mug, while observing a quiet time of prayer, watching the sun come up over the water.

It dawned on me I was actually in the Carribean.

Roosters were in abundance, definitely making their presence known in the early morning hours, long before daybreak. There were many dogs that roamed about. At times they were a problem when they got to barking.

One of the team, who I had spent some time with before coming to Helene, was always talking about how old she was and couldn't do much anymore. It was neat to see her reach back and find she had a lot more reserve than she realized. Serena, our only teen was a delight. She was eager to learn and while with us gave her heart to the Lord. Her grandparents were thrilled as we all were.

A big Harvest Celebration was held our last night and it was packed full of all kinds of things. Jen was gifted and blessed with a trained operatic voice. She worked with a group of teenage girls that sang. In just the few months she had led them there was notable improvement. Their performance was appreciated, a blessing to all. Lots of food and noisy celebrations took place into the late hours. We all were packed and ready to go the next morning. Our return to Roatan was on two flat boats with planks to sit on. It turned out to be delightful. I had requested a few people back in Sequim to pray specially that when I had to be on the boat to and fro from Roatan that the seas would be quiet. The water was perfectly calm. The return trip the boats tended to hug the shoreline and I found it interesting to see the homes along the way. When docking in Roatan, everyone wanted to go out in a glass bottom boat to see the fish. Unfortunately, I was miserable from the swaying motion and had to rush up on deck, upchucking over the side of the boat.

We then all flopped into some lounge chairs and were refreshed before another lovely dinner that finally I was able to eat a small amount. The next morning was Saturday, September 8th... smooth going through Customs both in Honduras and Houston. Of course our stuff had diminished, actually I could fit one bag inside the larger one after unloading all our supplies we left at the Mission. A long day of travel and Steve and Ginny, friends from the church, (SPC) were a welcome sight when we landed late at SeaTac.

back home in Sequim

Tuesday, a few days later was 9/11. The shock of that day was staggering and in response the church held a prayer vigil. Many folks sought the comfort of meeting together. The following Sunday, Scott scrapped his anticipated sermon and gave a meaningful message. Attendance was notably larger than usual. In checking with Denise she shared all three of the kids had a reaction. The next day, going to school, Shane put one of his stuffed animals in his back pack. Cole put on his fastest sneaks in case he had to run and Jessi needed to be reassured her dad would not have to go to war.

I managed to get out to the coast to have some reflective time. My plate was overflowing as well as my emotions. The whole mission trip experience had been a bumpy one for me. Starting with the prep, processing the mixed messages on site and my debilitating sickness.

Friday night the mission team gathered at Lois' and planned for our presentation at a pot luck, after church. What fun we all had telling about the trip. Andy proved to be a most capable MC. My contribution was to have the team, all armed with wash cloths, sing one of the kids' songs. Much laughter ensued as we flicked off non-existent mosquitoes on one another.

Returning to Bernice, I was glad to now be there for her. We found ourselves dealing with the mixture of feelings that her son and wife stirred up in both of us. The next months my little nest would be occupied and I would be making several moves, thankfully housesitting. Seemed like my little place was needed more and more. This caused Ruth Barnes distress as she would come knocking on my door, having to tell me that they had received a call from someone wanting and/ or needing "my" place." This upset her, sensing it was difficult for me being displaced. The Lord was always faithful providing me with house sitting, but it did seem I was back to making continual moves since lots of the house-sitting arrangements were "quickies", a week or two here and there. Once again a familiar "family" ache returned making me wonder whether the Lord was preparing something.

full schedule...

My new ministry challenges were exhilarating, but also demanded significant changes. First challenge was the beginning of a Women's Bible Study. Fortunately I had spent time in the summer and chosen some Serendipity material I had used before in other places, that involved lots of "around the table" interaction. This material would not require lots of preparation on my part. It worked perfectly our first few weeks, helping me over the hump.

Bernice continued to need more attention. She seemed to be very irritated with several friends who had helped her in my absence. This made me wonder whether her health and/or meds was a factor as this was not typical for her. Her bad mood continued until I was able to encourage her to talk about her feelings. She realized as we talked, that she was hurting because the class she had taught many years started up without her, leaving her feeling left out and useless. Bernice did come to my new women's study and was welcomed into her small group who very much appreciated her wise input. Janie, her leader, I handpicked knowing that combination would be blessed. That was more than true.

The upcoming Sunday would be my turn to be in the pulpit. My custom was to set aside a day to just be quiet and focus on the Lord. On the drive out to the coast, while praying, I asked the Lord about my car that now had lots of miles on it. Also, it was a two door and BJ's friends couldn't use the back seat plus I was having a dickens of a time getting Bernice's walker in. Was it time to get another car?

After spending a wonderful day at my favorite beach in La

Push I started home. When I began to approach the curvy winding road along the lake, it had begun to sprinkle. The tires hit a slick spot and the car spun out, crossing over into the other lane and hitting the guard rail. I know God was protecting me because during those moments no traffic was coming in that lane. A young couple stopped and helped me to move the car to a nearby spot off the road. Then they called for a policeman but he was engaged with another person who also had just spun out. They willingly followed me as I headed back to Sequim. I was able to drive the car, even though the front was all smashed, as were the headlights. I was not injured just shook up and soon pulled over to both thank them again and to tell them I was fine and they could go on.

Sunday morning went well. Thankfully I was calm and energized by the Lord's presence. Many folks, with a twinkle in their eye, counseled me to be more careful about what I prayed for. Certainly had a clear answer about needing a new car. In a few weeks I found the car for me at a good price. I wanted a four door, stick shift with air. Air conditioning wasn't available but my car served me well, the next few years.

The next big event on my calendar was the retreat at Alderbrook. Our plans were progressing nicely. The members of the committee were pleased and anticipating the approaching weekend. It was scheduled for the end of October and when the big day arrived we found ourselves blessed with outstanding weather and lovely autumn foliage. Our facility provided a large and attractive main building as well as cozy cottages. Most of the women were in the cottages with only a few in the main building. A few ladies from the church's Worship Teams led us in singing. Our featured speaker Barbara was a perfect fit. Everyone responded to her teaching and insightful presentation of the scripture.

On Saturday, after the meetings, we had a fun night. The

committee had arranged to have different activities in designated cottages that the women could pick and choose which of the activities they wanted to join. The whole area was alive, full of laughter and chatter as we moved from place to place. Some other guests mentioned to us that they had wished they were apart of the group we were having so much fun. Sunday morning we had our own Worship Service and communion. Afterwards when the committee met to debrief we felt enriched and deeply blessed with the entire experience.

difficult changes...

The ensuing months were full, passing quickly. My schedule was packed... teaching the weekly women's study... meeting with the retreat committee now planning another event for the Fall... being involved in a small group.... numerous one on one conversations... caring for Bernice. She was turning ninety on April 14th and I arranged a birthday celebration to follow the eleven o'clock service. Some friends stepped in setting up and arranging the food and cake and handling other details. We ushered her in to the crowded Fellowship Hall and sat her down. People lined up and came to her one by one with lots of hugs and happy birthday wishes. I couldn't help thinking that this just might be the last people would be able to see her and I relished the wondrous moment. BJ was radiant and beautiful. She delighted in all her cards when we returned home and savored the morning together.

Bernice then had another celebration, a reception at the Fifth Avenue, her residence. Paul had contacted relatives and folks from the church in Steel Lake near Tacoma, where she and her husband had ministered for years. She was thrilled to see dear people, and was especially surprised when her sister- in- law and family walked into the room. Unfortunately she had minium energy and the party was difficult. In those last few weeks there had been a noticeable decline. I couldn't help thinking this was probably a goodbye for everyone.

Keenly aware of her weakening condition, I felt it was urgent to have her new doctor see her. The doctor agreed with me and while we sat there had her nurse call Seattle and arrange an immediate appointment. We then traveled to Virginia Mason and was seen by the surgeon. The spleen was growing rapidly, her feet and legs were swollen and she was experiencing shortness of breath. He took one look and said we need to operate. She was put on his schedule to operate.

Paul, Jo and I were facing the real possibility that she might not come through the operation and it might be the time she would go home to be with the Lord. It hurt to watch her have to struggle. "God you know what's best". I had booked a trip to Alaska and it was looking more and more that I would be there when the surgery took place. I was conflicted about the whole thing, but as I prayed the Lord was leading me to proceed with my plans. I was beginning to sense that the family, especially her son needed to step up and be the significant decision maker. I had been bearing the brunt, the one running interference and now Paul was needing to take responsibility for her welfare.

Plans were made and it was decided Lori, BJ's granddaughter would come to pick her up and take her to Paul's. He would bring her to some pre- exams and take care of her. Significant people from the church came to say good bye, that weekend. Bernice had her hair done and I washed and packed her things. Janie thoughtfully brought her small group over to visit. BJ was touched by their love.

The clock was ticking and we were faced with a good-bye. It may be for a few weeks or it may be until I caught up with her in heaven. My heart ached. I wanted to go with her. This time she was leaving me and I had to be brave and let her go. I was glad that she and her family would have this time together. Sunday afternoon Lori came. We all walked down the long hall way into the foyer and out the front door. She climbed into the front seat looking small and frail. We hugged and shed some more tears. As the car pulled away neither of us realized this was goodbye for her, from her home in Sequim.

Monday night Bernice called me to tell me all her tests had gone well and she's was okay for surgery. I went over her apartment and straightened it up and fussed about. There were conflicting emotions; in some ways I felt her presence and that was comforting, but I was forced to acknowledge the emptiness was haunting.

Alaska

Alaska was awaiting, but my usual enthusiasm was lacking. The flight was an easy one and blessed with clear skies. The pilot flew over Sitka pointing out Mount Edgecomb. That was a treat for me. I picked up my gear and then rented a car. The house was easy to find conveniently located close to the airport. I moved into my empty place and was greeted by Tinkerbell the family dog who was happy to have company. As usual my instructions were to help myself to any available food. Later I made my way to downtown Anchorage and then took a short walk at Earthquake Park, on the waterfront. I called Paul, anxious for news of Bernice, but had no luck. Saturday was the surgery. I was optimistic expecting my dear one, once again to come through the surgery and be all right.

My next day I enjoyed wandering around downtown, checking out the Imax Alaska Experience and browsing in some shops. As I stepped into one of them I was greeted with the pungent aroma of Russian tea that added to the ambiance of the store. For lunch I had to have salmon! Yummy as always. Paul called and filled me in with a good report. Thank you, Lord.

Saturday, Whittier was my destination. The scenery was

gorgeous. In order to reach the tiny town I had to drive through a two and a half mile tunnel. The population of the tiny village was one hundred sixty-seven. There I boarded an excursion boat, a catamaran. Lunch of halibut was part of the trip. Enjoyed seeing eagles, otters, seals, plus a killer whale. The captain maneuvered the boat close to the glaciers.

When the boat turned around, the sky changed from clear to dark and became threatening. My trip was enjoyable, but rather disappointing. There wasn't as much animal life, especially whales that are typically seen on that trip.

Sunday, I was up early and off to Fairbanks. It was Mother's Day and on the very long drive I was treated to awesome views of Mount Mc Kinley, also known as Denali, the "High One" the name the native Athabascan people call her. That was a privilege because most of the time she is shrouded in clouds. I stopped in the park, enjoyed the displays in the Visitors' Center and then drove out on a road that was told was a good viewing spot only to find the mount now was engulfed in clouds. After leaving Denali, it took a few hours more of driving to reach Fairbanks. There were long stretches of sameness, rather baron areas. My not being sure of pit and gas stations, added some stress.

Weary but excited I arrived in the city, found a place to eat before locating "my bed and breakfast". It was a lovely house with gorgeous views and a very comfortable room. The house was tastefully decorated, clean and uncluttered. I loved the many quilts on display. My homey surroundings made it was easy to settle in. I was eager to look in a phone book to see if I could find the phone number of a second cousin who lived in the area. Deb and her adopted Chinese daughter had lived in Fairbanks for a few years and always sent me a Christmas card. I hadn't received one the last Christmas and had wondered if she had moved. I found the number and eagerly dialed it only to have to leave a message. I decided against that and then looking through the yellow pages found her work number and address.

At the breakfast table the next morning, the hostess asked the guests what their plans were for the day and my reply was to find my second cousin. My hostess asked who she was and when I gave her name she said she knew her. With great enthusiasm she told me, "we all love her, she is doing so much for this city." Deb was involved with developing the city's tourist trade.

First stop was at Deb's office and the receptionist became excited when I told her my story. Obviously it would be extremely rare to have a relative just happen to stop by saying, "I was in the neighborhood, thought I stop by". Deb was in a meeting, but would be free in an hour. She promised not to tell her about me. When I returned there was another person behind a desk and they both were a buzz. She took me into the room since the meeting had ended. Deb and I looked at each other and recognized we were family. Quickly I identified myself and explained what I was doing there. She laughed and then took me out to have coffee and conversation.

Later she met me at my place and took me out to dinner. On the way we picked up her daughter, Izzy. What a darling and what a talker. Deb said she usually brings earplugs for the guest. We both wondered how Izzy and my sister would make out together as both of them are talkers. The next day was full of sight seeing. It was capped off as Deb brought me to her house for a superb salmon feast. I loved her cozy nest and was thrilled to see some of Aunt Belle's things around. My aunt had been her grandmother and we both swapped pleasant stories. It certainly stirred many sweet memories from my childhood.

Deb tried to arrange passage on the mail plane up to the north pole, but unfortunately there were no seats available. On my return to Anchorage I stayed one night in Denali. Enjoyed sitting out on the deck of a restaurant and lodge sipping a mocha while inhaling the spectacular view. Back to Anchorage I stopped at the Native Heritage Center. It was entertaining watching a line dance, listening to the story telling and viewing exhibits both inside and out. A native person was at each display and patiently told about what life had been like. The whole experience was outstanding and my stop most worthwhile. So thankful I was able to make that trip. Alaska is overwhelming, still maintains the flavor of the frontier in the energy of its people, the vast open places and its rugged beauty .

necessary adjustments...

Back in Washington I was eager to visit Bernice in the hospital and see for myself how she was doing. She, I knew would be ready to see me, too. One of my calls to her family, I was told she was progressing physically, but emotionally was very confuse and troubled. She was fearful, suspicious and acting irrationally, even removing her catheter. I had witnessed before that she was apt to over react to anesthesia and pain medications and was hoping that was the probable cause. During one of my phone calls from Anchorage, Jo had told me that she was mentally unbalanced and would never come back to Sequim. I was numb. One of her friends had been in contact with Paul and Jo and were told the same thing. Oh Lord, help!

I went to the Fifth Avenue to meet with the director of the facility. She confirmed that the family had notified her that Bernice would not be returning. Her apartment would be emptied the end of the week. I was in shock and in tears. A person who was a table mate in the dining room, comforted me as he found me sobbing after verifying the information. He, too,was upset as he knew this was not what Bernice wanted. With tears in my eyes and a giant lump in my throat I walked down the long familiar highway to her empty apartment, picked up her mail and cleaned out a few things. My heart ached when I turned to leave and walk away from this "home". I knew I needed to make my peace with all this.

On Sunday, I attended the first service which now meeting in the new building. The music was beautiful, stirred my emotions and set off some tears. The drive to Seattle went quickly and helped me to process the events before seeing my BJ. When I walked into her room immediately she sat up and brightened. What a sweet reunion that was. Such a precious love we shared. Paranoia had moved in and I sensed her urgent needed to talk. She related all kinds of disturbing things she had experienced. I let her spill everything out and didn't attempt to correct her. It bothered her that her family discounted what she was telling them. I reassured her helping her to relieve the bottled up emotions. We both had faced the reality that she might die during the operation. But now, on a lighter note, I teased her saying, " either the Lord is making you some extravagant house or you've done something really bad you need to correct".

Her next step was to a nursing home in Puyallup. This was an ideal location as Paul could stop by on his way home. It also worked for me, not being too far off of I-5. I was able to get permission to take her out to eat. Paul told her they had found her an assisted living apartment. He also laid it on as to the therapy and facilities were much better than Sequim could provide. The family and close friends also were telling her how great to have her close, now they could make frequent visits.

12

My Final Year '02 to '03

...once someone/s has/have been in your life, you keep that person despite the agony of the loss, as long as you had faith that you could bring the sum of all your hours together in one shining moment..

Once again I was flying home to enjoy some time with my grandkids in North Carolina and then travel to Connecticut to visit family and friends there. My sister and her husband were celebrating their fiftieth wedding anniversary and I certainly wouldn't miss that. Both of us had been married in the same year so of course there were some sad feelings to deal with. Jim and family had come from North Carolina to their home in the Poconos. The place was alive with the many cousins, many meeting for the first time. My girlfriend from grade school came with her husband, my cousin Wayne. I was so happy to visit with them and hear that she had been teaching Bible studies.

Brother Doug had taken his old movies and put them on a tape. Laughter broke out as we gathered around viewing family times when Mom and Dad were alive and the kids were young. I had come with John, Gretchen and Kristen and was thankful I didn't have to drive back to Connecticut in the dark and heavy rains.

While in Connecticut, Ginger, John's family dog had been

sick the last month or so and John had to put her down. I felt his grief as he buried her in their backyard. This stirred memories of burying our beloved Rascal in the woods years ago. Our pets give us so much joy while becoming part of the family, part of us.

My visits complete, it was once again time to return to Seattle. Friends of Bernice had invited me to stay overnight with them upon my return and then make a short trip to visit Bernice in her new place, an assisted living apartment complex. Another frantic move made without any preparation. Paul and Jo settled BJ into her new place and stored things in their garage that would not fit. The apartment was somewhat smaller, but pleasant. In addition to her home being cleaned, her laundry was taken care of. She now had to see the nurse to be given her meds. It was painful as I observed her loss of independence and sense of self-sufficiency. Paul had taken over her checkbook and didn't include her in on any information about her finances.

Back into Sequim I was settling in while facing all the emotions that went with Bernice's relocation. There were lots of meetings and catching-up with people. My getaways to the Spit continued to be a balm to my spirits. The vigorous walks and spotting my special seal, Smitty as he unexpectantly would pop up his head, continued to tickle me. I always felt that was one of God's many blessings the ways he provides my entertainment. The Terrace View group continued to meet monthly. I appreciated our times together keeping abreast of each other's happenings.

Pastor Scott and Claire invited me to move in while they vacationed the month of July. I took on the care of their cats and weeded and watered the garden. Their oldest son, David was living independently in the trailer out in the yard. The most comfortable house was endowed with a great view of the Strait.

It was fascinating watching the many ships making their way to the Puget Sound.

my own home...

Andy and Judy had relocated from their log house and moved to Three Crabs Road into a module home on the beach. They told me about an garage apartment they owned and wondered if I might be interested. When I saw it I knew that this was meant to be. Yes, my place. a place of my own. They charged a modest rent that I could manage. The apartment was in a large barn they had constructed. It was divided in three sections. One part provided a place to keep their RV. The middle portion was a place to store some furniture they weren't ready to part with. The third section was a finished apartment. It was carpeted and furnished simply. Of all things there was a four poster bed with a canopy and lovely dressers for me to use and lots of space to hang up my clothes and stash my gear in the middle section. There were a few old rugs on the part of the space that would be my "bedroom". The finished part was one long room with a counter and cabinets over them at the far end. They provided a microwave and a hot plate. The only sink was in the adjacent bath that also had the washer and dryer in it. Challenging yes, I was given table and chairs and a frig that was much larger than I needed. It was a delight moving into my own place the beginning of August and putting some of my things around. This felt like a giant step in many ways and made me wonder about its significance. It seemed that perhaps God was preparing me ... easing me into having more responsibility about my own affairs... perhaps getting closer to owning a home all my own. I had a modest rent to pay, my own phone, had TV cable installed. Hm....

During the last year I enjoyed a growing and deepening relationship with one of the moms. She was struggling with wanting another child and not having it happen. She and her husband were opening up to adoption, echoes of Watsons. We shared many times together. I began to call her my adopted daughter as she had shared that I was her mom. They soon adopted a daughter.

Betty, one of the woman in the church had reached out to me in friendship and had taken me on delightful walks. She had done lots of hiking and been part of a hiking group enabling her to introduce me to new places. A favorite of mine was a trail along the Elwha River.

Paul called to tell me his mom had broken her hip and was in the nearby hospital. Bernice had gone out on the bus the facility uses to take trips and had to sit near the back where she bounced around so much she had broken her hip. I was able to visit her the day they were moving her from the hospital back to the same nursing home she had been in previously. This time she was in a room by herself. It hurt me to see her in pain later that day when the nurses got her up on her feet. Once again her grit and determination were evident as she struggled to her feet and was able to take some steps. Her sister had been confined to a wheel chair in her last years and Bernice vowed that would not happen to her. We had been planning a visit back to Sequim, obviously that was out for a while.

a new reality...

This new reality was closing in on Bernice. She was consumed with loneliness, feeling very alone. Her hearing problems were worsening causing her great difficulty in deciphering voices on the phone and in the dining room, isolating her even more. In Sequim she had people who cared about her in addition to our relationship. The last thing she had ever wanted was to leave except of course to go to Heaven. No thought had been given as to making the transition easier. When she tried to talk about her feelings she felt she was being told she needed to face the facts and tough it out. There seemed to be little understanding of her need to grieve, while dealing with the multiple physical and emotional changes. Sadly, the promised visits were sparse.

There had been no contact made or efforts to see about her getting to church. She was told to attend the one on the campus, but it was on the other side of the complex requiring a long walk. She made it once only to be disappointed. It didn't feel like church. Now it was October and when I came to visit, after doing some asking and looking, I checked out a Presbyterian Church located close to her. The building was closed, but had an upbeat look and feel about it . Obviously there were young families as there was playground equipment on site and a youth pastor listed on the sign. Scott was more than willing for me to miss a Sunday so I could take Bernice to a service to see how she liked it. We went and the young pastor came up to us afterwards to chat and I filled him in with the situation. He promised he would contact members of the church and they would arrange transportation each week and bring her to the services. Shepherd of the Hill did follow through and even though she had some hearing difficulties it meant a lot to her to go and feel connected to a church. Her whole life had been centered around church. It was hard for me to understand some of the decisions.

eventful happenings...

The Leadership Summit is an annual event held at Willow Creek Church, near Chicago. Bill Hybels, the pastor is the dynamic force that launched the conference and keeps it going. He is committed to supporting and developing leaders and chooses significant speakers that bring a broad range of expertise and inspiration to the podium. The Willow Drama and Worship teams were inspirational and used to full advantage .

I attended this conference in Bellevue, near Seattle where

a large group of hundreds had gathered to witness this event on satellite. In '02 this event was viewed in fifty-one locations. Being part of a large group you quickly forget you are watching all this on a screen. We all laughed and cried and applauded at the appropriate times.

Having read one of Hybel's books and hearing much about him, I was eager to hear him speak. The staff had gone to Willow to a conference when I was in Scotland so when I asked if I could go to the Summit, Scott was more than glad to arrange to cover all my expenses. Bill is a dynamic speaker, but even more impressive was his humility that permeated whatever he did. He started the conference by talking about his Dutch upbringing. In his culture people don't say much to each other or express their feelings. But when someone dies the whole community gathers in the home and sing songs for the grieving family. He related how the Sunday after 9/11, that is what they did at Willow. For thirty minutes the lights were dimmed as the vocal group gathered around the piano. Everyone sang well known and simple, beloved songs. He then shared his desire to start our conference the same way. It was a precious time of worship, a time for the Holy Spirit to begin his work and be keenly aware of his presence.

There was so much that was stimulating to both my heart and mind. During the next sessions, I began quietly to sense that very possibly it was time to go home and be there with my family. This would be a traumatic decision, one that would demand more reflection and intense prayer.

Meanwhile my short hops between my motel and church were disturbing. Friday morning I arrived at the church after experiencing difficulty with my car. I inquired hoping to find someone who might help me diagnose the problem. One of the ministers on staff during the break came out to listen to my engine. He thought it was my distributor and that I should be able to make it back to Sequim. Was I relieved and glad to relax and enjoy the remainder of the day. When leaving as I approached a major intersection packed with cars, my car died and would not restart. It was five o'clock on a Friday night. The absolute worst time and place to have this happen. A willing "angel" jumped out of his car to push mine over and around the corner and into a large strip mall parking lot. Shaking and scared I called Triple A. I was told that a tow truck would meet me the next day after the summit ended.

Fortunately there was a restaurant in that mall where I was able to relax and have dinner. The owner called a taxi to take me to my motel. It picked me up the next morning driving me to the conference. My contract with Triple A was proving to be a good investment. I was informed that a tow truck would come about one o'clock. Yeah, I didn't have to miss out on any of the conference, especially as one of my heroes, John Ortberg was speaking.

One of the woman at the conference after the session was completed drove me down to where my car was parked. I had been told my policy covered towing up to one hundred miles. If we took the ferry I knew the distance would be less that the limit, but if the driver chose to "go around" using the Narrows Bridge that would be much longer. After I climbed up into the new truck with the driver and a buddy I asked which way we would be going and he answered, " Oh I never take the long route, always use the Edmonds ferry." Thank you Lord.

It was a pleasant ride, another new experience, out to Sequim and to my auto service place. Janie came to pick me up and brought me to her home to relax and enjoy amost delicious salmon dinner.

The next week I was scheduled to speak and felt the Lord leading me to speak on James 1... *consider it pure joy, whenever you face trials of many kinds, because you know that the testing of your faith develops perseverance."* Couldn't help but grin, *"Lord you are too much you know".* I had just experienced those words, had a real live test under fire and was rejoicing that it hadn't taken anything away from my Summit experience. I had been open and received all the Lord had planned and provided for me.

After I finished my message and came down the steps to greet people I saw a familiar woman with a giant smile approaching. She was Corky, one of the gals who had been in my young moms group in Sitka. We both shared our surprise.

She and her family had just moved to Sequim and they had begun the search for a church home. She couldn't believe when she saw me up front leading the service. How sweet is that. The family loved the church and It blesses me when I see her stepping up in various capacities serving the Lord.

Fall '02

The second women's retreat was in early September. During the enrollment phase we had some bumps, but they had smoothed out and all systems were on go. The quality of the retreat was even better than the first. There's nothing more profitable than experience. Barbara returned as our speaker and we all continued to feel that special connection. We changed the location of our small group time to the cottages and that worked well. Communion was a blessed time as there were some that went forward for prayer.

TNT was up and running with nine new ladies. Janie had prayerfully switched to lead the young moms and that was a good move. The first year their leader had complications at home that prevented her was getting there so had decided to step aside. The group leaders were wondering about my insistence at having six groups, but that decision I knew was one the Lord had led me to make. Almost immediately the places filled up and we were glad we were prepared for the growth.

Another new venture I started was a committee of women that would be committed to Women's Events I had dubbed it WE. Our meetings progressed nicely while we were planning a November event that was named Holiday Inspiration and would have a definite Christmas Fair flavor. We hoped this would draw people into our new facility, providing an opportunity to check us out and hopefully return to Worship on a Sunday. Ken, one of the men who worked with visuals and filming was great at doing videos of events and packaging them for viewing. I asked him to take some tape of all the on- going women's activities. He was pleased with the challenge. After my viewing them and with a little fine tuning I was more than pleased. He surprised me by stating that he thought I should narrate it... that got "my juices" going.

Now that Bernice was over on the Seattle side of the Sound it became an all day event to go and spend time with her. She was back in the nursing home for a long stretch due to a staph infection. On my visits I always would push her outside in her wheel chair so she could feel the sun and the fresh air on her skin. Paul was scheduled to take her to see her doctor and hopefully she would be able to return to her own place. He was always available to take her to those appointments, but didn't realize how BJ longed for him, just to sit down and visit a while.

making a decision...

I noted in my journal that of having more thoughts about moving to Concord. My grandkids were growing up fast and my window of opportunity to have time with them was decreasing. I was struggling with the realization of how hard this move would be for Bernice as well as myself. My weight was a problem continually and I needed a super injection of self control in that area. The reoccurring car problems were troublesome, making me uncertain.

Beginning of October, I visited in Connecticut. Kristen was working diligently while enjoying her college courses at Johnson and Wales in Providence. John's work often took him to the eastern part of the state and this made it easy to drive to Kristen's and take her occasionally to dinner. They both looked forward to these visits.

In making my usual round of visits I headed up to Maine to see the Baileys and as always was blessed. I shared with them I was considering retiring and hoped they would think about coming in the summer to visit me in Sequim. Expenses were a consideration of course, but when Gale turned to Gary and said she would really like to go, I felt the deal was sealed.

On my return trip, I was able to meet Susan who was spending some time on the coast about an hour or so south of Baileys and squeeze in a visit. It was October and the area was depleted of people so walking her beach provided ample doses of solitude and reflection. I had run by my three sets of friends my thoughts about coming home to live and was getting no "red flags"... nothing but positive comments.

I returned to the west coast and quickly got back into the groove. Scott took me out to eat at the Oak Table. It was time to tell him about my decision. After discussion about ministry concerns I shared that after much thought and prayer, I felt God was wanting me to move back to be near family. My thoughts led to a decision that leaving in September '03 would be most appropriate. This would provide me the opportunity to end my various commitments and have new leadership in place. He was understanding of this news and generous in his support. I explained that this needed to be secret until January, until after I had told Bernice about my plans. She would be visiting me in December and we would have a few days together. I felt that setting would be less painful for her rather than telling her on a day trip and then having to leave her all alone in her sorrow. He understood and agreed that was wise.

Rose invited the retreat committee to her house to enjoy a lovely lunch. She thoughtfully included Teresa who had served on the first committee. Such a wonderful sweet time. It was tough keeping a lid on my decision, that isn't my style as I tend to be very open. I was beginning to realize that this would be a "last" for me. Alderbrook, our retreat center was in process of selling and the deal was about to close. It was known they would be closing down for a year to remodel and update the facility. I was able to arrange with them a commitment that we all could hold another retreat at the same price when they reopened. What a deal that was and it pleased me, how the Lord had led through the negotiations.

The women's study and plans for the holiday event kept me busy as they both required my attention. The Holiday Inspiration was very rewarding. We had great support with several men showing up both to help us before and after the event. There were several stations; candle making, decorating, massage, wreaths, to name a few. I had given a welcome and a prayer and then mid-morning we showed Ken's video of women's events. We had a group of carolers dressed in old English garb that sang and then circulated through the crowd engaging in conversations. Our refreshments were in an adjacent room where we had tables and chairs set up so people could sit down to take a break. The attendance was substantial and we felt all our efforts were more than rewarded.

The challenging process of going through my stuff and giving away some books had begun. I now called my family and shared with them my decision about moving in the Fall the news was received with great enthusiasm.

Both Jo and Paul in conversations with Jeri, a dear friend of Bernice's were negative about their mom's mental state. She and

I had many upsetting phone calls as she needed to pour out her dismay. I wanted to bring BJ home to visit in December and called to clear that with Paul. He was comfortable with that. Also mentioned that we would be going to church so she could see so many precious people. Thankfully they took her to a beauty salon and treated her to a haircut, wash and perm. This was such a morale booster as she had always been fastidious about her hair. Then they treated her to dinner and brought her some comfortable shoes. She had also seen her doctor at Virginia Mason after complaining of general fatigue. He was concerned that there was internal bleeding and prescribed a colonoscopy. More ordeals...

My garage apartment was a success, but I was beginning to realize the winter months would be a challenge getting into my four-poster bed in the unheated bedroom. I toughed it out that winter, but think I would have purchased an electric blanket if I had stayed. On the same property was a modular home with a young couple living in it. I had chatted with them and had them for a dessert one night. They seemed pleasant. One night Jill came down knocking frantically on my door and shared that her husband had been drinking and had been abusive to her. She told me this had happened before. I became her support system and arranged a move to the Barnes in the Dome after explaining the situation to Bob and Ruth. With my encouragement she finished up her last weeks at Peninsula College and then with a car jammed full of stuff moved back to be with her folks in the midwest.

Andy and Judy were traveling again, and once again I had the joy of enjoying their house on the beach. So many delights ... the weather... the water.... and of course Fendie, my dog.... plus the agreement was... I didn't pay rent when house sitting. What a deal! God graciously was blessing me while reaffirming his call to go back east.

telling BJ...

Now, it was time to share my decision with Bernice. I picked her up at her apartment getting the various prescriptions from the nurse. She was excited about the visit. I was dealing with extremely mixed feelings of my joy at having her with me while dreading the news I would be sharing with her. This would be painful for both of us to think of being separated from each other.

I had decorated a small tree and bought a turkey to cook and food I knew she especially liked. When we arrived at the house after enjoying dinner at the Red Lobster, there was a very strong fierce wind coming off the water. We were faced with a long path to walk before getting into the porch and house. What a struggle. I was almost beside myself, even needing to push her, in order to reach the door. She was always game, determined to make it. Exhausted and relieved we relaxed in our warm house by the sea. Friday night we attended the Christmas Program at the church which as always was awesome. Folks lined up after the program to give Bernice a hug and tell her how much they missed her.

The next day, I knew I had to struggle to tell her my decision. That was tough. We both cried as we hugged each other. She said she wasn't shocked and understood my need to go home. Of course Bernice had always sought and followed God's will in her life and even though painful, knew he would never fail. We had more than a day together to talk, hug and cry some more. My decision was to not leave until September and I promised we would have lots of good times before our goodbye. She had the joy of going to church in the morning and again, receive lots of love from dear folks.

After taking Bernice home I began to experience pain in my knee and leg. I'll never know what caused this, but while we were together BJ needed my assistance to help her get up off the couch or chair and also help her to use the facilities as the toilet was too low for her to get up from. Each time I now walked the dog, the pain became more intense. I started taking some ibuprofen and keeping my leg elevated and iced. By Christmas I could hardly walk Fendie at all. Alwynn, my of my young moms had invited me for Christmas dinner and when she and her husband, Eric saw me, they became concerned. I had shared with Scott before the Christmas Eve service my problem and he suggested seeing an orthopedic doctor. When I called to make an appointment there were no available appointments for more than a month. Eric had told me if I had difficulty getting in to see the doctor to call him and he would use his clout as a person on the hospital staff to get me in.

The last time the gang from Terrace View met in Edmonds we had decided that we would celebrate my 70th birthday at Anthony's a favorite dining place of mine. It is situated right on the waterfront with a great view of the ferry as it crosses the Sound. Usually I left my car on the west shore, but the walk on and off the ferry is a long one and I knew I couldn't make it. My only other recourse was to take the car over to Edmonds. Well, another one of those happenings, Alwynn had a free ticket on the ferry she happily gave me. I shared with the group my news about leaving Sequim in September. Their reaction was one of a understanding...one of loss. I certainly could relate to that.

knee problems...

Early January, I made my visit to the doctor. He had my knee X-rayed and gave me a most devastating diagnosis that I should only walk on smooth level surfaces and at most a mile only. I wasn't to expect I would ever be able to walk like I was accustomed to. I had some loss of cartilage that he anticipated would worsen. He prescribed Viox, an ibuprofen, and glucosamine chondroitin.

This news devastated me. Walking provided more than

exercise, it was a precious time with the Lord. Pastor Bill had told me once that he pictured me walking along hand in hand with Jesus on the Spit. Prayer which for me encompasses worship... reflection... processing... listening...just being... nourished and replenished me. Certainly I prayed many places and times, but my favorite was when I walked.

When the new year began, I laid it all at the Lord's feet and cried out to him to reveal how he wanted me to live. Once again he had a "growing" for me to experience. I began to realize that the time had come to finally deal with my weight. It now involved more than looking and feeling better, it just might be helpful for my knee.

One day while sitting by the window, I focused on a bold and solitary seagull perched on one of the huge logs that had come ashore in the storm with its howling winds and rough waves. He or perhaps, she had come two days in a row and was content to sit there, letting the stiff breezes blow in her face. Where were the other guys? I identified with the single bird knowing that I would be leaving alone, moving into the next phase of my life. Leaving very special people and deeply satisfying ministry seemed overwhelming. this time I would be stepping into a vacumn not knowing what laid ahead. Hearing God's whisper of reassurance, promising me that there would be more precious ministry was a precious gift that nourished my soul. Later some other gulls joined my friend and playfully coasted on the winds out my window.

Warm wonderful memories swept over me while I cleaned "my house" that morning. A multitude of precious days the Lord had blessed us with here. How I loved having Bernice with me sharing the ever changing views of the water and the sky, while demonstrating my love in tangible ways. She ate with such pleasure. It was good to see Bernice once again vital and radiant as people came to show their love and respect. Oh, dear one I don't know what our Lord has for you, but both of us know we can trust him with our hearts.

The end of January I went to Harriet, my nurse practitioner, for a checkup. Filling her in on the trouble I was having with my knee and the prognosis I was given, she smiled and told me shaking her head, "Ruth, he doesn't know you, you'll be walking like you want to." He also didn't know what the Lord would do.

transition time...

My mind and heart were engaged in seeking God's leading in first of all staffing TNT for the Fall. There were capable teachers, but I sensed none of them would be willing to take the full load of teaching every week. I began the search for three that would rotate, sharing the responsibility. Also, I needed someone to be the coordinator, another key person. It was reassuring to know this was God's program and he would fill these positions.

Another "biggy" was the right person to head up the WE events. That one was easy as the Holy Spirit was already speaking to the right person to step up. I love the way God works in our hearts. Arlene already had heard his call. The third big area was the retreat that was scheduled for the Fall of '04. Once again the Lord had the person ready to be asked.

Later when I visited Armenta, an older, friend from '85, my first time in Sequim, she remarked as I was telling her how things were falling into place, "my goodness Ruth, just look at all the people you had to get to do all the things you were doing alone." I loved her typical sweet and sharp affirmation.

a major nudge...

When TNT started up again in January our attendance increased and we were now consistently in the forties. What a personal joy recognizing the Lord had used me in birthing this ministry to the women in our church as well as a few that attended from other churches. The small group leaders met an hour prior to the general meeting. Together we would work through the lesson of the particular morning sharing trouble spots and special insights. I thoroughly enjoyed these meetings and loved the nourishment I received from these gals, appreciating their support before teaching the day's lesson.

One of the group leaders had committed to a low carb diet. Each week she would excitedly tell that both her husband and she were losing weight. I was catching the vision. Soon after that I took a drive to enjoy the ocean view and lunch at Kaloach. When I checked out the menu I decided to splurge on some salmon. My waitress shared she loved salmon too and had even enjoyed some at breakfast that morning. She went on to inform me she was on a special low carb diet and salmon was a good breakfast for her. I had to laugh telling the Lord on my drive home that was overkill. I love his sense of humor. The guidance was there, it was time to get serious and to begin.

But first I needed to use my airline senior coupons before they were no longer allowed. I used one to fly to Florida and visit Dan the end of January. He treated me to a visit to the Holy Land in Orlando, a fascinating experience for both of us. Then I had booked a flight to San Antonio to use my remaining lone coupon on my return. It was March and upon my arrival I was told at the car rental that the city was anticipating an unusual ice storm, especially at that time of year. Fortunately I was able to purchase some food, plus a diet book before settling into my room. In the morning many of the roads were unpassable, by mid-day the ice had melted freeing me to get out and do some exploring. I was interested in visiting the Alamo. My first impression shared by many is how small and undistinguished the place seems until you walk through the building and area reading the information and observing the displays. You find your opinion changes and you walk away inspired.

Next I was eager to see the River Walk. As I strolled along the walk I made multiple stops in a variety of shops. The Mexican flavor intermingled with a cowboy presence. I chose to indulge in Mexican food and enjoyed a tasty lunch. On my second visit my choice was a thick Texas steak followed by the River Cruise that was a must. I also hopped a trolley that took me to the Institute of Texas Cultures that I had read about. The displays, many of them staffed with demonstrators were outstanding. The happy sound of school kids enjoying their outing added to my enjoyment.

On my last day I drove away from the city to visit Fredrickburg out in the hill country. Here everything was German, a total change from San Antonio. I devoured some great sausage and sauerkraut and as I strolled along the main street I wished I had more time to explore the various art and gift shops.

After bidding farewell to Texas, I returned to Sequim, ready to begin my diet. This challenge brought success and by early summer I had lost twenty-five pounds, meeting my goal.

more blessings...

One of the ladies that was involved with the Bible Study and had attended the retreats struck a cord in me. I had taken note of her and wished there was an opportunity to know her better. Unbeknown to me she had a similar yearning. We just "happened" one day to be in the church office to use the copier at the same time. I felt led to ask if she might be interested in getting together and that led to a meeting at my place. We knew we wanted to continue our sharing and prayer on a weekly basis. What a sweet friendship developed.

There were several individuals that I would connect with for a while . That ministry was rich and I cherished it. One of the things that made it all worthwhile was knowing the Lord was using me to stimulate spiritual growth.

Plans for the summer were happening. I had offered both Jim and John and their families to come to Sequim to visit in the summer. We all knew that would be their last opportunity since I would be moving East. I also extended my invitation to two sets of friends. When everyone was telling me they were making plans I knew there was no way my garage apartment would accommodate my guests. I stopped in at the Barnes to ask if I might move back the beginning of July and stay until I left mid-September. Bob with a twinkle in his eye said "yes, come home, all is forgiven for your running away."

A routine of visits evolved as the weeks slipped away. I would drive over to see Bernice every other Friday. When the day was sunny I was treated to awesome views of Mt. Rainier. Usually I took her out to lunch and was tickled with her appetite. One time she told me she needed a new night gown and could we shop. I got a wheelchair and pushed her around the mall going to a few favorite stores. She surprised me as she purchased several items. When I questioned her about how much she was spending, with a gleam in her eyes and a feistiness I hadn't seen in a long time, she whipped out her credit card. Her son had been telling her she was getting low on funds, but she had control for the moment at least.

There were new cottages on the coast at La Push and three of us planned an overnight treat. Just a day prior to our going I woke with an intense pain in my neck. As the day progressed so did the pain. I was taking ibuprofen and that helped some, but the day we were to leave it hurt so much I was even apprehensive about driving. Betty willingly drove. The pain in my neck and left shoulder was so intense during the night I even dreaded getting up. Some day I hope to be able to go to that beach again. The cottages were both attractive and cozy.

The next week Winnie told me about her chiropractor and I quickly made an appointment. The doctor was both warm and cheerful, but sad to give me the news after looking at my x-rays. I had scoliosis. Many appointments paid off for me as he adjusted my back. It worked, I have not had a reoccurrence of that pain.

"Gleanings from Ruth" was the title of the retreats I led both for Terrace View and Okanogan women in the spring. As I dug into the Book of Ruth I was richly blessed not only with the beautiful love story, but impressed with the beautiful relationship Ruth had with Naomi, her mother-in-law. My trip to Okanogan was my first good bye. It was precious and painful, rich in many sweet memories. The toughest goodbye was with Tollie and Woody.

last times...

More "last times" were happening. TNT meetings always ended the first weeks of May. On our last Tuesday, I felt both humbled and thankful as I was presented special gifts and multiple words of appreciation. My gifts included a small replica of the lighthouse on the Spit, a lovely book on the names of God and a handmade banner of the lighthouse. The next ending was my Small Group. Before we said our goodbyes they gathered around me and prayed, asking especially that my knee would be healed.

Scott was going to be gone all summer on his long planned and awaited sabbatical. Just before he left we had my last staff meeting. All of these endings were hard, sorrowful. This whole experience had been so deeply rewarding, full of challenges and rich rewards. Being a part of SPC's amazing growth and working side by side with this vital staff was a privilege I will always hold dear. Thankfully I was bathed with the peace that only comes from above, knowing I was right where God wanted me to be.

My organizing gifts were now in high gear as I was weeding

and eliminating, while packing up things I knew I didn't need that summer. Arlene helped me ship my foot locker of winter things and some personal articles.

John, my good buddy from Connecticut days had urged me to use his place in Santa Barbara, CA. I invited Winnie to join me and her answer was an enthusiastic yes. We flew into LA and boarded a bus for Santa Barbara. When we pulled into the stop we were met by a friend of John's who then drove us around, helping to orient us and then onto our place. What a great house it was, most homey and comfortable. We each had our own bedroom and bath. Our apartment was on the second floor and we loved eating out on the deck while looking down at the large yard complete with flowers and some veggies growing. We also had use of a van .

Winnie is a great garden lover and mapped out her agenda each day. I of course was drawn to the lovely beaches, lapping up the sun and fresh air. I was still experiencing limitations on my walking so to sit on the beach and watch the ocean while reading a good book was what I needed. It was beneficial emotionally while I processed the events and "last times" of the past few weeks. Also I needed to plan and prepare for all the company I was about to have.

In spite of my walking problems I was able to sight-see around the town and visit the mission. On Sunday we attended Calvary Chapel. The church had been a warehouse and now was creatively transformed. When we approached the entrance we noted the high tables and stools where folks gathered with their expresso and doughnuts. Then as we walked into the open and airy Worship area there was a sense of the beach. Over the platform area was posted the church's motto, 'Worship the Son", most appropriate for a beach town full of sun worshippers.

While listening to the sermon that morning I caught a vision of Bernice. She was surrounded with angels, free of all her ailments, smiling and radiant. What a joy and a comfort that was. I felt the Lord was reassuring me, while releasing me to leave her in September.

The pastor in his sermon said, *if you want peace start with the focus on grace and the peace will follow.* Good advice, life is full of challenges and lots of tough times. *We pay now but reap later. The world reaps now but pays later. Faith is the anchor and needs to hook onto something to be secure. An anchor by itself is worthless.* Powerful words for my needy heart.

After the service ended I continued to stay seated, praying, laying before the Lord my troubled soul pertaining to the unknown future condition of my knee and joints. My prayer was "Lord , you know how much I love to walk. Right now help me as I put that love in your hands. I trust you with my life and know that whatever lies ahead you will use it for your glory and will surround me with your care and keep me in your grace, Lord trusting that where and what you want is where I want to be." Facing the unknown next phase of my life and in the "not knowing" I affirmed that God has always known and provided what was best. I will trust and not be afraid. Precious words from a teenage favorite, I'll go where you want me to go dear Lord.....I'll be what you want me to be, flooded my heart and mind. I walked out of that service richly blessed and encouraged.

That afternoon Winnie and I strolled around the lovely gardens located on the campus of Westmont College up on the hillside that overlooks the city. There were many places to sit and quietly reflect in the midst of the flowers. This was a perfect place to share our hearts and love for our God.

Winnie had heard about a Healing Room Ministry nearby and one evening we went to investigate it. We were given directions to go in and sit in the sanctuary and be in prayer while waiting. There were two teams of people who came for you and led you to another room. There was a solitary chair that I was directed to and then a team of three surrounded me. My group asked me a few questions about myself and then inquired about what needs I wanted them to pray about. I had been sharing with great joy about my ministry in Sequim when they stopped me to relate they were puzzled by a deep sorrow they were sensing. Then I talked about my love and concern for Bernice and how painful the leaving would be. They lovingly engulfed me in pray and affirmed, an abundant ministry awaited me.

Such blessings, the beach time was so rich and deep, preparing, fortifying me. I loved the reflective time it provided. The Holy Spirit was leading me again and again to portions of Romans as it is stated in the Message.

> *Don't burn out; keep yourself fueled and aflame. Be alert servants of the Master, cheerfully expectant. Don't quit in hard times; pray all the harder. Help needy Christians; be inventive in hospitality.*

Bernice, having all sorts of medical problems was very lonely and sad. She, though down, was not defeated, but was reading "The Message", a most contemporary version of the Bible, and loving it. Her whole life, she had been saturated with the scriptures and that never ceased.

Reflections........ as I remember that holy time in Santa Barbara. What a rich oasis...... What a way to begin my summer parade....... Rested... relaxed... restored, actually filled to overflowing.... bursting with your love. God touched me in my hurting over BJ. Such an expectant heart I came back with... striving to walk in that gift of grace. Incredible how my Lord weaves the strands of my life to make continuous beauty.

> *Beauty for ashes the oil of joy for mourning the garment of praise for the spirit of heaviness. Isaiah 61:3*

It was summer now, and in a few weeks my parade of company was to begin. I had hoped to have Bernice for a last visit to Sequim, but she needed more surgery. Once again she came through fine and was surprised when I showed up at the hospital. Of course her next step would be another time in the nursing home, before she would be able to return to her apartment.

Friends helped me to move and settle back into my cottage at the Barnes. This had been my first home when I came to Sequim and it made the perfect place to complete my time there. My first visitors were my family from North Carolina, Jim, Denise, Jessi, Shane and Cole. What excitement when I picked them up at the airport. We drove into Seattle, grabbed a bite to eat at the waterfront and took the ferry across. The next day was brilliant, certainly a Mount Rainier day so we took off bright and early. We enjoyed our picnic lunch up at Paradise and then the family hiked the steep trail to the spot at the edge of the snow where only hikers with equipment are permitted to continue. Unable to join them I remained in the lodge keeping my leg elevated. They returned breathless and excited at their experience.

On our way back we popped into Bernice's nursing home around nine p.m. and was she thrilled! My dear grandkids all gave her great hugs even though they didn't really know her. She was radiant. and looked like a kid on Christmas morning. BJ knew my family was visiting and had hoped she would get to see them, but I had made no promises to her, uncertain how our schedule would evolve.

My family loved everything, the Spit, making a fort of the logs... Hurricane Ridge... Lake Crescent.... Beach 2 where the tide pools were at their best..... downtown Seattle and a Mariners game...both the boat trip and the sightseeing in Victoria. What a great time, worth my investment.

After a short break my Connecticut family, John, Gretchen, Kristen, Matt and Lindsay came. We did basically the same things, but I wisely sent them off to visit Victoria on their own so I could have a long day home to myself. We also popped in to see Bernice, this time she was back in her apartment. When John asked how she was her reply was just fine, except this "crazy" person kept bringing company at late hours. I love it.

We all took in a Seattle Storm, WNBA basketball game while in the city. The main attraction was one of the players, Sue Byrd, the former UConn great. Matt was a delight to have in our group. He was so appreciative of everything and extremely interested.

Gary and Gale, my friends from Maine came next. I always look forward to our times together through the years and enjoyed the privilege of showing them places they had never experienced before. We, also stopped in to see Bernice.

Friends from Mount Lake Terrace wanted to arrange a time for our group to be together before I left. Dick and Christine extended an invitation to the gang for all of us, husbands included, to come to dinner at their house. It was a fitting way to be with the pastor and folks that helped to launch my whole volunteering ministry. I again thanked Dick and everyone. Terrace View Church had been willing to take a risk, climbing out on a limb. Little did any of us ever dream that my volunteering would extend to twenty years and all the places I would go.

September had begun, but my roster of visitors wasn't complete. Pastor Scott had returned from his summer sabbatical and was approaching his 50th birthday. A committee had planned all summer long in his absence to give him a surprise party he would never forget. I was able to bring Bernice to Sequim for her last visit and to coincide with the big event. The staff took him out to dinner and included Bernice. Scott was rather cocky thinking that he knew everything that was going to transpire, but when we all returned to the church the plan had been for him to attend a Keenagers' event, instead he was confronted with a packed house at the Fellowship Hall. He was then escorted up to the platform and sat down in an overstuffed chair. The evening unfolded as the committee did a "This Is your Life" having old friends appear on stage and tell stories about him. What fun! He was already on overload and shocked speechless when presented keys to a new sports car he had his eye on.

Bernice's presence also was celebrated as folks lined up to wish her well and send her off with warm hugs. Once again I saw her radiant, energized and more mentally alert than I could have imagined.

The last time in the pulpit for me was two weeks before leaving. I was blessed with a calm and a flow that comes from the Lord. A light touch was added to the service as Scott did the parts of the service I usually did for him, the prayers and scripture reading. I quipped, how do you all like my new assistant and everyone broke out laughing.

My last guests were the Chuvalas and that was a fitting climax for my eventful summer. They had taken Am Trak, cross country, fulfilling a dream of Bob's. We had a special time and it meant a lot to be sharing my last Sunday. They had been there in many significant times through the years. It was fitting that they were with me when I completed my ministry as a Volunteer In Mission.

Scott called me up in both services and after giving a generous thank you he presented me with a fabulous check from the church as a farewell gift. He had been sensitive to my need to purchase furniture as well as other household items when I settled into my own home. After the first service he asked me to return the envelope so he could present it at the second service. When he gave it to me the second time I couldn't resist asking him if I could keep it this time. There was a wave of laughter that rolled across the pews.

Cards and hugs, words of appreciation were abundant.

Their overflowing love and thanks touched my deep places. The worship team came and sang a song for me that made me struggle to hold back the tears. One of the sound men who was rather reserved came to me on my last sermon day, and shared that he and his wife always arranged their schedule so they would be home and not miss my sermons. He told me my words on several occasions had spoken to him with great impact.

It was time to take Bob and Ruth Chuvala to Seattle to the train back to Connecticut and then onto to say a final goodbye to Bernice. This time I stayed over night and we enjoyed a deep sharing time.

My last day in Sequim, I went to church for goodbyes, only to find a woman in tears. We went into the sanctuary to talk. Her husband had been abusive and she had moved out, staying in a friend's house with her two kids. When I told her I was leaving the next morning and would see if she could move in at the Barnes she was thrilled. Lord you blessed me, even as I was leaving.

Morning dawned and I drove down the familiar driveway and over to pick up Betty, my hiking pal. She had offered to travel with me to Banff and Jackson Hole. We then took off to Port Townsend to take the ferry to Widby Island, a favorite ride of mine. Then we drove north into Canada, through BC and into Banff and Lake Louise. This had been the only place I hadn't visited that I had listed seven years ago on my must list. I had been somewhat undecided as to whether to go or not, but our gracious Lord who supplies more than we could ever ask or think had given me the nudge. "Don't be foolish, Ruth. I have this special experience to bless you with."

Even after all the beautiful awesome places in Washington and Alaska, I found the beauty of the Canadian Rockies especially breathtaking. We enjoyed a few days there before heading south crossing back into the states near Glacier. We spent an overnight in Missoula and then continued south to Jackson Hole to my niece's, Peggy. The loveliness of the Tetons completed this trip. After a few days of sightseeing it was time to put Betty on the plane back to Sequim and continue East... on my own to North Carolina.

Post Script

This time I knew that I was not only going home, but I was leaving "home". My roots had gone deep into the soil and they would never be completely uprooted. I was driving away from family... a family of forever friends... deep relationships that were precious to me and a ministry that blesses me still. What an incredible journey I had experienced.

It's February '09 and at long last I'm finishing this book. It's been a struggle at times as well as a great joy. I never have considered myself a writer, but I experienced a clear calling to write this story.

> Writing ..was a way in which I could taste life twice...gave opportunity to savor life again from different and unique angles..go beyond appearances to unwrap the essence of my experiences.
> Tim Hansel.."You've Gotta Keep Dancing"

In case you are wondering about a few things... yes, after renting for a year I am now a proud condo owner. What a delight furnishing my own place with both splurges and hand-me -downs. My home sits on a side of a hill overlooking a large pond where I enjoy watching the changing seasons as well as a variety of ducks and geese. I'm also blessed with daily visits of many cardinals who like to eat at my feeder.

How deeply satisfying it is to welcome loved ones in this home that my Heavenly Father provided me... riches upon riches.

Lots of family time... grandkids school events ...celebrating holidays...having reasonable access to my other sons... friends in New England.. PLUS annual visits home to Sequim.

Yes, I'm still walking, usually two to three miles and sometimes more.

My dear Bernice went home to be with our Lord In January of '04. When I find myself missing her I switch the picture and focus on how full of joy she is in Heaven.

In February of '06, I met a wonderful man who loved me dearly and although our time together was much too brief I will always cherish our time together. I was his *sweet lady* and he was my loving man.

Although I miss the challenges of ministry I was blessed with I know that I am right where my Lord wants me and that he will continue to always bless me with new challenges *God is not so interested in what we are , as he is in what we are becoming.*

Printed in the United States
145900LV00004B/2/P

9 781438 968568